DIGITAL DEMOCRACY:

POLICY AND POLITICS IN THE WIRED WORLD

edited by
Cynthia J. Alexander and Leslie A. Pal

Toronto   Oxford   New York
OXFORD UNIVERSITY PRESS
1998

Oxford University Press
70 Wynford Drive, Don Mills, Ontario M3C 1J9
http://www.oupcan.com

Oxford New York
Athens Auckland Bangkok Bogotá Buenos Aires
Calcutta Cape Town Chennai Dar es Salaam Delhi Florence
Hong Kong Istanbul Karachi Kuala Lumpur Madrid Melbourne
Mexico City Mumbai Nairobi Paris São Paulo Singapore Taipei
Tokyo Toronto Warsaw
and associated companies in Berlin Ibadan

Oxford is a trade mark of Oxford University Press

Canadian Cataloguing in Publication Data

Main entry under title:

Digital democracy : policy and politics in the wired world

Includes bibliographical references.
ISBN 0-19-541359-8

1. Political science. 2. Policy sciences. 3. Information technology - Political
aspects. 4. Communication - Political aspects. 5 Democracy. I. Alexander,
Cynthia Jacqueline, 1960- . II. Pal, Leslie A. (Leslie Alexander), 1954- .

JA71.D533 1998   320   C98-931180-5

Cover & Text design: Brett Miller

1 2 3 4 - 01 00 99 98

This book is printed on permanent (acid-free) paper ∞.

Printed in Canada

Contents

□

DEDICATION

To my parents, with love and respect

— Cynthia J. Alexander

For Mary, always

— Leslie A. Pal

Acknowledgements

---------------------- ☐ ----------------------

The seeds for this book first germinated during a meeting between the editors at a conference in 1996. Alexander was organizing the Atlantic Provinces Political Science Association meetings and invited Pal to present a paper on what was to him a new and exciting area of research—politics in cyberspace. The original idea was to have one panel of papers at the conference, but it soon grew to several panels and ultimately became a main subtheme of the conference itself. We were fortunate to have such an accomplished and knowledgeable roster of contributors from Canada and the United States. Several agencies and organizations helped support that segment of the conference dealing with digital democracy: Industry Canada, the Department of Foreign Affairs and International Trade, the government of Nova Scotia, MT&T, IBM, and Marriott Hotels. Acadia University also provided support through the Office of the President and the Alumni Visiting Lectureship Fund. We would also like to thank our colleagues in the Department of Political Science at Acadia University for hosting the conference, and especially the conference co-chairs, Drs Agar Adamson and Ian Stewart. Leanne Wells, the department secretary, provided us with invaluable logistic support. We greatly appreciated the scores of graduate and undergraduate student volunteers at the conference, and particularly the Politics and the New Metamedia class for its poster demonstration.

Euan White of Oxford University Press was consistently supportive of the project and expressed early interest in publishing this book. Phyllis Wilson steered the manuscript through to publication with a firm but gentle hand, and Richard Tallman gave us a new definition of professional editing—infusing grace under pressure. We also benefited greatly from the help of research assistants Daniel Hosseus and Alia Tayyeb. Leonard Preyra reviewed the entire manuscript and was both generous and perceptive in his suggestions for changes and improvements.

Our greatest thanks, however, are to our contributors. The demands of an edited volume can sometimes be onerous, and each of our authors was consistently enthusiastic and professional. This book is no doubt only a first effort at trying to sketch the contours of the digital democracy that seems to be emerging in our midst, but we are convinced that it performs its task of exploration and signposting quite well, establishing themes and offering arguments and analyses that will help set the terms of discussion for those who follow.

□

DIGITAL DEMOCRACY
OR
POLITICS ON
A MICROCHIP

□

Edwin R. Black

Computers are changing our governments as well as our electoral politics. Not only do they change the way parties conduct elections and the way we watch election returns, they are changing the choices our elected representatives make for us and the way that public servants deal with us in implementing those choices. It's happening right under our noses, it's important, and not enough people are paying attention.

Casting your bread upon the waters does not sound like the 'done thing' in the days of digital democracy, real or hoped for. Sometimes, though, a few crumbs of bread tossed timidly out before a bunch of academics do come back—in loaves, fishes, whole bakeries even. This book is the evidence. The stimulating inquiries reported here come some time after a preliminary reconnaissance sketched out the government and computers territory in the presidential address at the annual meeting of the Canadian Political Science Association in 1983.* These changes in government were so significant, I noted at that time, that students of politics and government should be paying much closer attention than they were, which at the time was hardly at all. Now, thanks to the stimulus of the two editors of this book, Cynthia J. Alexander and Leslie Pal, we are beginning to see some of the things that are happening to us and our governments.

Information and communication technologies are changing more than just national governments. City councils, legislative assemblies, provincial governments, and public regulatory authorities are all acting differently because of changes in the business of public collection, manipulation, and computerized manufacturing of 'facts' about our affairs. What is involved goes far beyond fancy record-keeping and data bank matching. It means a rapid evolution in some of the most important aspects of the state:

- the political legitimacy of representative government versus 'direct democracy';
- the ways in which the opinions of interest groupings and various sectors of the voting public are determined and assessed;
- the operation of new biases or sets of values in what appears to be the mechanics of information handling;
- the importance assigned in budgetary battles to quantified approaches to developing and delivering 'soft services';
- changing bureaucratic subcultures that deal with the framing, phrasing, and weighting of policy choices.

In short, the ever-spreading use of digital information technologies is transforming both how we are governed and the institutions of that governance.

---

* Some of these ideas were first suggested in 'Politics on a Microchip', the author's presidential address to the Canadian Political Science Association, which is reprinted in the *Canadian Journal of Political Science/Revue canadienne de science politique* 16, 4 (Dec. 1983).

Whether these developments are for the better remains to be demonstrated. Before we can do that, we must know where to start and what the right questions will be.

What, then, should people be looking for, and what would a preliminary reconnaissance of the territory look like? First of all, one should be clear that whatever the spread of office automation, of the World Wide Web or Internet, of Apples and other computers in the schools, or of expensive games in the home, revolution is not the scene. While for a time some commentators felt sure that computer specialists would rise to new-found public importance, that is not happening. The only discernible change in domestic authority structures is the sight of new money and business acumen muscling in for a share of the élites' political power and position. What must be examined closely is not revolution but the consequence of new modes of data collection, transformation, and transmittal, of élite and special public communication, and of the implication of current fascination with digital technologies for the system of governance.

Those with interests in government and politics should keep an eye on at least two sets of phenomena. The first is the most likely to be neglected: the rapid changes in our political institutions, processes, and subcultures set in motion by the exploitation of information technologies in all phases of political life. No communication system can exist shorn of power, purpose, or organization. Although seldom recognized because of their spurious claim to scientific neutrality, information and communication technologies (ICT) are as subject to social values and partisan biases as the 'worst' state or provincial highway proposal. More likely to attract a student's attention—as demonstrated by the work in this book—are the second sorts of phenomena: the public policy issues. These relate to automation and employment, public access to public information, law and public morality, the health or survival of a host of trades and industries, the financial and educational spheres, and, ultimately, to questions of national security.

Particular, and often new, sets of social biases operate at all these levels. Information specialists and senior government officials will protest in vain; it is difficult for any student of society to agree that processing systems in use on today's scale could be neutral in their effects on either policy or administration. Not only would that be difficult to believe, it would be impossible in practice.

The centralization of information facilitated by computers raises questions of security, privacy, sovereignty, accountability, and many other political issues involving publicly held stores of data. Cross-border data flows represent only one of many geopolitical centralization questions we should confront. In the international sphere, for example, competition relates not simply to trade. The governments of some countries are amassing huge information-processing resources while others have little at all. The latter are doomed to growing ineffectiveness in many areas of interstate activity. It was not mere patriotism that led the US government to treat computer power as an important resource not only during the Cold War but through the following trade wars. At the subnational level, ICT resource inequities among state, provincial, and central governments will worsen the bargaining resources of small administrations.

If governments are disadvantaged in their dealings with other governments, think how much worse off are the disadvantaged 'clients' of computerized government services. Public scrutiny of administrative actions is becoming even more difficult in the information society despite the well-meaning attempts of some public servants to make their ICT systems more 'user-friendly'.

Part of the problem in analysing and adjusting to enormous technological changes in the creation, manipulation, and transmission of data is that we scarcely understand the nature of information and its social role. This causes major problems for policy-makers because information is not easily quantified and assigned numerical weights. More difficult to grasp are the distinctions to be drawn among data, information, meaning, and knowledge. The old catchphrase tells us 'knowledge is power'. The possessor of knowledge, however, unlike the owners of many commodities, does not necessarily lose value by sharing the information or giving it away. Today the question is not so much who possesses particular information as it is a question of who has access to certain stores of data and who has the skills to turn it into exploitable knowledge. For all of the egalitarian impulses allegedly inherent in some conceptions of digital democracy, nobody has yet shown how these qualities will do anything other than to make the badly-off even worse off in comparison to the better-educated.

Theoretically, computer simulations and model-building could lead to innovative and progressive policies. That has been the promise of other technologies in the past. That seldom happened. New tools lend themselves much more readily to consolidating the power of the well-established people and values. What you build into a model is more likely to be an abstraction of today's power arrangements than it is of some ideal or even realizable liberal democracy.

Bureaucratic and ministerial power resources continue to expand, thanks largely to ICT. Does that leave much room for the people's elected representatives to improve significant public control over our government in between elections? The answer is no, not if past Canadian and American experience is any guide at all. If present trends go very far—and they will if there is not more examination of the issues presented here in *Digital Democracy*—the computerization of government could mean the end of meaningful public interest in representative government and its replacement by a plebiscitarian dictatorship under the guise of direct democracy. The triumph of converging information technologies married to digitized entertainment systems is busy stripping representative legislatures of their last shreds of dignity and threatening all governments in their attempts to shape popular culture. The authors of the studies that follow have done much to explore the dimensions and implications of some of the matters raised in this Preface. Their successes will be measured in the extent to which they bring you to see aspects of government in new and interesting ways and then inspire you to pursue these important questions even further.

Chapter 1

□

INTRODUCTION: NEW CURRENTS IN POLITICS AND POLICY

□

Cynthia J. Alexander and Leslie A. Pal

———

A new technology is opening up new vistas for democracy, education and personal enrichment, a magazine predicts. 'The government', it says, 'will be a living thing to its citizens instead of an abstract and unseen force. . . . Elected representatives will not be able to evade their responsibility to those who put them in office.'

The new medium will be like a gigantic school, the magazine declares, and 'have a greater student body than all our universities put together.'

The year was 1922, radio was the new technology, and the magazine was *Radio Broadcast.*[1]

———

Digital Democracy: Issues and Implications

In the 1990s the parameters of our political lives are increasingly circumscribed by the bits and bytes of information and communication technologies (ICT). Individually and collectively, as consumers and as citizens, our lives are increasingly computer-mediated. While we readily and even enthusiastically embrace these technologies, we know much less about their political or policy impacts. Similarly, the sheer speed of technological development has surpassed our ability to design and implement policy responses that effectively grapple with the host of legal, ethical, sociopolitical, and economic implications of ICT. Sissela Bok states that 'our technological advances have been so extraordinary that they have to some extent left us behind when it comes to the wisdom of using all that we are capable of using.'[2] The essays in this collection advance our understanding of the ways in which technological change introduces new possibilities and new risks in our political and policy worlds, with particular attention to Canada and the United States. Rapid technological innovation in the field of informatics has contributed to the seismic shifts altering our intellectual foundations, political institutions and processes, and local, national, and international economies.

The essays in this volume show that the changes in our midst have an importance that goes beyond our academic, intellectual interest. Each of us has a personal stake in the new technological order, since we are all being processed into the bits and bytes of the wired world, as recipients of health care and other public services, as activists waving electronic placards, as indigenous peoples seeking to build digital libraries or as women's groups striving to build local and global networks, as citizens filing electronic tax returns, assessing and comparing international on-line news sources, or seeking on-line information about today's debates in the House of Commons or Congress. The reader is introduced here to some of the emerging challenges and choices in Canadian politics and government in the new wired world. At the core of technological change one detects the 'stuff of politics': power and influence, value dilemmas and policy choices, issues of identity and of community. The process of technological innovation can be characterized by conflict, agenda-setting, and consensus-building. At every level of politics, at stake is the allocation of a new power resource with the potential to redefine the winners and the losers in the wired world. The title of this book reflects our sense that democratic practices may be substantially affected by the digital technology revolution. The advent of digital democracy has potentially both positive and negative implications for us as citizens, as well as clients of public services.

Discussions about information and communication technologies typically make reference to a range of developments, including personal computers, parallel processing systems, faxes, satellites, and the development of knowledge or expert systems, intra- and extra-nets. In the nineties, significant software developments are increasingly evident beyond the defence sector or 'hard' policy sectors such as finance, and into the so-called 'soft' policy fields such as health and education; indeed, 'software is rapidly exceeding the ability of any human to grasp both the overview and the detail of the most complex programs.'[3] The introduction of sophisticated technological systems into our policy worlds is altering our roles as 'clients' and as employees of re-engineered public-sector organizations. At least two key questions merit consideration when one considers the issue of connectivity between the array of information and communication technologies: (1) Who will create the new world information order? (2) Is the new world to be characterized by disorder? Three categories of forces will affect the way we address those questions by the year 2005:

1. Those who control information.
2. Those who control the pipelines to the information.
3. Those who control the software that gets the information to, through, and out of the pipelines and onto your screen.[4]

Beyond helping us understand the quest for control by multinational corporations such as Microsoft, addressing the questions above in the context of political and policy processes may help us understand how technological innovation will affect the public goods and services we receive as well as the ways in which they are delivered. For example, in the health care sector the application of computer networks and other ICT introduces new policy issues ranging from concerns about the confidentiality of our patient records to quality-of-work issues for health professionals, to the integrity and comparability of data and information available to public policy-makers, to the legal implications of medical expert systems. As citizens, we are increasingly targeted by political parties and interest groups that may use computerized demographic information systems to help them identify our individual socio-economic status, our interests as political consumers, and other data and information to allow them to construct the messages they think we want or need to hear. This book explores the political promise and policy options that technological prowess proffers. Assuredly, we have the potential to use the technologies in ways that extend our democratic processes, advance the nation's economic competitiveness and global security, enhance labour relations, and minimize ethnic, gender, and other socio-economic and political divisions. However, it will take more than hardwiring our governments, military institutions, schools, and hospitals to realize such ambitions. Harnessing our technological capabilities to advance human progress depends on political leadership and policy acumen; the willingness to rethink our institutions and processes with more than narrowly defined notions of efficiency in mind; the character and pervasiveness of our collective values and aspirations vis-à-vis those assumptions, values, and priorities that dominate our institutions and processes—and the technological systems used within them.

Never before have some of us enjoyed such immediate access to a wealth of on-line news sources, government documents, and other information sources from around the world. Increasingly, one can submit on-line contributions to, or simply read, the contributions made by interested citizens and various policy stakeholders to policy documents posted by different government departments and agencies. Justice Canada, for example, is a partner in the Access to Justice Network (ACJNet Information Services): 'Through an open discussion forum you can ask questions on law and justice. These questions are monitored and will be answered by ACJNet staff and visitors of the forum. ACJNet staff consists of librarians, educators and researchers that specialize in providing justice and legal information and referrals.'[5] Consider another example. Neither one's provincial or state legislature's library nor one's university library would have had easily accessible information in their stacks about the US federal government's efforts to use information technology to enhance government services to the nation's indigenous peoples. However, using an on-line search engine, it takes only a minute or two to discover the electronic gateway to such information—'Codetalk',[6] as well as a host of other related information sources—from the Aboriginal Rights Coalition in British Columbia[7] to the Centre for World Indigenous Studies' Fourth World Documentation Project,[8] to the Web site of the indigenous peoples of Hawaii outlining their efforts to restore the island's independence.[9]

'Access' in the new 'information order' remains, however, a profoundly important and controversial political issue. Consideration of access issues involves an examination of the barriers to access to services available on-line and barriers to access to servers, which allows one to disseminate data and information. The gap is widening between the 'information rich and poor', both with reference to the ability to access information and to produce and disseminate it. Figures released in January 1997 of a survey undertaken by a research firm in Texas, Matrix Information and Directory Services, ranked the top countries or regions with the most Internet hosts for each 1,000 people. The results, offered below, may surprise some readers.[10]

Some reasons why Finland might be a leader in its citizens' Internet use include the country's high education and literacy levels, its ethnically homogeneous citizenry, and the government's spending in basic research.[11] The five Nordic countries were among the top 15 countries in terms of having the most Internet-connected computers per capita.

There are growing concerns in Canada and the United States that the benefits of technological change are not improving the lot of those who reside in isolated and/or rural communities. Jeremy Rifkin concludes:

□ Table 1:   Internet Hosts, Various Countries, 1997

Country	Hosts per 1,000
1. Finland	62
2. Iceland	42
3. United States	31
4. Norway	30
5. Australia	24
6. Sweden	23
7. New Zealand	23
8. Canada	23
9. Switzerland	18
10. Singapore	18
11. Netherlands	16
12. Denmark	15
13. Britain	11
14. Austria	10

Global corporations are now capable of producing an unprecedented volume of goods and services with an ever smaller workforce. The new technologies are bringing us into an era of near workerless production at the very moment in world history when population is surging to unprecedented levels. The clash between rising population pressures and falling job opportunities will shape the geopolitics of the emerging high-tech global economy well into the next century.[12]

From this vantage, the world is increasingly dominated by an information élite and an unemployed, technologically displaced majority. Access and equity are both national and international issues. Within nations such as Canada, the question is whether women, indigenous peoples, and other underrepresented segments of the population will fall outside the parameters of the information society, while internationally, the question is whether and how divisions between nations—particularly between nations in the northern and southern hemispheres—will be aggravated rather than alleviated. As well, the 'access issue' is not merely a problem of access to hardware and software (although that is a significant consideration); it also involves literacy, defined in conventional terms as well as in terms of the new technical literacy requirements of this new era. Charles R. McClure states:

There is an educational disconnect between the rapidly developing communications technologies and information resources available to the public, and the public's ability to use these resources—our education system seems largely oblivious to the widening gap between the network literates and illiterates. . . . Federal policy and planning has been inadequate to assist the public with accessing these new repositories of information—will the networked society result in excluding a range of services and opportunities from those who, for whatever reason, cannot participate? How will the public make decisions about technology that will affect them, when a large portion of these individuals have little or no concept of its importance? How we address and resolve these issues will have a significant impact on how society evolves, how notions of literacy and a literate society evolve, and the degree to which social equity can be enhanced in this country.[13]

However sophisticated a system may be, technological change offers no easy 'solution' to alleviate complex social and political problems or ameliorate sociopolitical and economic cleavages. Indigenous peoples, women, and other underrepresented citizens in our political system have not yet found quick-fix technological 'solutions' to the challenges of economic dependence, weak political influence, and social inequity. We should not expect any technological silver bullet to deal with such complex and recalcitrant issues. For example, Canada's indigenous peoples could benefit greatly from the information highway. But their information requirements go far beyond the need for news sources; the high cost of travel, isolation, and the lack of health and social services mean a national information infrastructure is required if they and others residing in northern and remote areas are to benefit socially and economically from the communications revolution. While there are some indications of policy actions that further this objective, such as (in the economic area) Aboriginal Business Canada,[14] it is often the case that our technological know-how remains more advanced than the political will necessary to 'make change'.

It will take more than digital systems to spark the political interest of an increasingly cynical citizenry. Fostering an 'attentive' public will involve much more than the nationwide installation of hard drives and modems. When politicians or pundits talk about teledemocracy, what kind of electronic commonwealth are they envisioning? We know from other efforts to achieve on-line democracy, such as Santa Monica's public electronic network or the PEN system as it is called, that the introduction of ICT can serve to amplify the voice of those citizens who are already politically active.[15] While ICT can give pressure groups a relatively inexpensive and immediate alternative to inform, mobilize, and recruit membership, the technology can also serve to fragment the citizenry further along narrow, issue-specific interests.[16] We live in a period in which policy stakeholders are increasingly vocal in their quest to get a share of the public pie. One major obstacle, however, is that technological developments do not automatically enhance our communicative competence, not just in terms of communicating our own views and assumptions, but equally important, in terms of our willingness to hear alternative perspectives and perhaps to acknowledge their legitimacy.

While the potential of new telecommunities has often been extolled, less consideration is given to the negative temporal implications of borderless communication. For example, the new instantaneous communicative environment may imperil democratic deliberation. Taylor and Saarinen caution: 'if politics is the art of negotiation, speed is the death of the political. Negotiation takes time . . . negotiation and deliberate decision become impossible. Speed privileges certainty and assertion. . . . It is not possible to slow down long enough to allow time for uncertainty and questions.'[17] There is potential for the technology to facilitate communication between individuals dispersed across geographical and temporal boundaries; however, the quality of the dialogue within and between these discussion groups merits serious examination before we can state that the technology exposes individuals to a broad diversity of perspectives, fosters rational, constructive discourse, generates an exchange that stimulates greater understanding, and cultivates consensus between diverse and/or opposing interests. In the 'global village' we may be less—not more—communicatively competent. In the Information Era, we may possess a more impoverished, not a more enhanced, understanding of world issues, events, and ideas.

Clifford Stoll concludes that computerization does not contribute to the enhancement of our civilization: 'The heavily promoted information infrastructure addresses few social needs or business concerns. At the same time, it directly threatens precious parts of our society, including schools, libraries, and social institutions.'[18] We can, however, choose to embed objectives such as the realization of greater social justice into the new wired systems that dole out social assistance, just as we can choose to construct systems that realize a higher degree of paternalism and an increased capacity for surveillance.

Students of politics learn a key phrase in an introductory course: to govern is to choose. This collection provides insight into some of the choices being made in the new wired world. This is a book about politics and policy, with consideration paid to issues of structure, such as a national information infrastructure, and to questions of substance, such as pornography on the World Wide Web. The volume offers analyses of issues that range from those that have been persistent and growing policy challenges in the past quarter-century, such as privacy issues, to those that have only recently emerged, such as the ethical and legal implications of medical expert systems. *Digital Democracy* identifies and assesses the political promise and the peril of our wired world, as well as a representative selection of public policy options and constraints, so the reader will gain an understanding of the range of 'current' issues and the stakeholders whose interests may be affected by the process of technological innovation. The different dimensions and implications of technological change are clarified as a result of the range of perspectives the authors bring, from legal to philosophical. Further, the diversity of approaches represented in this book suggests that the process of technological assessment is, in most organizational contexts, a multi-stakeholder consensus-building initiative.[19] Certainly, such an initiative will involve discussion about hardware and software considerations. However, a common theme throughout this volume is that technological change is much more than a debate about bandwidth and browsers. The foundation for successful innovation involves clarification of the values, ideas, and ideals behind any initiative, the identification and consideration of alternative structures and processes that technology can facilitate, careful consideration of the implications for the host of stakeholders involved, and a consensus-building process to ensure that all the stakeholders have an opportunity to consider, accept, or contest the policy options.

Organization of the Book

This book is broadly divided into essays on political processes and on specific public policy issues. Several key themes, however, cut across these divisions and the papers themselves. One broad theme is participation and empowerment. A second is the way in which ICT affect the balance of power among institutions and individuals. A third is the impact of ICT on services that depend to a great degree on technology, such as health care; in an era of scarce fiscal resources for public services, a key question is whether the cost for innovation is worth the benefit.

Ronald Deibert's chapter addresses these themes in their broadest terms, providing a synoptic overview of the field of ICT and their political effects. His thesis is that the 'hypermedia environment' (digital-electronic communications) is altering the conventional landscape of world politics. The new technologies are creating new opportunities and social forces that are shifting the centre of political gravity away from states towards corporations, non-governmental organizations, and activists. States remain an important organizing framework for contemporary politics, but the new technologies are decentralizing power to a variety of non-territorial domains. He explores this argument through an analysis of four areas: transnational production, global finance, civil society networks, and state-security practices.

In terms of production, we are in the midst of a shift from national to transnational organization, that is, from making things largely within one nation-state to making those same things in complex co-operative arrangements in various states. The hypermedia environment makes it possible to co-ordinate these complex arrangements by allowing the transmission of vast amounts of data and participation in far-flung research and development efforts. In addition, this environment enables business to respond to localized consumer tastes and even permits small, locally oriented firms to reach out to a broader global market. The same technology makes possible a tightly integrated, global financial system that sees vast amounts of capital rocketing around the world in fractions of a second. Much of this is 'virtual' money—bits and bytes that flow across computer screens rather than money that is physically rooted to any one place.

The same forces are affecting non-governmental organizations and state-security practices. While global social movements have existed for at least a hundred years (e.g., the anti-slavery movement), the new technologies are making the emergence of a global civil society possible for the first time. Environmental and human rights organizations, for example, can co-ordinate and combine into networks that span the planet. As Deibert points out, these same organizations now have access to satellites and surveillance technologies that would have been inconceivable only a decade ago. Whereas some argue that the new hypermedia environment uniquely privileges state authorities by providing them with the technical capacity to penetrate citizens' privacy, Deibert suggests that, on balance, the new technologies are actually undermining state power by distributing these technical capacities broadly among non-state actors. Ultimately, this is the broadest impact of the new hypermedia environment: it 'unbundles' sovereignty and is creating a 'multi-centric' world where states are no longer the key organizing framework for political action.

Catherine Alexander addresses many of the same themes concerning sovereignty and the contemporary role of the state in her chapter on national security issues. During the Cold War, the contours of national security policy were more sharply defined, largely in conventional military terms—that is, weapons systems that were developed by a domestic arms industry. Today, however, most of the technologies important to the military are being developed first for commercial products, and are often produced through international co-operative arrangements. The new ICT are posing a fundamental challenge to how we conceive of state power, sovereignty, and appropriate military policy. The definition of what constitutes a security threat has had to change with the development of what is called 'dual-use technology', or technologies that have both military and non-military applications. Indeed, the centrality of technology and innovation to economic development means that power relations among states are changing, too: the country with the biggest guns may be less influential than the country with the brightest brains or the best technologies. This in turn has implications for economic statecraft and how states see their competitive advantage. Security may be less about arms and military might than about encouraging innovation, technological development, and political and market stability. The relative positions of states in the international arena may be altered by their technological prowess; relative technological asymmetry between nations, therefore, is increasingly affecting the international security system and the priorities of nation-states.

Like Deibert, Catherine Alexander emphasizes the decentralizing impact of the new ICT. Strategists now talk of 'information warfare' in which countries with relatively small reserves of conventional military resources such as armies and weapons could none the less pose grave threats by infiltrating sensitive computer systems. Of course, it may not be states at all that pose the threat, but non-state actors such as hackers or terrorist organizations. The nature of threat in this new security paradigm is thus changed. What changes, too, is what it means to pursue or reinforce security. In the conventional military model it means building reserves of domestic military strength; in the model being driven by ICT, it may mean enhancing technological capacities. But since those capacities depend increasingly on research and development in the commercial sector, these 'dual-use' technologies cannot be home-grown in the old military-industrial mode. Indeed, technology and the knowledge industries on which it depends are notoriously fluid, and questions of technology transfer and trade are becoming central to discussions of national security.

Michael Ogden critically examines the forces that lie behind the communications revolution. He reminds us that unless we recognize our own responsibilities and obligations in helping build the National Information Infrastructure and/or Global Information Infrastructure (NII/GII), we may end up with a system that serves only certain interests and is largely beyond public control. If the hype about the impact of new communications technologies on politics and society has even a grain of truth in it, then our societies will be radically transformed in the next decades, just as the Industrial Revolution and railroads transformed the nineteenth and twentieth centuries. Ogden invites us to think through various scenarios and understand their implications. After describing the nature of new technologies and the current American government vision of the NII/GII, Ogden assesses some of the more likely scenarios. He points out that the NII/GII will not likely be a single entity but more of an aggregation of different networks, and its emerging shape is open to question and struggle. One possibility is what he calls the 'Information Society' scenario as promoted by governments and private interests: a world of happy telecommuters, virtual consumers and citizens, and electronic learners attending virtual schools in which information becomes the key to economic and social interaction. It is a vision of expansive participation and services. The second scenario is what Ogden calls 'Couch Potatoes in Cyberspace'. This is a darker vision of the NII/GII, one in which business interests dominate, and those interests will focus on providing 'infotainment' to largely captive and passive audiences. As a primarily commercial medium, few efforts will be made to expand its capacity for social and political exchange and governance. The third scenario is 'Stage Transition' wherein the NII/GII proceeds in measured stages to respond to the needs—both commercial and social—of the public. The evolution will be driven by an ethic of interactivity and connectivity, and whatever enhances this will be attractive and supported. Even this scenario has to be treated cautiously, however. Ogden explores the dynamics of 'cyberdemocracy' (also see the chapters by Davis, Pal, and Cross on these issues), pointing out that instant democracy can make for unbridled majoritarianism that is as thoughtless as it is instant. He observes that in this emerging political context, it is all the more important to reflect on basic principles of civil rights and responsibilities and the constitutional protections required to actualize them.

Dineh Davis and Leslie Pal offer perspectives on the impact of ICT on the political mobilization of political communities. Pal looks at the mobilization around the US Communications Decency Act, or what one writer has called the 'Stamp Act of the Net'. In a medium noted for its fractiousness and fragmentation, the CDA fight welded together thousands of individuals and organizations in defence of the Internet. Pal analysed over 100 Web sites associated with the CDA issue and asked two questions: (1) who mobilized around the issue; and (2) what strategies were used in the campaign? Davis takes another approach, one of participant-observation and reflection on women's organizations and their mobilization in and through the Net around the Fourth World Conference on Women. Whereas the CDA was primarily a US issue, Davis explores an issue with global significance that attracted activism from around the world. As well, the chapters contrast a more traditional human rights issue—free speech—in the context of the Net, with cutting-edge concerns about social justice and the advantages and limits of networked technologies to deal with the challenges faced by the international feminist movement.

Davis places her analysis of the Beijing conference in the context of social movements. She notes that communications technologies have often been crucial to the growth and development of these movements. Recent analyses of social movements have stressed the need to go beyond traditional paradigms and frameworks, and Davis underscores the degree to which the women's movement has had to address unique issues such as systematic wartime rape, genital mutilation, and other gender-specific human rights violations. Understanding the contemporary global women's movement requires some of the tools from social movement analysis, but the scope and depth of the challenges faced by the movement also require a grasp of the proportions of the global concerns that have to be mobilized by that movement. The Fourth World Conference on Women provided a unique opportunity for women across the world to connect—and they connected in unprecedented ways through modern communication technologies. Davis analyses the key Beijing Internet mailing lists and uncovers some interesting gender patterns. Her chapter offers a series of sharp vignettes of various women at Beijing and their experiences. The key question that emerges in these very human stories is, why? Why travel to Beijing to connect when one could—and indeed, did—connect electronically in rich and varied ways?

Like Bill Cross and Leslie Pal, Davis addresses the problem of collective action through the Internet. Pal's chapter evokes a simultaneous sense of connectedness and disconnectedness; the Web sites were linked, but did this mean that a viable, collective movement was actually created? Cross is less equivocal in questioning the impact of ICT on collective action. Davis captures yet another dimension to our understanding of technology and community action: the persistent feeling among women that face-to-face interactions were necessary to mobilization and empowerment. This feeling was grounded, Davis argues, in some of the perils of 'electronic travel'. The potential to disguise identity and agendas, the impediments of high access costs and fee structures, limited access time, and language barriers—not to mention literacy—often make the Internet a less than perfect instrument of political mobilization. She concludes with reflections on the different way men and women might approach the new electronic media—differences that should give pause to those who see ICT in completely gender-neutral and culturally neutral terms.

Pal's chapter deals with the CDA, or Title V of the US Telecommunications Act of 1996. The CDA primarily focused on the Internet, though it embraced telephony as well. It defined virtually any communication relating to the sexual organs as lewd and obscene, potentially embracing passages from the Bible and Shakespeare as well as safe sex manuals and videos. Internet defenders were enflamed, and the psychology of their outrage doubtless was rooted in two factors: firstly, the sense that 'they' (the world of traditional communications media) were out to get 'us' (the new community based on the new technology), and secondly, that the Internet would be treated like television (which historically has attracted more government regulation) rather than print media. Various civil liberties organizations immediately launched lawsuits, and a coalition quickly formed to mobilize 'netizens' against the legislation. In reviewing the Web sites connected to the issue, Pal notes that they were almost exclusively anti-CDA. Like Cross's analysis of the impact of teledemocracy, Pal's chapter shows that participation actually consists of a narrower spectrum than one might anticipate. The chapter also indicates that the anti-CDA coalition consisted of both almost 'pure' netizen organizations (like the Electronic Frontier Foundation) and 'real world' organizations like the American Civil Liberties Association. In terms of strategies, Pal outlines court manoeuvres, on-line registration techniques, electronic letter-writing campaigns, 'Black Thursday' (Web pages were darkened in protest), and icons and images.

The CDA struggle illuminates several aspects of electronic mobilization, according to Pal. While the numbers are not overwhelming (and this accords with Cross's analysis from a different context), Pal argues that numbers are less important than the nature of the network itself. It is precisely the distributed networks of coalitions or organizations and information that the Internet facilitates. In this sense, the mobilization around the CDA was indeed unique. While tactics and strategies borrowed heavily from conventional mobilization, there were features (live feeds of court proceedings on the Internet, the sheer capacity to point people to mountains of information) that readily distinguished the CDA struggle from typical mobilization. Like Cross, Pal ends on a somewhat ambiguous note; yes, the technologies clearly made a difference in how this political issue evolved, but it is unclear whether the CDA experience can be transferred to other policy domains.

Bill Cross's chapter explores the issues of teledemocracy and the use of ICT by Canadian political parties and politicians. The issues have had only limited exploration in the Canadian political science literature.[20] Other treatments are mixed. Almost 40 years ago the American political scientist Robert Dahl expressed the optimistic view: 'Telecommunications can give every citizen the opportunity to place questions of their own on the public agenda and partici- pate in discussions with experts, policy-makers and fellow citizens.'[21] A con- temporary version of this thesis is Lawrence Grossman's argument that the 'big losers in the present-day reshuffling and resurgence of public influence are the traditional institutions that have served as the main intermediaries between government and its citizens: the political parties, labor unions, civic associa- tions, even the commentators and correspondents in the mainstream press.'[22] A darker side has been proposed by other authors, who fear that ICT in the hands of political parties will give them unprecedented power to manipulate the electorate. Cross points out that there are several political benefits posited for ICT applications in the service of public decision-making. The technology potentially makes direct participation possible because it overcomes the prob- lems of large, dispersed populations. Moreover, more citizens can participate because many of the burdens of participation are lowered, and this in turn will increase equity in public decision-making. Other proponents have highlighted the increased number of voters who will participate, as well as better commu- nication and information flows ICT can facilitate between the electorate and policy-makers.

Cross critically assesses all these claims through an analysis of four types of teledemocracy experiments: (1) the Reform Party's use of cable and telephone technology to communicate with voters; (2) the use by individual members of Parliament of telephone polling of their constituents; (3) MPs' use of the Inter- net; and (4) provincial parties' use of telephone technology for leadership selec- tion. The results are mixed. But it is precisely the value of Cross's analysis that he deals with a wide variety of attempts to use the technology and assesses each attempt on its own merits, since the technologies are quite different. Participa- tion rates across all the technologies have not been particularly high. Contrary to expectations, for example, leadership selection conducted by phone does not have significantly higher participation rates than traditional conventions. This is partly because of the ways in which these technologies are applied on the ground. Many people do not watch cable TV shows; many do not have access to the Internet; many (about a quarter of the population) do not have cable TV.

On the other hand, while participation may be disappointingly low, Cross discerns a greater degree of representativeness among those who participate than has traditionally been assumed, although they may be a better indicator of the intensity of opinion on some matters than a reflection of the population at large. Cross's greatest concern, however, is with the potentially fragmenting effect of the technology; while it may in some instances provide information to voters, it does so in a manner that discourages collective deliberation and consensus-building. Cross ends on a hopeful note, however. Teledemocracy still has the potential to make an important contribution.

The second theme of the balance of power between individuals and institutions is picked up in the essays by Julie Thorburn and Michael Mehta. At first blush it may seem difficult to discern this theme in a chapter on intellectual property and a chapter on pornography, but both chapters explore how technology provides new capacities as well as challenges for individuals and organizations. Thorburn's chapter underscores the degree to which the nature of information has changed with new technologies, and how both this change and the sheer importance of information to the modern economy create the need for new legal frameworks. Patents and copyright are two ways in which intellectual property has traditionally been regulated, with patents governing creations of a commercial nature and copyright protecting those whose creations were considered more aesthetic than commercial. As Thorburn points out, that distinction is now blurred with the rise of entertainment, communication, and computer industries. Information and privacy legislation has been a complement to these instruments, protecting information and records of public institutions and of individuals. Again, the needs of the computer industry have outstripped the capacity of these instruments to protect confidential information.

Thorburn argues for a new conceptualization of confidential business information as property, given the limitations of both the existing legislative instruments and the common law. She points up some of the limits to this approach as well (e.g., information that is shared is still retained by the originator), and briefly addresses the feasibility of developing a distinct category or concept of confidential information. Canada is somewhat behind both the United States and the United Kingdom in developing a uniform treatment of information as a commercial resource.

Michael Mehta's chapter addresses one of the most contentious aspects of the Internet, as well as a key issue in the realm of privacy, confidentiality, and the obligations and rights that governments have to regulate and censor information. Pornography on the Net was the stimulus to the Communications Decency Act, and almost every critical discussion of the Internet eventually comes around to expressing concern about the ease with which individuals (especially minors) can access adult-oriented materials. As Mehta points out, pornography itself is not a new problem. What is new is the capacity that ICT provide for the production and dissemination of these materials. While the materials themselves are not new, the ability to generate huge amounts of that material and distribute it via computer networks at virtually no cost to the distributor and its consequent accessibility are new. Like the other chapters in the book, one of Mehta's key contributions is the empirical analysis of something that is usually debated or discussed in somewhat fuzzy terms. How much pornography is actually on the Net, and what is its character? This study is an extension of an earlier analysis of pornography on the UseNet. That study found differences in theme and presentation in materials on the Internet from commercially available adult magazines and videos. In a finding that is sure to generate debate, this earlier study confirms some of the findings of the infamous Rimm study of pornographic images on the Internet; Rimm actually studied private bulletin boards, but his analysis has conventionally been dismissed by Internet aficionados as being far too narrow. Mehta also refers to more recent data that have tracked the impact of commercialization on the availability of pornographic images on the Net. His conclusion is that the impact has been discernible and, moreover, that the continued growth in the availability of adult-oriented materials illustrates the difficulty, if not impossibility, of using traditional command-and-control techniques to regulate the Internet.

The second half of Mehta's chapter discusses the appropriate regulatory regimes for the Internet. As he points out, the centrality of the Internet in the new information economy has encouraged two dynamics. The first is one of deregulation, as regimes that made sense for television and telephones are reconsidered in light of the needs for a seamless global infrastructure of electronic communication. The second dynamic is reactive—once the seamless web has been built, should any content whatsoever be available on it, or should there continue to be some social oversight of materials distributed electronically? Numerous information and privacy issues arise with the growth of the Internet, and pornography has become the 'sacrificial lamb' in the debate, a sort of testing ground as to what is technically feasible and socially acceptable. Technically, the problem is that the impulse of the Internet is to be dramatically decentralizing, while the traditional impulse of regulation has relied on central authority to develop and apply rules. This traditional paradigm is difficult in the face of the technology, and various alternatives that rely on self-regulation have been offered. Filtering and blocking software are examples, as is the development of codes of conduct for Internet providers. Mehta also gives some examples of public institutions that have begun to monitor Internet account use internally, a development that makes him somewhat uncomfortable.

Privacy issues also form the core of Ann Cavoukian's chapter. She points out that freedom and privacy are mutually supporting; we cannot have one without the other. Debates over and definitions of privacy have had a long philosophical history, but modern technology raises several unique and unfamiliar problems. 'Information privacy' becomes an important feature of any free society where large organizations, both public and private, have two new advantages. Firstly, they have access to quantities of private information about individuals that literally were inconceivable even a decade ago: what we buy, where we like to eat, what movies we enjoy, where we travel, and whom we phone, not to mention the usual mountain of medical, legal, and other types of information that we all now routinely give out when asked to contribute to the shape of our electronic footprints. Secondly, however, modern technology has made it possible to combine these bits of information in new ways, rapidly and inexpensively. A simple database and search program, for example, can match demographic, economic, and geographical information to give remarkably precise accounts about consumption patterns across any city. Cavoukian argues that there is an intimate link between information and identity; the information that others have about us also defines who we are. While there was always the potential to 'steal' identities by stealing information about others (e.g., robbing someone's passport or driver's licence), the concern is much greater today. Ironically, the very dependence of modern communication and information systems on 'user IDs' of some sort (credit cards, numbers, passwords, etc.) makes those IDs more valuable, and hence more susceptible to theft and fraud. Governments and private organizations, despite deep discomfort among the population with universal identity schemes or cards (an issue also explored in the Alexander and Stafford chapter), will continue to press for such things. Part of the answer in striking an appropriate balance is to make the distinction, as Cavoukian does, between all-purpose ID cards and special-purpose ones. The latter are more acceptable because they actually protect an individual's claim to certain benefits or services (e.g., a health card). Theft or fraud in this case does not risk exposing every facet of one's identity. Privacy commissioners have steadfastly resisted all-purpose cards, but have looked benignly on the special-purpose variant.

Of course, the nature of the new technologies is that they are interactive and on-line, and so privacy needs to be considered in this context as well. The second half of Cavoukian's chapter discusses the nature of public-key encryption efforts. These work through a combination of a private key (that only you know) and a public key (that everyone can know about). Cavoukian also discusses the next stage in the discussion about electronic privacy: privacy-enhancing technologies that decouple the personal identifier from a quantum of information. When that is done (e.g., when your health records cannot be linked to you personally), then the information becomes anonymous. Privacy enhancement is not the same as security enhancement, since the latter might still insist on identifying individuals. However, Cavoukian makes a convincing case that all that is required for better security—since no system is fail-safe—is the authentication of identity, not its revelation. Ending on an optimistic note, Cavoukian points out that information technologies contain the potential both to undermine our privacy and to enhance it. We may be at a stage where technologies can be devised to serve the needs of individuals as well as organizations.

Cynthia Alexander and Sue Stafford address similar themes in their chapter on technological developments in health care. Most of us are aware of high-tech medicine, even if only through watching *ER* or *Chicago Hope*. However, as their chapter makes clear, there are huge consequences that follow from the use of ICT for data acquisition, record-keeping, data analysis, communication, health monitoring, decision support, and education. One of the most important features of their analysis is the context they provide for an understanding of the impacts of technology on health care. For example, these technologies have largely been introduced as measures to enhance efficiency and reduce costs. This does not necessarily yield better care. As well, the gender imbalances that already exist in the health care system might actually be exacerbated rather than ameliorated through the introduction of some of these technologies.

The bulk of Alexander and Stafford's chapter examines the application of informatics in the health care system. The health care system has actually been quite slow in making effective use of information systems and decision-support technologies. In part this has been due to resistance from the medical profession itself, but also from the embedded institutional features of our health care system, which has tended to discourage information-sharing. However, the health care system is now undergoing major changes as the informatics industry pushes its products and governments look for savings. The introduction of standardized information and computer systems, however, raises the same privacy considerations addressed by Cavoukian. A June 1992 Supreme Court of Canada decision for the first time outlined patients' rights to view their own health records, and provincial privacy legislation is gradually ensuring that sensitive information of this type be strictly controlled. The need for care in these matters is amply illustrated in the detailed case study Alexander and Stafford provide of the APACHE (Acute Physiology Age Chronic Health Evaluation) III system. It is one of the most developed 'expert systems' available in the health care field, but even so it is clearly quite fallible. Beyond the problem of fallibility is the larger moral issue of how we wish key health-related decisions to be made. We should not be implementing technological solutions before we are aware of both the limits of those technologies as well as the range of stakeholders and interests that will be affected by that implementation. Technology is never neutral.

Jim May deals explicitly with the theme of empowerment and the potential that the new ICT have for helping one constituency that has often been disadvantaged through modern technology—indigenous or Aboriginal peoples.

May provides a fascinating overview of the communicative traditions of Aboriginal peoples, and while he is well aware of the toll that television and telecommunications are taking on traditional Aboriginal culture, he argues that, if properly used, these technologies can actually be turned towards the preservation and even enhancement of those same cultures.

May points out that Aboriginal peoples have two kinds of information needs, internal and external. The internal needs are primarily about preservation of Native languages, literature, art, and science. The external needs are keyed to sharing information as well as access to various storehouses of data beyond the Aboriginal communities. The chapter illustrates the possibilities in a variety of examples drawn from indigenous experiences and policy from around the world. May argues that these examples of information generation and sharing through various networks actually reflect some fundamental trends in contemporary communications technologies that are of some benefit to Aboriginal peoples. These include the rapidly emerging graphical interface of most computer systems, thus making them more accessible, and the falling costs of information technologies and publishing media. Trends, however, do not guarantee results, and May's chapter closes with some concrete initiatives that can be undertaken at the tribal, national, and international levels to ensure the informational robustness of indigenous cultures.

This range of authors, subjects, and approaches is deliberately wide and eclectic. The problem with assessing the impact of information technologies is that, because those technologies are so deeply entangled with every facet of society, it is quite conceivable that everything will be affected. It is hard to study everything, and so the usual approach is to take one slice of reality and examine it closely. To some extent we have adopted that approach by encouraging a focus on democratic politics and policy issues. However, since political science is only beginning to think carefully about the impact of ICT, we believe a wide-ranging collection of essays can be more helpful in stimulating insights and debate. We hope we've succeeded in that goal.

Internet Resources

Below is a short list of some Internet resources that will be of help in pursuing some of the issues raised in this chapter and throughout the book. Every effort was made to ensure that these links are current, but some addresses may have changed in the period between writing and publication.

On-line Resources for Political Scientists

Political Science and Technology
http://www.emory.edu/POINT/9.10.96/9.10.96.2.html

Electronic Resources of Interest to Canadian Political Scientists
http://www.sfu.ca/igs/CPSA.html

Berkeley's List of Political Science Resources on the Web
http://www.lib.berkeley.edu/GSSI/poliscie.html

Poly-Cy: West Virginia's Web Resource List for Political Scientists
http://www.polsci.wvu.edu/PolyCy/

Web sites on National Parliaments
http://www.soc.umn.edu/~sssmith/Parliaments.html

Federal Government of Canada
http://www.cpac.ca/english/resources/fedwww.html#info

CPAC Canadian Provinces Sites
http://www.cpac.ca/english/resources/provwww.html

Thomas—Legislative Information on the Internet (US)
http://thomas.loc.gov/

Worldwide Parties on the Web
http://www.geocities.com/~derksen/parties.htm

Internet en Français
http://www.uqat.uquebec.ca/~wwweduc/franc.html

VPAC-International
http://www.carleton.ca/~schwartz/vpaci.html

Understanding Technology: General

An Atlas of Cyberspace
http://www.geog.ucl.ac.uk/casa/martin/atlas/atlas.html

CyberWire Dispatch
http://cyberwerks.com:70/1/cyberwire

The Media Studies Centre
http://www.mediastudies.org/factsheet.html

Media Awareness Network
http://www.schoolnet.ca/medianet/

Wired Magazine
http://www.wired.com/wired/

University of Iowa: Digital Media
http://www.lib.uiowa.edu/gw/comm/digitalmedia/

Marshall McLuhan Links
http://www.law.pitt.edu/hibbitts/mcl.htm

Harold A. Innis Biography
http://www.regent.edu/acad/schcom/rojc/mdic/innis3.html

Howard Rheingold's Homepage
http://www.well.com/user/hlr/index.html

Sherry Turkle
http://web.mit.edu/sturkle/www/

Gender Considerations

Webnetworks WomensWeb
http://community.web.net/womensweb/index.html

Women Leaders Online
http://wlo.org/

Canadian Women's Internet Association
http://www.women.ca/

Cybergrrl
http://www.cybergrrl.com/planet/

Feminist Activist Resources on the Net
http://www.igc.apc.org/women/feminist.html

Voices of Women Online
http://www.voiceofwomen.com/

The Christian Science Monitor's Cybercoverage
http://www.csmonitor.com/mixed_media/mixed_media.html

Computers and Democracy

World-Wide E-Democracy Page
http://www.freenet.msp.mn.us/govt/e-democracy/e-demos.1.html

Electronic Democracy Library
http://www.e-democracy.org/intl/library/

The Center for Democracy and Technology
http://www.cdt.org/

Highway1
http://www.highway1.org/

Democracy.net
http://www.democracy.net/

The Network Observer
http://communication.ucsd.edu/pagre/tno.html

US Online News Citizen's Toolbox
http://www.usnews.com/usnews/wash/people.htm

Project Vote Smart
http://www.vote-smart.org/

The Jefferson Project
http://www.voxpop.org:80/jefferson/

Electronic Frontier Canada
http://insight.mcmaster.ca/org/efc/efc.html

Policy Issues

Cyber-Rights and Cyber-Liberties (UK)
http://www.leeds.ac.uk/law/pgs/yaman/yaman.htm

IT Security
http://www.rcmp-grc.gc.ca/html/tss-2-e.htm

Defence and Security Institutes
http://www.umanitoba.ca/centres/defence/institut.htm

Information Warfare
http://www.umanitoba.ca/centres/defence/institut.htm

Net Law News
http://www.mindspring.com/~moceyuna/

World Intellectual Property Organization
http://www.wipo.int/

Privacy Commissioner of Canada
http://infoweb.magi.com/~privcan/

The Industry Canada and McGill University Telehealth Study
http://www.arts.mcgill.ca/gpc/telehealth/

First Nations Peoples

The Assembly of First Nations' Links
http://www.afn.ca/links.htm

Center for World Indigenous Studies' Fourth World Documentation Homepage
http://www.halcyon.com/FWDP/fwdp.html

Innu Nation
http://www.innu.ca/

Index of Native American Resources on the Internet
http://hanksville.phast.umass.edu/misc/NAresources.html

Aboriginal Business Canada
http://strategis.ic.gc.ca/sc_mangb/abc/engdoc/homepage.html

Codetalk (US)
http://www.codetalk.fed.us/cdtk.html

For Fun

The Red Rock Eater
http://communication.ucsd.edu/pagre/rre.html

Doonesbury Electronic Townhall
http://www.doonesbury.com/

Political Site of the Day (US)
http://www.penncen.com/psotd/

Portraits in Cyberspace
http://persona.www.media.mit.edu/1010/Exhibit
/Prizes.html

Notes

1   Steve Lohr, 'The Great Unplugged Masses Confront the Future', *The New York Times Online*,
     CyberTimes, 21 Apr. 1996.
2   Sissela Bok, 'Grappling with Principles', in Rushworth M. Kidder, ed., *An Agenda for the 21st
     Century* (Cambridge, Mass.: MIT Press, 1987), 12.
3   John E. Midwinter, 'Convergence of Telecommunications, Cable, and Computers in the 21st
     Century: A Personal View of the Technology', *Crossroads on the Information Highway: Conver-
     gence and Diversity in Communications Technologies*, the 1995 Annual Review of the Institute
     for Information Studies, a joint program of NORTEL and The Aspen Institute, Queenstown. URL:
     http://www.aspeninst.org/dir/polpro/CSP/IIS/95/Midwinter.html [06/06/97].
4   Ashley Dunn, 'Big War in Cyberspace. What if Nobody Wins?', *New York Times Online, Cyber-
     Times Extra*, 7 Apr. 1996.
5   http://www.acjnet.org/info/infoserv.html
6   http://www.codetalk.fed.us/cdtk.html
7   http://www.com/~arcbc/
8   http://www.halcyon.com/FWDP/fwdp.html
9   http://www.hawaii-nation.org/index.html
10   Youssef M. Ibrahim, 'As Most Wired Nation, Finland Has Jump on 21st Century', *New York
     Times Online, CyberTimes*, 20 Jan. 1997.
11   Ibid.
12   Jeremy Rifkin, *The End of Work: The Decline of the Global Labour Force and the Dawn of the
     Post-Market Era* (New York: G.P. Putnam's Sons, 1995), 207.
13   Charles R. McClure, 'Network Literacy in an Electronic Society: An Educational Disconnect?',
     The Knowledge Economy: The Nature of Information in the 21st Century, the 1993–4 Annual
     Review of the Institute for Information Studies, a joint program of NORTEL and The Aspen Insti-
     tute, Queenstown. URL: http://www.aspeninst.org/dir/polpro/CSP/IIS/93-94/93-94.html
     [06/06/97].
14   Industry Canada, *Aboriginal Business Canada*, URL:
     http://strategis.ic.gc.ca/sc_mangb/abc/engdoc/abc_serv.html [06/06/97].
15   See C.J. Alexander, 'Plugging into New Currents: The Use of New Information and Communica-
     tion Technologies in Party Politics', in Hugh G. Thorburn, ed., *Party Politics in Canada*, 7th edn
     (Scarborough, Ont.: Prentice-Hall, 1996), 594–610.
16   See William T. Stanbury and Ilan B. Vertinsky, 'Assessing the Impact of New Information Tech-
     nologies on Interest Group Behaviour and Policymaking', in Thomas J. Courchene, ed., *Technol-
     ogy, Information and Public Policy, The Bell Canada Papers on Economic and Public Policy*
     (Kingston: John Deutsch Institute for the Study of Economic Policy, 1995), 293–379.
17   Mark C. Taylor and Esa Saarinen, *Imagologies: Media Philosphy* (New York: Routledge, 1994), 6.

18 Clifford Stoll, *Silicon Snake Oil: Second Thoughts on the Information Highway* (Toronto: Double-day, 1995).

19 See Edward Wenk, Jr, *Tradeoffs: Imperatives of Choice in a High-Tech World* (Baltimore: Johns Hopkins University Press, 1989).

20 See Leonard Preyra, 'Changing Conventions: Plebiscitarian Democracy and Party Leadership Selection in Canada', in Thorburn, ed., *Party Politics in Canada*, 7th edn, 213–24.

21 Robert A. Dahl, *Democracy and Its Critics* (New Haven: Yale University Press, 1989), 339.

22 Lawrence K. Grossman, *The Electronic Republic: Reshaping Democracy in the Information Age* (New York: Viking, 1995), 15.

Chapter 2

ALTERED WORLDS: SOCIAL FORCES IN THE HYPERMEDIA ENVIRONMENT

Ronald J. Deibert

Beginning around the fifteenth and sixteenth centuries in Europe, during what
has now become known as the medieval-to-modern transformation, patterns of
human collective organization underwent fundamental change.[1] Driven by
environmental, technological, and social factors, the overlapping and multiple
layers of feudal authority gave way to a more rigid demarcation of political
space—territorially distinct and legally autonomous political communities. The
principal embodiment of this new form of collective organization was state sovereignty. It affirmed the legal independence of states from each other, thus formally dissolving all but a few shared cultural traits (e.g., Christianity) as overarching links between them. The absence of political authority at the
international level became the norm.

This mode of organizing political space spread gradually over the entire
planet by the twentieth century, and it was strongly reaffirmed following decol-
onization in the mid-1950s.[2] Today it stands as the dominant paradigm of
world order at a global level, reinforced daily by a wide range of social, political, and economic activities. At the most basic level, the overwhelming majority of people around the world vote in a single state, carry passports of a single
state, and consider themselves to be citizens of and thus subject to the government and laws of a particular sovereign state. Breaches of sovereign territorial
boundaries are still strongly condemned, and the majority of independence
movements around the world still overwhelmingly define their political goals
in terms of sovereign aspirations.[3]

While this modern 'paradigm' runs deep in social and political practices,
the advent of digital-electronic telecommunications—what I call the 'hypermedia environment'—is altering the landscape upon which world politics unfolds,
creating new opportunities and constraints for social forces with major consequences for the way political authority is ordered at a global level. The old paradigm is giving way to new post-modern configurations of political space. In
this chapter, I sketch out social forces in four areas—transnational production,
global finance, civil society networks, and state-security practices—that I see
flourishing in the hypermedia environment, and how these, in turn, are contributing to a fundamental shift in world order.[4] Whereas once political authority was parcelled and segmented into territorially distinct and mutually exclusive sovereign states, today such authority is dispersing and decentralizing to
multiple, non-territorial domains—to corporations, bond-rating agencies, and
non-governmental organizations and activists, as well as to states. Such a fundamental reordering of political space puts into serious doubt the continued
utility of much of our thinking about world politics. In the hypermedia environment, traditional ways of seeing the world are fast becoming dysfunctional,
if not obsolete.

From National to Transnational Production

In the modern world order, economic production has generally been a 'national' affair undertaken in a 'national' context, and has been shaped and driven by a desire for self-sufficiency and autonomy. Of course, national economic production has never been completely insulated from the world economic system. But, in general, it has been organized, planned, measured, and thus overwhelmingly contained within discrete sovereign-territorial boundaries.[5] As Kurtzman notes, 'most of the world's economy [during the nineteenth century] remained as separate islands only tangentially linked by slowly moving steam- and sail-powered ships, trains, and (beginning in 1844) the telegraph.'[6] Prior to the development of hypermedia, trade among states—which often reached proportionately high levels relative to gross national product (GNP) during times of stability—was predominantly of the 'arm's-length' variety, with nationally produced goods and commodities being transported across state boundaries.[7] In the hypermedia environment, however, the organization of production is quickly diffusing across territorial boundaries, creating a complex web of transnational production arrangements. There are three main reasons for this 'fit' between transnational production and the hypermedia environment.

The most obvious way in which the hypermedia environment favours the transnationalization of production is by providing a way to communicate vast amounts of voice, text, and image data instantaneously throughout the world. Such capabilities encourage what Hepworth has called 'multilocational flexibility' by reducing the prior constraints associated with the risks and costs of operating over large distances.[8] One increasingly popular example of multilocational flexibility is the segmentation of different components of the firm's production process into multiple national locations. This not only neutralizes swings in currency differentials among national economies, but also takes advantage of 'niche' regulatory climates or labour pools that favour specific processes (e.g., marketing, management, 'back-room' data-processing, and/or research and development). For example, United Technologies operates more than 120 manufacturing plants in 24 countries, with sales and service offices in 56 countries. Production of its Elevonic 411 elevator exemplifies the segmentation of production: the French branch built the door systems; the Spanish division handled the small-geared components; the German subsidiary handled the electronics; the Japanese unit designed the special motor drives; and the United States/Connecticut group co-ordinated the systems integration.[9] Perhaps the most common example of this transnational disaggregation is data-entry, 'back-office' jobs—a phenomenon that has given rise to the term 'global office'.[10]

The hypermedia environment not only favours the transnationalization of production internal to individual firms, it also facilitates it among multiple firms. By making it easier to co-ordinate strategic alliances, joint ventures, and joint production arrangements among separate firms, regardless of the geographical distance that separates them, the hypermedia environment provides a way for individual firms to spread out the risks and costs of research and development. This provides an entry into foreign markets that might otherwise be precluded by tariffs or other regulatory restrictions.[11] Although examples of these types of arrangements can be found prior to hypermedia, they have flourished since their development, becoming a much more dominant feature of the global economy. According to James and Weidenbaum, 'The pace at which cooperative strategic alliances between firms occur is accelerating, particularly in high-tech, high-growth industries, such as computers, semiconductors, telecommunications, electronics, chemicals, and industrial equipment.'[12] In the aerospace and automotive industries, 'every major company has formed alliances with foreign competitors in an effort to spread the costs and risks of developing new products, as well as to ensure access to overseas markets.'[13] Through desktop teleconferencing systems, faxes, and computer networks (in particular, electronic mail), transnational collaborative arrangements can be as closely co-ordinated as if they were in the same building. Today, it is not uncommon for design teams located thousands of miles from each other to work on the same project in real-time over computer networks.

These types of collaborative ventures have also transformed the nature of subcontracting and traditional supplier-client relationships, with suppliers being drawn more closely into the research and design of their clients' products. Inventories can be adjusted electronically in what has been referred to as 'just-in-time' delivery of parts and products. Just-in-time interaction could not take place without the use of electronic data interchange, or EDI, which maintains a constant electronic link between companies like Wal-Mart and one of its major suppliers, Procter & Gamble; or Domino's Pizza, which uses a computer network called 'Domilink' to co-ordinate supplies among its 1,100 suppliers located at 28 North American distribution sites.[14] Such complex electronic links reduce the constraints of operating supplier-client relationships over large distances since inventories can be constantly monitored from afar and delivery times adjusted. These electronic connections link companies from all parts of the production chain, both domestically and internationally, into a rapid-response/mutual-adjustment system that often begins the moment the bar-code is scanned at the point of purchase.

A second way in which the hypermedia environment favours the transnationalization of production is by allowing more flexible production keyed to the vagaries of local consumer tastes. As hypermedia provide knowledge-intensive/software-based production lines, rapid and abrupt shifts in production output or major changes in advertising campaigns become feasible. These shifts can be highly sensitive to 'localized consumer preferences and national political constraints without compromising their economic efficiency'.[15] This particular capability contradicts the widespread belief that globalization of production necessitates homogenization.[16] To the contrary, in order to operate successfully, transnational corporations have to be willing to accommodate local conditions: a strategy captured by the former head of Sony, Akio Morito, who called it 'global localization', and a pervasive concept within the multinational business literature today.[17] With computer-assisted consumer profiles and other market-surveillance mechanisms, firms can maintain a constant watch over disparate localities around the globe, enabling diversified responses to local conditions, as well as rapid adjustments in advertising campaigns to influence parochial consumer tastes.

A third way in which the hypermedia environment favours the transnationalization process is by enabling small, locally based firms to reach a global audience. While globalization is generally associated with massive, multibillion-dollar transnational enterprises, hypermedia increasingly allow small firms with niche products to reach a global market and thus compete with industry giants in select areas. The best example of this phenomenon is the rapid commercialization of the Internet, where individuals or small firms with low initial investment can market products to a rapidly increasing, global Internet audience through the mere posting of Web-site advertisements.[18] Everything from floral arrangements to pizzas, from computer software to legal consultation, is now marketed on the Internet. Initially, security concerns among credit card companies limited the scope of Internet commercialization. However, innovative credit solutions have been made to sidestep these concerns ('Digicash' and 'Cybercash' are the two most prominent examples), while credit card companies are sponsoring research to devise better encryption technologies.[19] What might be called (in an inversion of Morito's phrase) 'local globalization' could not take place on such a large scale without the low-cost, planetary reach afforded by hypermedia to the average individual producer. As the Internet continues its exponential growth around the world, and as more private companies flock to the Net, the connection between a considerable portion of the production, marketing, and sale of goods and services will become detached from 'place', existing only in the non-territorial 'space' of globally linked computer networks.

The result of this convergence between the hypermedia environment and the transnationalization of production is the rapid emergence of a much more complex and cross-cutting non-territorial organization of production. Not only are new corporate structures emerging that are less hierarchical and more 'web-like', but firms all over the planet are now embedded in a global 'networked' environment composed of overlapping and complex transnational production arrangements ranging from formal equity-sharing or co-production arrangements to informal alliances and joint ventures. Although we are still far from a completely 'borderless' economy, the changes that have already occurred are significant and growing, suggesting important consequences for the architecture of political authority.

The Emergence of Global Finance

The movement of money across borders is not a new phenomenon but has developed along with modern industrial capitalism.[20] However, as with production, finance has been predominantly a national affair, with whatever money moving across borders being closely tied to the financing of international trade. Only sporadically was it also used to channel capital into overseas investment. Right up until the 1950s and 1960s, 'international finance served to lubricate trade flows and to finance the operations of transnational firms and governments in a relatively controlled system.'[21] The subsidiary role of finance to production and trade throughout this period was a product of both technological constraints, which limited the mobility of finance capital, and deliberate policy initiatives designed to keep finance the 'servant' of production.[22]

The rise of a globally integrated financial sector has had a host of causes, making it futile to identify any one 'prime mover'.[23] Although the hypermedia environment is considered to be crucial to this process, it is virtually impossible to disentangle its impact from other factors.[24] One such factor was the transnationalization of production discussed above: as production became global, so did banks and financial institutions. Transnational banks in particular became more widespread in the 1960s and 1970s to service the demands of multinational corporations.[25] A second factor was the creation of new financial instruments, especially the creation of the so-called 'Eurodollar' market. Originating in London's less regulated and more highly sophisticated financial climate, the Eurodollar market exploded after the 1973 oil crisis, allowing investment of petro-dollars by oil-producing states where they were 'untaxed, anonymous, and profitable'.[26] The result was a sudden explosion in the volume of financial capital circulating around the globe—'a gigantic pool of quasi-stateless mobile capital, not subject to political authority or accountability'.[27] A third factor was the liberalization of domestic capital controls—a process that can be traced back to the collapse of Bretton Woods in 1971, the closing of the 'gold window', and the subsequent removal of controls over the flow of money across borders.[28] The change 'redefined money', created 'enormous arbitrage possibilities and set the stage for the invention of a myriad of new financial products'.[29] International finance suddenly became, in Strange's apt phrase, 'casino capitalism'.[30]

None of these factors can be divorced from the development of the hyper-media environment. In fact, finance capital and communication technologies have had a symbiotic relationship dating back to the telegraph. The 'fit' between global finance and hypermedia is not difficult to understand when one considers the important relationship between time and money. In the United States alone, on an average day, 14,000 banks transfer about $2.1 trillion over their local data networks to settle account balances. The cost for a bank of financing an internal deficit, even if it is only for overnight, translates into strong incentives to develop networks that are efficient and quick.[31] One recent study showed that a major investment in hypermedia systems gave one major US bank a 10-second advantage over competitors—a powerful advantage that meant gains on the order of billions of dollars.[32] The ultimate goal, according to banking technology experts, is 'just-in-time' cash, or what has been called a 'disappearing float'—a real-time clearance of balances that would be incon-ceivable without hypermedia.

The consequence of the 'time is money' imperative for the financial sector has been an explosion of hypermedia applications, as innovations in informa-tion technology saturate the industry—each new product and service provid-ing yet more information with more speed, and more computing power than before, on a global scale. Stock exchanges now no longer require a physical trading floor as electronically linked exchanges operate globally in a 24-hour marketplace. Examples are numerous and increasing, and include such systems as: the Stock Exchange Automated Quotation (SEAQ) of London; the US-based NASDAQ network; the electronic trading system Globex, developed jointly by Reuters and the Chicago Mercantile Exchange; and the Computer Assisted Trading System (CATS) centred in Toronto. These larger systems are now joined by on-line trading 'clubs' on the World Wide Web, which allow trading to take place remotely from PCs located anywhere in the world at any time. Complex artificial-intelligence software systems are then developed by securities firms to handle vast, complex stock portfolios that react instantaneously to slight shifts in the market.[33] On-line services, such as Reuters, Telerate, and Quotron in the United States, and Extel and Datastream in Europe, plus smaller, hand-held devices like Quotreks, compete with each other and with global television net-works, such as CNN and Asian Business news, to provide the most up-to-date information on international trading activities.[34] Financial institutions now invest heavily in transnational communications infrastructural projects to help facilitate global trading activity as a whole.[35] Leased lines or specialized elec-tronic transfer services, such as the Society of Worldwide Interbank Financial Telecommunications (or SWIFT), then provide the ever-intensifying, real-time links among these institutions.[36]

Like the tightening of a knot, each advanced application of hypermedia in the financial sector furthers and deepens the global integration of capital markets in a planetary web of complex speculative financial flows. In ways that are similar to the overlapping layers of transnational production, the players in this 'casino capitalism' market represent a complex montage of both massive global enterprises and small entrepreneurs with a planetary reach afforded by hyper-media. The 'big' players—financial institutions like Citicorp, Chase Manhattan, Merrill Lynch, Salomon Brothers, Barclays, National Westminster, Warburg, and Nomura—have offices around the world and dominate trading: typically, the top 20 institutions in a market account for between 40 and 60 per cent of worldwide transactions.[37] Because of the way the hypermedia environment links the globe into a 24-hour market, companies like Salomon Brothers, which can trade up to $2 trillion US in stocks, bonds, and commodities in a single year, are 'always open, everywhere'.[38] Stocks, bonds, and other instruments of debt are continuously traded, bounding from exchange to exchange in response to slight shifts in the market—often without human intervention as computer programs handle portfolios for traders. In the words of Thrift and Leyshon, 'we might conceive of the international financial system as an elec-tronically networked, constantly circulating, nomadic "state", operating 24 hours a day around the world.'[39]

The entire volume of capital speeding through hypermedia currents is thus truly staggering, and at times seems almost incomprehensibly large compared to more readily identifiable figures. Kurtzman offers the following startling comparison:

> Every day, through the 'lobe' in the neural network that is New York, more than $1.9 tril-lion electronically changes hands at nearly the speed of light. These dollars—and the cares, hopes, and fears they represent—appear as momentary flashes on a screen. . . . Every three days a sum of money passes through the fibre-optic network underneath the pitted streets of New York equal to the total output for one year of all of America's companies and all of its workforce. And every two weeks the annual product of the world passes through the network of New York—trillions and trillions of ones and zeros representing all the toil, sweat, and guile from all of humanity's good-faith efforts and all of its terrible follies.[40]

CS First Boston, a leading global bond trader based in New York, trades more money each year than the entire GNP of the United States.[41] As will be shown below, these volumes assume a special significance when they are considered in relation to state autonomy over macroeconomic policies.

In response to this massive, global 24-hour marketplace, new spaces and flows are arising, and centres and 'hubs' have emerged that may provide a glimpse of the evolving architecture of the post-modern world order. Large cities, such as New York, London, Tokyo, Singapore, and Hong Kong, are assuming more importance as 'command centres' in the global 'finanscape'—what an *Economist* survey referred to as 'Capitals of capital'.[42] According to

Thrift and Leyshon, these 'ordering centres' arise because 'the interdependent connectedness of disembedded electronic networks promotes dependence on just a few places like London, New York and Tokyo where representations can be mutually constructed, negotiated, accepted and acted upon.'[43] They act not so much as national cities as they do world cities—interfacial nodes in the global hypermedia environment.

Also assuming more importance are the many 'offshore' micro-states that 'have been transformed by exploiting niches in the circuits of fictitious capital.'[44] The term 'offshore' is especially significant: in Ruggie's words, it signifies the way emerging financial practices strain our current vocabulary, 'as though they existed in some ethereal space waiting to be reconceived by an economic equivalent of relativity theory.'[45] Likewise, Roberts notes that 'these offshore financial centres are sites that dramatically evince the contrary and complex melding of offshore and onshore, of national and international, and of local and global.'[46] For example, because of its strategic time-zone location and lax regulations, the tiny Cayman Islands 'house' 546 banks from all around the world, of which only 69 maintain any kind of physical presence.[47] The quintessential 'offshore' market is the Eurodollar or Eurocurrency market. Martin calls the Eurocurrency market 'stateless' money.[48] The prefix 'Euro', as Roberts points out, is a misleading vestige of an earlier time; today, the Eurocurrency market involves a dynamic new geography of flows 'stretching from Panama to Switzerland and on to Singapore and beyond'.[49]

The changes to global production and finance outlined above have undermined the effective power of state regulatory systems within territorial-political jurisdictions.[50] Firstly, states around the world are increasingly conforming to a particular model of governance—variously called the 'transmission belt' state[51] or the 'competition' state[52]—which defines itself and its interests according to the pressures and values of global capitalism. Governments at all levels—provincial, state, and regional—now engage in competitive deregulatory and re-regulatory 'locational tournaments' designed to attract global investment.[53]

The second consequence has been the creation and emergence of multiple and overlapping layers of authority designed to respond to and govern globalizing economic forces. Most states now find themselves enmeshed in an ever-widening network of informal and formal international institutions, regimes, organizations, and regional trading blocs that have arisen in reaction to the transnationalization of production and finance outlined above. Examples of these layers of global 'governance' are numerous, ranging from more informal bodies, such as the Trilateral Commission or the G-7 economic summits, to more formal bodies, such as the recently created World Trade Organization, to regional bodies and agreements, such as the European Union, the North American Free Trade Agreement, and the Asia-Pacific Economic Council, to more specialized, functional bodies, such as the World Bank, the International Monetary Fund, and the Bank for International Settlements.

Global Civil Society Networks

A third set of social forces thriving in the hypermedia environment is transnational social movements with multiple, overlapping, and often competing interests. These new movements represent the emergence of what Lipschutz has called a 'global civil society': that is, transnationally organized political networks and interest groups largely autonomous from any one state's control.[54] In ways that are similar to the transnationalization of production and finance outlined above, the rise of a global civil society presents fundamental challenges to the modern world order paradigm by diffusing a dense network of social and interest group activities across territorial-political boundaries. Although hypermedia do not generate these new social movements, they do create a communications environment in which such activities flourish dramatically. As computer networks have grown, transnational social movements have exploded, forming complex non-territorial-based links that defy the organization of political authority in the modern world order.

To some extent, there have always been social movements throughout modernity whose interests transcend political boundaries. A good example, outlined by Nadelmann, is the nineteenth-century anti-slavery campaign initiated by the British and Foreign Anti-Slavery Society.[55] Founded in 1839, the Society lobbied to abolish slavery around the world, calling international conventions and mass meetings and circulating petitions and propaganda to élites in foreign countries. Movements like this continued to grow in the nineteenth and twentieth centuries, spurred by new liberal principles of human rights and a burgeoning middle class.[56] These movements continued to grow such that by the 1980s they were becoming a common feature of the world political landscape (though one that was generally overlooked by traditional international relations theorists). For example, human rights non-governmental organizations (NGOs) alone increased from 38 in 1950, to 72 in 1960, to 103 in 1970, to 138 in 1980, to 275 by 1990.[57] The Union of International Associations now recognizes some 14,500 international NGOs.[58] Their visibility in a wide variety of international forums and conventions, and their growing influence on both international and domestic policy, make them hard to ignore. As an illustration of the growing importance of some of these groups, NGOs provided $8.3 billion in aid to developing countries in 1992—13 per cent of development assistance worldwide.[59]

The movements that together comprise this emerging global civil society are not homogeneous in their orientation or organization, but rather consist of scores of 'heteronomous' networks of political associations.[60] The causes around which these movements are formed are equally varied. Examples are numerous and include groups in issue-areas such as the environment (e.g., Greenpeace, Earth First!), human rights (e.g., Amnesty International), indigenous peoples' networks, gay and lesbian movements, and women's rights associations. As Spiro notes, 'Environmentalists, human rights advocates, women, children, animal rights advocates, consumers, the disabled, gays, and indigenous peoples have all gone international.'[61] The majority of these transnational social movements do not operate through the traditional lobbying procedures and political channels of participation as defined by state structures.[62] Most of them cannot be characterized as political parties campaigning for government office. Indeed, their very importance as a challenge to the modern world order paradigm lies in their willingness to sidestep traditional political structures and sovereign boundaries 'to address international problems, and to reflect a global sensitivity'.[63] They are 'decentred, local actors, that cross the reified boundaries of space as though they were not there',[64] seeking to organize activities, and educate and motivate populations directly.

The rise in the visibility and density of these transnational social movements cannot be divorced from the communications technologies that have empowered them. As Spiro notes, 'this explosion in nongovernmental activity reflects the dramatically heightened permeability of national borders and improvements in communications that have allowed territorially dispersed individuals to develop common agendas and objectives at the international level.'[65] Although telephones and faxes have long been staples for international co-ordination, computer networks—in particular, the Internet—have vastly transformed the scope and potential of these transnational movements. In fact, transnational environmental groups were among the first to realize the potential of the early computer networks as facilitators of their organization. EcoNet, for example, was formed in 1982—long before the popularity of the Internet—and now spans over 70 countries.

Today, EcoNet is only one part of a vast web of networks operating through the Internet and linked together under the broad umbrella called the Association for Progressive Communications (APC). The APC is a non-profit consortium of 16 international member networks serving approximately 25,000 individuals and NGOs in 94 countries.[66] According to Sallin, it is 'the most extensive global computer networking system dedicated to social and environmental issues'.[67] The member networks comprising the APC include Alternex (Brazil); GreenNet (England); Nicaro (Nicaragua); NordNet (Sweden); Pegasus (Australia); Web (Canada); Comlink (Germany); Glasnet (Russia); Equanex (Ecuador); Chasque (Uruguay); SangoNet (South Africa); Wamani (Argentina); GLUK (Ukraine); Histria (Slovenia); and LaNeta (Mexico). One of the larger members of the APC network is the US-based Institute for Global Communications (IGC), which itself is an umbrella organization encompassing a wide variety of social and environmental movements, subdivided into five main specialty networks: EcoNet, PeaceNet, ConflictNet, WomensNet, and LaborNet. Together, these linked networks share enormous databases containing everything from government department phone numbers and addresses to scientific studies and from calendars of events to various government regulations and accords, all hyper-linked and searchable by keyword. Over 80 'alternative' news and information services are available through the APC, including the Third World InterPress Service, the UN information service, and Greenpeace News. Members engage in electronic conferences, communicate directly through electronic mail, and distribute information, including urgent human rights or environmental violations. Almost every environmental, human rights, or issue-oriented NGO is now either affiliated with, or can be accessed through, the APC network.

Of course, not included in the formal APC network are the many informal transnational social movements linked through Internet bulletin boards, newsgroups, and mailing lists. For example, Asian democracy activists (and any other potential interested party, for that matter) exchange information through computer mailing lists such as BurmaNet (strider@igc.apc.org); China News Digest (cnd-info@cnd.org); Vietnam (viet-net-info@media.mit.edu); and Indonesia-L (apakabar@clark.net). Separate UseNet newsgroups typically centred on human rights issues can be found in such areas as soc.culture.burma, soc-culture.saudi-arabia, and soc.culture.china. Countless other 'private' exchanges take place through regular electronic mail and in similar discussion groups on private computer networks such as Compuserve, Prodigy, and America On-Line.

Although computer networks form the vital backbone of transnational social movement communications, their day-to-day activities are complemented by other components of the hypermedia environment as well. For example, Greenpeace (which has over 40 offices in 30 countries) has its own satellite communications link, called 'Greenlink', that connects its ships and offices.[68] Desktop publishing capabilities provide these movements with more effective (and affective) means of distributing pamphlets and newsletters on a grassroots level. In this way, local nodes in global movements can tailor their strategies and messages to match local conditions. Some elements of global civil society rely on the properties of particular components of the hypermedia environment more than others. Consider the use of fax machines and hand-held video cameras by dissident groups to publicize their activities abroad. While the most often cited example is the Tiananmen Square massacre in Beijing, where radical students were able to reach a global audience through fax machines, these technologies have long been staples in the 'urgent action' strategies of human rights organizations such as Amnesty International, which rely on speedy transmissions to publicize human rights violations to various national and regional centres.[69]

Of course, not all of these transnational social forces are working with the same goals in mind, and not all can be said to be working to the betterment of the human condition: such technologies have also facilitated the rise of transborder criminal activities, including pornographic distribution systems, terrorist activities, and the money-laundering schemes of organized crime. One of the more effective transnational social movements in exploiting hypermedia has been the neo-Nazi movement, which has gained a considerable following among younger generations in the United States, Canada, and Europe through the use of computer networks, faxes, video cassettes, and other electronic forms of communication. The Oklahoma City bombing focused media attention on the use of computer networks by transnational terrorist organizations and militia movements. The commander of the Michigan Militia, Norman Olson, called the Internet 'absolutely vital' to his cause.[70]

Less important (for the purposes of this chapter) than the values of these social movements, however, is the extent to which their interests are defined and their actions organized largely without respect to sovereign-territorial boundaries. By moving around and through political boundaries to influence populations, they undermine states' monopoly of legitimate authority over a territorially defined populace, which is one of the central ideas of sovereignty.[71] This is especially the case with respect to those movements that lobby to enforce the global institutionalization of norms and principles relating to universal human rights—a direct challenge to sovereignty. As Sikkink argues, 'human rights policies and practices are contributing to a gradual, significant, and probably irreversible transformation of sovereignty in the modern world'— a shift that 'cannot be explained without taking into account the role of transnational nonstate actors.'[72] The monopoly claims of territorial states over legitimate authority, in other words, are increasingly challenged by global civil society networks that buttress their actions on wider, universalist aspirations.[73] Whether motivated by these more humane values or not, however, the sheer density and complexity of contemporary transnational social movements, operating within the 'global non-territorial region' of computer networks, present a fundamental challenge to the modern world order paradigm.[74]

State-Security Practices

What type of security practices 'fit' the hypermedia communications environment? At first blush, it may seem that digital-electronic technologies enable 'Big Brother' surveillance by centralized authorities of their citizens. One of the most common forms this argument takes is in the image of the electronic

Panopticon—originally an eighteenth-century architectural plan for a prison devised by Jeremy Bentham, and later employed by the twentieth-century French social theorist Michel Foucault as a general theory of modern surveillance.[75] The Panopticon was designed as a system of constant surveillance where prisoners could not know whether they were being watched. Control was thus maintained by an omnipresent sense that every action was being watched and monitored.[76] Foucault argued that this model of surveillance was in fact a metaphor of how various social, scientific, and political techniques combine in the modern state to regulate even the most private corners of everyday life.

The evidence gathered in support of these arguments is considerable, detailing how the manipulation of information through computer databases and the use of electronic monitoring devices facilitate greater state control in such areas as policing, internal revenue, and other far-reaching facets of bureaucratic administration.[77] For example, Gary Marx has analysed the way American undercover police surveillance has been boosted by hypermedia technologies to such an extent that the United States is approaching a 'maximum security society'.[78] Similar observations are made by Stanley Cohen with respect to electronic tagging devices that monitor 'freed' criminal offenders.[79] Going further, Diana Gordon argues that state computer databases and computer matching techniques have become so sophisticated and penetrating that not only are criminals more easily tracked, but 'we are all enclosed in an electronic Panopticon.'[80] Indeed, the extent to which cross-matching and exchange of personal data have become much easier for government bureaucracies of all sorts in the hypermedia environment is hard to deny, as David Flaherty, Oscar Gandy, and others attest.[81] Perhaps the clearest illustration is the Financial Crimes Enforcement Network (FinCEN) of the United States, used primarily to track money-laundering activities.[82] FinCEN monitors large financial transactions and, through powerful artificial intelligence computer programs, compares such transactions with government, private, and foreign computer databases and then with 'profiles' of typical financial criminal activities. Through this process, results are obtained that 'flag' certain transactions as potentially criminal. Similar systems have been set up in other countries, which now share data with each other and with Interpol. While there can be little doubt that the hypermedia environment enhances bureaucratic surveillance along the lines outlined above, do such trends favour more authoritarian regimes? Do they signal the rise of an electronic Big Brother?

The most serious flaw in these analyses is that they tend to put forth a distorted image of contemporary surveillance that ignores countervailing pressures in the hypermedia environment that actually undermine illiberal security regimes. The obsession with 'the gaze'[83] obscures other forces. While governments are able to track and monitor individuals with greater ease in the hypermedia environment, they are less able to control the flow of information or at least prevent individuals from having access to certain types of information. As Neuman explains, 'The special character of the new media is that they can as easily be extended horizontally (among individuals and groups) as vertically (in the more traditional connection between the centralized authorities and the mass populace).'[84] The new technologies of hypermedia communications are smaller, more mobile, more amorphous, and thus less easy to track and contain. Consider mobile personal digital assistants—small pocket-sized devices that now allow wireless two-way communication of digital information through credit-card-sized modems. As these devices are linked into LEO satellites, such as those of the planned Iridium system, it will be nearly impossible for authorities to prevent communications from going in and out of their country. Perhaps the best example is portable satellite dishes—now as small as 18 inches in diameter—that provide links to satellite broadcasts for even the remotest of regions. Even though Iran has banned satellite dishes (which sell in the black market for as little as $400) an estimated 200,000 homes still receive television programs by satellite.[85] In China, even though private ownership of satellite dishes was banned in 1990, it was reported in early 1994 that about 11 million households owned dishes, with around 30 million people being able to receive Rupert Murdoch's Star TV either through direct satellite reception or by cable relay.[86] Elsewhere in Asia, where states have long maintained strict government controls over national broadcasting and in some cases, like Singapore and Malaysia, have banned satellite dishes altogether, many are now realizing the futility of their policies and reversing course. As Lee and Wang point out, the loss of advertising revenues and audiences from state-run television to illicit satellite broadcasts has forced regulatory changes to allow more competition in Malaysia, Taiwan, Thailand, and South Korea.[87] In India, the state-run Doordashan channel took similar measures, offering five new channels to independent producers after facing competition from Star TV.[88]

These control problems are only magnified by the economic changes outlined earlier in the chapter. As structural pressures increase to conform to liberal economic policies and allow the penetration of foreign investment from transnational corporations, it becomes more difficult for these states to keep a 'firewall' between information intended purely for economic reasons and other broader forms of social and political communication. This is especially the case as more transnational commerce takes place over the seamless webs of computer networks. Digital information moves through these networks by a system called 'packet-switching', which breaks transmissions down into a series of units and sends them along independent channels to the transmission destination. Even if a state chose to monitor such transmissions it would be a costly and difficult task, especially as widely distributed shareware encryption technologies and re-mailing systems allow anonymity and security of communications. Non-liberal states that hope to attract foreign investment must grapple with the risks of providing a globally networked communications environment on the one hand, while sifting out any politically sensitive information on the other. Although such a strategy can be maintained in the short run, both the technological constraints and economic costs of doing so are high. These contradictory forces are likely to be most pronounced in the coming decades in those states, like Singapore, where liberalizing measures have been made in the economic sphere and where a sophisticated information technology environment has been promoted by the state to attract investment (the 'intelligent island'), while centralized control over information is vigorously maintained.[89]

A second reason to be wary of the 'panoptic' metaphor is that in focusing only on the enhanced surveillance capacity of the state, it overlooks the way in which transparency in general has been raised in the hypermedia environment to such an extent that states themselves are caught in a surveillance web. In other words, rather than a single 'gaze', the hypermedia environment has dispersed and decentralized the centres of surveillance to a much wider domain. Evidence of this dispersal can be found in the many emerging forms of private surveillance, ranging all the way from large-scale, commercial data-gathering enterprises to security cameras in local shops, malls, and banks, to tiny handheld video cameras. The latter are selling at a rate of 2.5 million per year in what has been referred to as the 'democratization of surveillance'.[90] The Rodney King beating of March 1991 illustrated the potential power of these private camcorders as they filter into the hands of many more people. The beating was inadvertently captured by George Halliday's SONY minicam. Halliday sent his tape to a local television station, which then forwarded the tape to CNN. Within a day, the tape had been broadcast to a global audience.[91] So prevalent are these mini-sites of surveillance that news organizations now actually encourage and sometimes rely on 'amateur videos' to capture news items.

Even more significant are the proliferating space-based surveillance technologies. Today the earth is blanketed by a dense web of national, regional, and internationally operated military, commercial, and environmental space-based reconnaissance systems. These systems monitor the planet in every conceivable spectral mode, from infrared to optical to radar, from the macro-perspective down to resolutions measured in centimetres, from real-time images to 3-D simulations. Imagery and data once the secret domain of the superpowers' top secret intelligence agencies are now widely available on the commercial market and distributed over the Internet. With $3,000, anyone could now purchase a satellite image of any spot on earth that could resolve objects as small as a metre in length.

This dispersal of centres of surveillance has meant that there are many more 'eyes' watching multiple, intersecting sites—many of which, of course, converge on states themselves. Today, governments and politicians find themselves under an intense scrutiny by an ever-expanding 'pool of watchers' both internal and external to the state itself. Not only do these include the proliferating global news organizations, like CNN or the BBC, but also local television stations, investigative journalists, and talk television and radio shows, all of which are growing exponentially with the increase in distributional systems. Adding to these dispersed centres of surveillance are the burgeoning transnational social movements described earlier in this chapter, many of which now operate and thrive in the non-territorial regions of computer networks and who make use of portable camcorders and commercial satellite imagery. In Spiro's words, these non-governmental organizations monitor 'compliance as a sort of new world police force'.[92] Alarm bells rung by watchdog groups, like Amnesty International, now spread rapidly through hypermedia currents, putting into global focus state behaviour that deviates from widely accepted norms. In addition, the two-way, interactive nature of hypermedia has increased the potential not only for direct citizen feedback and participation in political processes, but also for the monitoring of government actions through databases, computer network discussion groups, and World Wide Web homepage modes of dissemination. One glance at some of the UseNet groups indicates a wide variety of unmediated discussions on such topics as alt.politics.clinton, talk. politics.medicine, soc.rights.human, and alt.politics.datahighway. The combined effect of all of these dispersed centres of surveillance, as one *Economist* survey put it, is that instead of 'Big Brother is watching you', 'Big Brother is you, watching.'[93]

Conclusion

What do these changes mean for the character of an emerging post-modern world order? Probably the most significant is the way considerable social, political, and economic practices are increasingly decoupling or 'unbundling' from sovereign-territorial spaces. In many respects, a 'space of flows' is coming to dominate and transcend a 'space of places' as the defining characteristic of postmodern world order. Certainly this describes the organization of the global economy, not only with respect to the transnationalization of production but particularly with respect to global financial trading activities. It also accurately portrays the interactions of the many heteronomous transnational social movements now operating through the global non-territorial spaces of computer networks. In fact, these movements may be but one manifestation of a larger 'demassification' of group identities fuelled by the hypermedia environment. The two-way, interactive nature of computer networks that has favoured transnational social movements is also contributing to a flourishing of multiple and overlapping transnational 'niche' or 'virtual' communities—what Howard Rheingold has aptly called an 'ecosystem of subcultures'. The values of these niche communities are multiple and contradictory and reflect widely varying aspirations, from religious fundamentalist groups to ethnic diasporas, and from functionally defined interest groups to terrorist organizations. What is perhaps the most significant aspect of these communities, however, is the extent to which they are not bound by traditional notions of territory or place as prerequisites for membership—an orientation that in many respects mirrors the decoupling or unbundling of economic and interest group practices described above.

Amid these wider changes, the purpose and forms of states themselves are being transformed. Although it would be conceptually misguided to portray these transformations as the 'withering away' of the state, it is true, as Spiro put it glibly, that the state is 'not what it used to be'. Perhaps the best way to characterize this transformation is that states are evolving from 'container' to 'transmission-belt' organizations designed to facilitate flows of information and capital and to provide an interface between multiple and overlapping layers of authority. While there is enough cultural and historical diversity among states to ensure a variety of separate trajectories within this process, nearly all states have taken similar liberalizing measures primarily in response to the structural pressures of global market forces. With the flourishing of both transnational corporate interests and transnational social movements, the locus of authority, once monopolized by sovereign states, has been disaggregated and diffused to a much wider domain—to what Rosenau calls 'diverse subnational and supranational sovereignty-free actors'. A quasi-feudal, multicentric system is emerging as the architecture of the post-modern world order.

Notes

[1] Portions of this paper are based on Ronald J. Deibert, *Parchment, Printing, and Hypermedia: Communication in World Order Transformation* (New York: Columbia University Press, 1997).

[2] See Gerrit W. Gong, *The Standard of 'Civilization' in International Society* (Oxford: Clarendon Press, 1984); Robert H. Jackson, *Quasi-States: Sovereignty, International Relations and the Third World* (Cambridge: Cambridge University Press, 1991). For a useful overview of the changes in the notion of 'sovereignty' as a world ordering principle, see J. Samuel Barkin and Bruce Cronin, 'The State and Nation: Changing Norms and Rules of Sovereignty in International Relations', *International Organization* 48 (Winter 1994): 107–30.

[3] Richard Falk, 'Sovereignty', in Joel Krieger, ed., *The Oxford Companion to Politics of the World* (New York: Oxford University Press, 1993).

[4] For a more comprehensive overview of my thoughts on these processes, see Deibert, *Parchment, Printing, and Hypermedia*.

[5] The most apparent evidence of this is that the vast majority of economic transactions have been internal or domestic as opposed to international. Part of this is related to the nature of capital throughout the modern world order period, which has primarily been fixed and/or concentrated within specific geographic regions, making it more 'captive' to state regulations and taxes. Richard B. McKenzie and Dwight R. Lee, *Quicksilver Capital: How the Rapid Movement*

of Wealth Has Changed the World (New York: The Free Press, 1991), ch. 2, 'From Captive Capital to Quicksilver Capital', 17–34.

6   Joel Kurtzman, *The Death of Money: How the Electronic Economy has Destabilized the World's Markets and Created Financial Chaos* (New York: Simon and Schuster, 1993), 207.

7   See Michael C. Webb and Stephen D. Krasner, 'Hegemonic Stability Theory: An Empirical Assessment', *Review of International Studies* 15 (1989): 183–98.

8   Mark Hepworth, *Geography of the Information Economy* (London: Belhaven Press, 1989), 94.

9   Harvey S. James, Jr, and Murray Weidenbaum, *When Businesses Cross International Boundaries: Strategic Alliances and Their Alternatives* (London: Praeger Publishers, 1993), 49; see also Amy Borrus, 'The Stateless Corporations', *Business Week,* 14 May 1990, 101.

10 See Richard J. Barnet and John Cavanaugh, 'Creating a Level Playing Field', *Technology Review* (May-June 1994): 46–54, who give a number of examples of transnational 'back-room' processing centres.

11 For an excellent, comprehensive overview, see James and Weidenbaum, *When Businesses Cross International Borders.*

12 Ibid., 63.

13 Ibid.

14 For discussion, see Thomas A. Stewart, 'Boom Time on the New Frontier', *Fortune* (Autumn 1993). For 'Domilink', see Peter H. Lewis, 'Trying to Find Gold with the Internet', *New York Times*, 3 Jan. 1995. See also Robin Mansell, 'European Telecommunication, Multinational Enterprises, and the Implication of "Globalization"', *International Journal of Political Economy* (Winter 1993–4): 83–104. As Mansell notes, 'In many cases, the reorganization of the production process involves the exchange of a vast array of information with respect to design, product and process innovations, competitor strategies, component supplier competencies, and consumer profiles. This may be supported by communications services ranging from the simple voice telephone to the high-speed exchange of computer integrated manufacturing design concepts.'

15 Christopher Bartlett and Sumantra Ghoshal, *Managing Across Borders: The Transnational Solution* (Boston: Harvard Business School Press, 1989), 9.

16 For a representative position, see Benjamin Barber, 'Jihad vs. McWorld', *The Atlantic* 269 (3 Mar. 1992).

17 For examples, see Bartlett and Ghoshal, *Managing Across Borders*; C.K. Prahalad and Y. Doz, *The Multinational Mission: Balancing Local Demands and Global Vision* (New York: The Free Press, 1987); Samuel Humes, *Managing the Multinational: Confronting the Global-Local Dilemma* (Englewood Cliffs, NJ: Prentice-Hall, 1993).

18 See Lewis, 'Trying to Find Gold with the Internet'; Peter H. Lewis, 'Companies Rush to Set up Shop in Cyberspace', *New York Times*, 2 Nov. 1994.

19 Personal interview, Herbert I. Phillipps, Jr, Vice-President, Strategic Solutions, Royal Bank of Canada, 12 Jan. 1995. See also John Markoff, 'A Credit Card for On-Line Sprees', *New York Times*, 15 Oct. 1994; Lawrence M. Fisher, 'Microsoft and Visa in Software Deal', *New York Times*, 9 Nov. 1994; Saul Hansell, 'Mastercard to Develop On-Line Standard', *New York Times*, 10 Jan. 1995; Kelley Holland and Amy Cortese, 'The Future of Money', *Business Week*, 12 June 1995.

20 See Charles Kindleberger, *International Capital Movements* (Cambridge: Cambridge University Press, 1987); Fred Hirsch, *Money International* (Middlesex: Penguin Books, 1967).

21 Stephen Gill, 'Economic Globalization and the Internationalization of Authority: Limits and Contradictions', *Geoforum* 23 (1992): 273.

22 As outlined, for example, by John Maynard Keynes at Bretton Woods. See Eric Helleiner, 'From Bretton Woods to Global Finance: A World Turned Upside Down', in Richard Stubbs and Geoffrey R.D. Underhill, eds, *Political Economy and the Changing Global Order* (Toronto: McClelland & Stewart, 1994), 163–5; Eric Helleiner, *States and the Reemergence of Global Finance: From Bretton Woods to the 1990s* (New York: Cornell University Press, 1994).

23 David M. Andrews, 'Capital Mobility and State Autonomy: Towards a Structural Theory of International Monetary Relations', *International Studies Quarterly* 38 (1994): 198.

24 Bryant writes that 'The technological nonpolicy factors were so powerful, I believe, that they would have caused a progressive internationalization of financial activity even without changes in government separation fences and the inducement of differing regulatory, tax, and supervisory systems. But I also conjecture that government-policy changes were important enough to have promoted a significant integration of national financial systems even if there had been no shrinkage in the economic distances between reservoirs due to nonpolicy innovations such as the fall in relative costs of the international communication of information.' R. Bryant, *International Financial Integration* (Washington: The Brookings Institution, 1987), 69. Bryant is also cited in Andrews, 'Capital Mobility and State Autonomy', 198–9.

25 John Langdale, 'Electronic Funds Transfer and the Internationalisation of the Banking and Finance Industry', *Geoforum* 6 (1985): 2.

26 Susan Strange, 'From Bretton Woods to the Casino Economy', in Stuart Corbridge, Ron Martin, and Nigel Thrift, eds, *Money, Power, and Space* (Oxford: Basil Blackwell, 1994), 58. See also Strange, *Casino Capitalism* (Oxford: Blackwell, 1986).

27 Gill, 'Economic Globalization', 274.

28 See Richard O'Brien, *Global Financial Integration: The End of Geography* (London: Pinter Publishers, 1992), 18; Kurtzman, *The Death of Money*, 51.

29 Kurtzman, *The Death of Money*, 51.

30 Strange, *Casino Capitalism*.

31 See Kurtzman, *The Death of Money*, 170–1; personal interview, Herbert I. Phillipps, Jr.

32 As cited in O'Brien, *Global Financial Integration*, 9.

33 Nigel Thrift and Andrew Leyshon, 'A Phantom State? The De-Traditionalization of Money, the International Financial System and International Financial Centres', *Political Geography* 13 (July 1994): 309. See also Maurice Estabrooks, *Programmed Capitalism: A Computer-mediated Society* (London: M.E. Sharpe, 1988); Robert X. Cringely, 'Fast Money: How Computers Are Used for Trading Securities', *Forbes,* 11 Apr. 1994.

34 Mark Hepworth, 'Information Technology and the Global Restructuring of Capital Markets', in Stanley D. Brunn and Thomas R. Leinbach, eds, *Collapsing Space and Time: Geographic Aspects of Communications and Information* (London: Routledge, 1990), 137–8. On Quotreks, see Kurtzman, *The Death of Money*, 112.

35 Every year for more than a decade the 300 or so major firms of Wall Street have invested in total about $3.4 billion US in hypermedia—a figure that typically accounts for about 20 per cent of their total outlays. See Kurtzman, *The Death of Money*, 26. See also Hepworth, *Geography of the Information Economy*, 174–5, who documents how leading financial institutions, such as Nomura Securities of Japan and Prudential-Bache Securities of the US, are the driving force behind major telecommunications developments around the world, such as teleports and fibre-optic installations.

36   For an overview of SWIFT, see Langdale, 'Electronic Funds Transfers'.

37   Ron Martin, 'Stateless Monies, Global Financial Integration, and National Economic Autonomy: The End of Geography?', in Stuart Corbridge, Nigel Thrift, and Ron Martin, eds, *Money, Power, and Space* (Oxford: Basil Blackwell, 1994), 261.

38   Kurtzman, *The Death of Money*, 109.

39   Thrift and Leyshon, 'A Phantom State?', 311.

40   Kurtzman, *The Death of Money*, 17.

41   Ibid., 77.

42   See 'Financial Centres: A Survey', *The Economist*, 27 June 1992; see also Nigel Thrift, 'On the Social and Cultural Determinants of International Financial Centres: The Case of the City of London', in Corbridge et al., *Money, Power, and Space*, 327–55; Ronald L. Mitchelson and James O. Wheeler, 'The Flow of Information in a Global Economy: The Role of the American Urban System in 1990', *Annals of the American Geographer* 84 (1994): 87, 91, 98; Manuel Castells, *The Informational City: Information Technology, Economic Restructuring, and the Urban-Regional Process* (Oxford: Basil Blackwell, 1989). The term 'finanscape' is from Arjun Appadurai, 'Disjuncture and Difference in the Global Cultural Economy', *Theory, Culture & Society* 7 (1990): 295–310.

43   Thrift and Leyshon, 'A Phantom State?', 312.

44   Susan Roberts, 'Fictitious Capital, Fictitious Spaces: The Geography of Offshore Financial Flows', in Corbridge et al., *Money, Power, and Space*, 92.

45   John Gerard Ruggie, 'Territoriality and Beyond: Problematizing Modernity in International Relations', *International Organization* 47 (Winter 1993): 141.

46   Roberts, 'Fictitious Capital, Fictitious Spaces', 92.

47   Ibid.

48   Martin, 'The End of Geography?', 259.

49   Roberts, 'Fictitious Capital, Fictitious Spaces', 94.

50   Andrew Leyshon, 'The Transformation of Regulatory Order: Regulating the Global Economy and Environment', *Geoforum* 23 (1992): 251; Stephen Gill and David Law, 'Global Hegemony and the Structural Power of Capital', *International Studies Quarterly* 33 (1989): 475–99. J. Goodman and L. Pauly, 'The Obsolescence of Capital Controls? Economic Management in an Age of Global Markets', *World Politics* 46 (1993): 50–82; Michael Webb, 'International Economic Structures, Government Interests, and International Coordination of Macroeconomic Adjust-ment Policies', *International Organization* 45 (1991): 309–42; Richard Cooper, *The Economics of Interdependence: Economic Policy in the Atlantic Community* (New York: McGraw-Hill, 1968); Andrews, 'Capital Mobility and State Autonomy'.

51   Robert Cox, *Production, Power and World Order: Social Forces in the Making of History* (New York: Columbia University Press, 1987).

52   Philip Cerny, 'The Deregulation and Re-regulation of Financial Markets in a More Open World', in Cerny, ed., *Finance and World Politics: Markets, Regimes, and States in the Post-Hegemonic Era* (Aldershot, England: Edward Elgar, 1993).

53   'Locational tournaments' is a term I borrow from Lynn K. Mytelka's talk at the Information Technologies and International Relations symposium, Department of Foreign Affairs and International Trade, Ottawa, 13 Jan. 1995.

54   Ronnie Lipschutz, 'Reconstructing World Politics: The Emergence of Global Civil Society', *Millennium: Journal of International Studies* 21 (1992): 398–420.

55   Ethan A. Nadelmann, 'Global Prohibition Regimes: The Evolution of Norms in International Society', *International Organization* 44 (Autumn 1990): 495.

56   An excellent historical overview is provided by Lipschutz, 'Reconstructing World Politics', 400–14.

57   Kathryn Sikkink, 'Human Rights, Principled Issue-Networks, and Sovereignty in Latin America', *International Organization* 47 (Summer 1993): 418.

58   Peter J. Spiro, 'New Global Communities: Nongovernmental Organizations in International Decision-Making Institutions', *The Washington Quarterly* 18 (1994): 47.

59   Ibid., 49.

60   The term 'heteronomous' is taken from Lipschutz, which, as he says, 'implies that these networks are differentiated from each other in terms of specialisations: there is not a single network, but many, each fulfilling a different function.' Lipschutz, 'Reconstructing World Politics', 400–14.

61   Spiro, 'New Global Communities', 45.

62   See Leslie Paul Thiele, 'Making Democracy Safe for the World: Social Movements and Global Politics', *Alternatives: Social Transformation and Human Governance* 18 (Summer 1993): 281.

63   Ibid., 280.

64   Lipschutz, 'Reconstructing World Politics', 390.

65   Spiro, 'New Global Communities', 47.

66   Susanne Sallin, *The Association for Progressive Communications: A Cooperative Effort to Meet the Information Needs of Non-Governmental Organizations* (A Case Study Prepared for the Harvard-CIESIN Project on Global Environmental Change Information Policy, 14 Feb. 1994).

67   Ibid., 1.

68   See William T. Stanbury, 'New Information Technologies and Transnational Interest Groups', paper prepared for delivery at the Information Technologies and International Relations symposium, Department of Foreign Affairs and International Trade, 13 Jan. 1995.

69   See Adam Jones, 'Wired World: Communications Technology, Governance and the Democratic Uprising', in Edward A. Comor, ed., *The Global Political Economy of Communication: Hegemony, Telecommunication, and the Information Economy* (New York: St Martin's Press, 1994), 145–64.

70   Jared Sandberg, 'Militia Groups Meet, Recruit in Cyberspace', *Wall Street Journal*, 26 Apr. 1995.

71   This point is made by Lipschutz in 'Reconstructing World Politics', 392.

72   Sikkink, 'Human Rights, Principled Issue-Networks', 411.

73   See Richard Falk, 'Challenges of a Changing Global Order', *Peace Research: The Canadian Journal of Peace Studies* 24 (Nov. 1992).

74   'Global, nonterritorial region' is taken from John Gerard Ruggie, 'International Structure and International Transformation: Space, Time and Method', in Ernst-Otto Czempiel and James N. Rosenau, eds, *Global Changes and Theoretical Challenges: Approaches to World Politics for the 1990s* (Lexington, Mass.: D.C. Heath/Lexington Books, 1989), 31.

75   See Michel Foucault, *Discipline and Punish: The Birth of the Prison* (New York: Vintage Books, 1977).

76   Good overviews can be found in David Lyon, 'An Electronic Panopticon? A Sociological Critique of Surveillance Theory', *Sociological Review* 41 (1993): 655–60; David Lyon, *The Electronic Eye: The Rise of Surveillance Society* (Minneapolis: University of Minnesota Press, 1994), esp. ch. 4.

77 The following section draws on Lyon's informative overview in 'An Electronic Panopticon?', 661–2. See also Stephen Gill, 'The Global Panopticon? The Neoliberal State, Economic Life, and Democratic Surveillance', *Alternatives* 2 (1995): 1–49, for a similar discussion.

78 Gary Marx, *Undercover Police Surveillance in America* (Berkeley: University of California Press, 1988).

79 Stanley Cohen, *Visions of Social Control* (New York: Basil Blackwell, 1985).

80 Diana Gordon, 'The Electronic Panopticon: A Case-Study of the Development of the National Crime Records System', *Politics and Society* 15 (1986): 387.

81 See David H. Flaherty, *Protecting Privacy in Surveillance Societies: The Federal Republic of Germany, Sweden, France, Canada, and the United States* (Chapel Hill: University of North Carolina Press, 1989); Oscar H. Gandy, 'The Surveillance Society: Information Technology and Bureaucratic Social Control', *Journal of Communication* 39 (1989): 61–76.

82 For a detailed discussion of FinCEN, see Steven A. Bercu, 'Toward Universal Surveillance in an Information Economy: Can We Handle Treasury's New Police Technology?', *Jurimetrics Journal* 34 (Summer 1994): 383–449.

83 Lyon, *The Electronic Eye*, 218–19.

84 W. Russell Neuman, *The Future of the Mass Audience* (Cambridge: Cambridge University Press, 1991), 13.

85 'Iran Prohibits Satellite Dishes To Bar U.S. TV', *New York Times*, 27 Dec. 1994.

86 Paul S.N. Lee and Georgette Wang, 'Satellite TV in Asia: Forming a New Ecology', *Telecommunications Policy* 19 (1995): 140–1; see also William Shawcross, 'Reaching for the Sky', *New Statesman and Society*, 24 Mar. 1995, 12–14.

87 Lee and Wang, 'Satellite TV in Asia', 141–3.

88 Ibid.

89 Subscribers to Teleview, Singapore's computer network, must agree not to use it 'for sending to any person, any message which is offensive on moral, religious, communal or political grounds.' ('Feeling for the Future: A Survey of Television', *The Economist*, 12–18 Feb. 1994, 16.) Victor Keegan notes the following with respect to Singapore: 'One irony is that the information revolution that Singapore is pioneering may become the Trojan Horse that upsets the political and cultural repression of the regime. How can a society that still bans satellite dishes and many foreign journals continue to do so when the global information highway will give its citizens instantaneous access to multimedia newspapers all over the world, not to speak of pornography?' Victor Keegan, 'Who's in Charge Here', *The Guardian*, 12 Dec. 1994.

90 Lili Berko, 'Surveying the Surveilled: Video, Space, and Subjectivity', *Quarterly Review of Film and Video* 14, 1–2 : 61–91.

91 Ibid., 73.

92 Spiro, 'New Global Communities', 45.

93 'Feeling for the Future', 17. *The Economist* attributes this quotation to Mark Crispin Miller. For a similar critique of the Panoptic metaphor along lines similar to my own, see Martin Hewson, 'Surveillance and the Global Political Economy', in Comor, ed., *The Global Political Economy of Communication*, 61–80.

Chapter 3

□

NATIONAL SECURITY ISSUES IN A WIRED WORLD

□

Catherine M. Alexander

The spectacular developments of this century—for example, the atomic bomb, intercontinental missiles, and the computer—can blind us to how much change occurred in the nineteenth century, as nations went from military reliance on animal and wind power to steam and gasoline engines, from hand-carried messages to the telephone, and from muskets to machine guns. But it is the creation of the institutional system for stimulating technological innovation and change, together with those more recent developments, that is so different from what came before.[1]

One of the most interesting and important developments for international politics in the 1990s is the implication of technological asymmetry for the international security system. With the collapse of the former Soviet Union and the end of the Cold War, the boundaries of security policy are changing. The lack of an identifiable enemy, coupled with economic recession, has contributed to a lack of consensus among states, international organizations, and non-governmental organizations on the nature and scope of global security. While the need to address the proliferation of weapons of mass destruction persists, the scope of security issues in the post-Cold War era increasingly includes issues such as: new kinds of warfare and operations other than war (OOTW); growing expectations for preventive diplomacy, including peacekeeping and peace enforcement; democratic transition; nationalism; regional, ethnic, and religious conflict; environmental problems, including population pressures; declining defence budgets and smaller force structures. Underlying such external and internal stresses are the evolving patterns of states' behaviour (particularly those with industrialized economies) towards technological development. This is a significant, evolving issue. Throughout the postwar era a common understanding has existed of the norms and principles of security (Cold War era bipolarity) and trade (namely, economic liberalism). An important feature of the current generation of military technology is that it is emerging in the absence of a specific threat to the United States or its allies. Instead, factors such as the globalization of production, the importance of scale economies, and cross-border partnerships increasingly determine the contours of technological development. The extent to which parameters of international security relations are changing is revealed in a United States Defence Science and Technology Planning paper located on the Internet. It states:

> Many technologies critical to future warfighting are being developed and matured, commercially and internationally. Therefore, in the future, if DOD [US Department of Defence] is to develop, field and sustain superior material, [the US] must rely increasingly on the same industrial base that builds commercial products.[2]

The implications of information and communication technologies (ICT) on the battlefield, as the subject of defence procurement decisions, and as vehicles that reinforce the trend towards increasingly open societies are all aspects of security that are drawing attention. An environment of new external and internal demands necessitates that defence departments pursue technological initiatives in new ways that will maintain and advance their military advantage.

This chapter examines some of the ways in which international security is being affected by the direction of technological change. It argues that the prevailing economic and technological environment requires that defence programs take advantage of the cost-conscious, market-driven commercialism of private industry. The changing conceptualizations of world power and new power resources—including new knowledge structures and global exchange systems built on digital technologies—is the first theme, with particular attention placed on the relation between military-political and trade strategies. The second theme explores why dual-use technologies (technologies with both military and commercial applications) are of growing importance to national security, particularly given the integration of dual-use technologies, such as semiconductor chips, which, as we approach the next millennium, permeate all dimensions of military capability, including nuclear weapons systems, surveillance systems, and the command and control of forces. In short, military systems are increasingly dependent on sophisticated information and communication systems. The final theme assesses why 'critical' technologies must be included as power resources in any calculation of state security; given that technological prowess is increasingly translated into power, we must not ignore the implications of this development in determining the relative positions of states. The chapter concludes that we are entering 'an era that recycles old security vocabulary to fit new issues: market share, protectionism, [and] relative gains from trade. An era, simply, that would reconceive the very character of security, redefine the international power game, and resituate its players.'[3] In the newly wired world, technological developments in the past decade have redefined the meaning and importance of state security, and have widened the number of actors—such as transnational entities—who can exert influence on the state.

Theoretical Considerations

At first glance, the concept of national security is most readily identified with a nation-state's possession of tangible military resources. Under this narrow light, military efforts are cited as being central to a state's security strategy. Examples of military security include: 'gunboat diplomacy', which historically involved the show of naval force for the purpose of coercing another state; a 'balance of power' scenario whereby military capabilities are distributed so no one state can dominate another or other states; the Cold War system of 'bipolycentrism', where two dominant powers maintain military bipolarity while their respective allies rely on the dominant powers for security. The current situation among the major powers is 'asymmetrical multipolarity' in which the United States is the strongest state; however, unlike a unipolar situation, the other major powers remain important actors, particularly in their own regions. For example, even though Japan does not have a seat on the Security Council in the United Nations, it remains a major power because it is the world's largest creditor nation and has considerable influence in the Asia-Pacific region. Since the collapse of the former Soviet Union, ideology is no longer held to be a divisive force in international relations. To a great extent, even nationalistic sentiment is tempered by the desire to build market economies. At its most basic level, national security incorporates military power as a central ordering principle in an international system. In part, military preoccupations maintain prominence in foreign policy agendas because democratic state actors must fulfil a responsibility to protect their citizens' well-being and their territory, and to ensure their nation's survival.

A second reason military resources are readily identified with national security is because many leaders understand the primary obligation of the state to be the acquisition of power and therefore consider that other objectives should be subordinated to this goal. According to this paradigm, military strength is of greater significance than economics for national security. Such a conceptualization is associated with the 'realist' school of thought, which regards military capability as central to a nation-state's power potential. This conclusion stems from the realist assumption that a state's ability to coerce is more important than non-military means of reward. The possibility of conflict cannot be fully discounted. Threats to the United States and other great powers emanate from rogue regimes such as North Korea and Iraq, as well as from transnational problems such as terrorism. Even though it is unlikely that the People's Republic of China or Russia is capable of mounting a broad strategic challenge to the US, potential conflict exists in the form of low-intensity challenges. Furthermore, weapons of mass destruction (WMD), such as nuclear, biological, or chemical attack, are considered by analysts to be the weapons of first choice for rogue states. However, although the scope and scale of strategic challenge are diminishing, information and communication technologies have enabled hostile states to circumvent US export-control policy, which restricts the sale of critical technology to non-signatories. Both China and Russia are nuclear powers and space powers with access to global communications. While licences are required for military-related sales of computers capable of at least 2 billion calculations per second, a state can obtain supercomputers if they are used for civilian purposes, such as weather forecasting, earthquake research, or other scientific research. Supercomputers, however, are also capable of testing nuclear weapons or developing code-breaking technology. For example, in June 1997 two incidents were investigated in the United States: firstly, Secretary of State Madeleine Albright reported to Congress that investigators were checking whether supercomputers sold to private Chinese companies may have been used for nuclear weapons testing; secondly, the US Justice Department began investigating 'three sales of supercomputers overseas—two in Russia and one to the Chinese Academy of Sciences'.[4] The civilian application of technology has created a situation in which future opponents can invest in resources that are highly capable of force but not immediately considered to be a challenge to global order.

The diffuse challenges now confronting the US and other great powers— ranging from declining public-sector budgets that have constrained defence procurements to escalating internal ethnic tensions, to the growing reliance on sophisticated electronic expert systems—have contributed to a rethinking of political and conceptual frameworks. The subfields within international relations (IR) are becoming increasingly interdisciplinary. The subfield of security studies has traditionally focused on the phenomenon of war and peace; however, during the Cold War this subfield stressed the military domain and the superpower arms race. Another subfield of IR has been international political economy (IPE); analyses within IPE examine how markets 'constitute a means to achieve and exercise power, and [how] the state can be and is used to obtain wealth. State and market interact to influence the distribution of power and wealth in international relations.'[5] What is notable, not only in IR literature but also in defence strategy documents from the US Defence Department, is that security analysts are moving away from 'state centric assumption' where states are considered the most important actors in the international system. It is misleading to maintain that state power has eroded to the point that it does not have the ability to use coercive force. However, the state is no longer the only relevant actor in international relations. This conclusion offers a profound conceptual transformation because the focus for states shifts from what can be gained by the state to how state identities can be sustained and operate amid the growing activity and influence of non-state actors. Transnational problems, such as international terrorism and crime, drugs, and massive refugee flows, challenge the notion of sovereignty as exclusive territorial control. The distinction that sovereignty places on external and internal forces may be antiquated in an era in which international borders are porous to capital mobility and global telecommunications. The visibility of transnational forces is exemplified by the ease with which information can be disseminated across borders using new information and communication technologies; the actions of transnational entities, such as Microsoft, are sparking new 'currents' in the wired world, in the form of the bits and bytes that are the core of transborder data flows and via new knowledge systems flowing within and across territorial boundaries.

Putting the Byte on National Security: Low Politics as Security Issues

Until very recently, the impact of ICT on international affairs has not been included as an aspect of the politics of war and conflict, but rather has been seen as a form of interaction with little bearing on the core of state relations. While ICT such as the Internet are not identified as instruments that can dictate the outcome of events, their ability to decentralize and globalize information is having an impact on state action. Table 1 identifies some of the new forms of warfare that information and communications technologies can facilitate.[6]

Underpinning the new forms of information warfare as we approach the year 2000 is the Internet: a global network of networked computers where

☐ Table 1:   Information Warfare—What's New, and What Is Effective

Form	Subtype	Is It New?	Effectiveness
C2W [Command and Control Warfare]	Antihead	Command systems, rather than commanders, are the target.	New technologies of dispersion and replication suggest that tomorrow's command centres can be protected.
	Antineck	Hard-wired communication links matter.	New techniques (e.g., redundancy, efficient error encoding) permit operations under reduced bit flows.
IBW [Intelligence Based Warfare]		The cheaper the more can be thrown into a system that looks for targets.	The United States will build the first system of seeking systems, but, stealth aside, pays too little attention to hiding.
EW [Electronic Warfare]	Antiradar	Around since WW II.	Dispersed generators and collectors will survive attack better than monolithic systems.
	Anticomms	Around since WW II.	Spread spectrum, frequency hopping, and directional antennas all suggest communications will get through.
	Cryptography	Digital code-making is now easy.	New code-making technologies (DES, PKE) favour code-makers over code-breakers.
Psychological Warfare	Antiwill	No.	Propaganda must adapt first to CNN, then to Me-TV.
	Antitroop	No.	Propaganda techniques must adapt to DBS and Me-TV.
	Anti-commander	No.	The basic calculus of deception will still be difficult.
	Kultur-kampf	Old history.	Clash of civilizations?

continued

☐ **Table 1:** **Information Warfare** (continued)

Form	Subtype	Is It New?	Effectiveness
Hacker Warfare		Yes.	All societies are becoming potentially more vulnerable but good housekeeping can secure systems.
Economic Information Warfare	Economic	Yes.	Very few countries are yet that dependent on high-bandwidth information flows.
	Techno-Imperialism	Since the 1970s.	Trade and war involve competition, but trade is not war.
Cyber-Warfare	Info-Terrorism	Dirty linen is dirty linen whether paper or computer files.	The threat may be a good reason for tough privacy laws.
	Semantic	Yes.	Too soon to tell.
	Simula-warfare	Approaching virtual reality.	If both sides are civilized enough to simulate warfare, why would they fight at all?
	[William] Gibson-warfare [Neuromancer]	Yes.	The stuff of science fiction.

individuals are connected worldwide via their desktop computers and can exchange electronic mail, read complex documents including government documents, or read multimedia documents on World Wide Web sites consisting of text, graphics, sound, and video. In the wired world, nations 'do not have to be military superpowers with large standing armies, fleets of battleships or squadrons of fighters to gain a competitive edge. . . . Instead, all they really need to steal sensitive data or shut down military computers is a $2,000 computer and modem and a connection to the Internet.' Indeed, the US Senate Subcommittee on Investigations heard testimony in the spring of 1996 that more than 120 nations are reported to be developing 'information warfare techniques' that could 'allow our enemies to seize control of public networks which [US] Defense [Department] relies upon for communications' and reported that 'Defense's computer systems are particularly susceptible to attack through connections on the Internet, which Defense uses to enhance communication and information sharing.'[7] Via the Internet, one can participate in on-line or real-time discussions with large groups of individuals anywhere in the world. Most significant for the state is the fact that there is no central authority managing the flow of information on the Internet. This situation has proved challenging for authoritarian regimes since the Internet can circumvent imposed information controls or allow dissidents to build coalitions and networks. For example, the Association for Progressive Communications (APC) is a non-profit, non-governmental umbrella organization that provides Internet access to networking activists. In October 1996 a notice was posted on APC that 'a well-known Nigerian environmentalist was sentenced to be executed for treason. Within two days, environmental groups all over Hungary had used the APC to issue a collective statement to the Nigerian government to stay the execution and hear an appeal. The accused traitor was put to death as planned.'[8] In democratic states, analysis ranges from the optimistic view, which anticipates an increase in political activism brought about by the sharing of information and organization of activities, to the pessimistic view, which fears the potential manipulation of information by political élites.

For security analysts, one question is how the state can control extensive communications networks both within the military hierarchy (i.e., satellite reconnaissance) and on the Internet (i.e., transfer of information from or to hostile states). It is no longer sufficient for research agendas to consider technology within a military 'black box' since states and transnational forces are often competing for the same leading-edge technology. The global economy is characterized by an international web of supply chains and alliances, and just as firms seek global alliances to provide access to foreign technology, defence departments are increasingly seeking research alliances with their foreign allies' defence departments. The rapid development of ICT in the commercial sector of the economy has created areas of mutual interest for defence departments and industry. That is, many of the technologies that provide a military advantage on the battlefield are also being actively pursued by industry to meet the demands of the commercial marketplace. By consciously designing future weapons systems with commercial products and processes where possible, the pace at which improvements are incorporated into defence systems increases, and the costs of those military systems are reduced because the same competitive pressures and market-driven efficiencies that lead to the accelerated development and savings in the commercial products have been incorporated. However, by exploiting technological gains in commercial technologies, defence systems are more closely linked to the production processes of commercial development in other states. For example, commercial production facilities in other states may be subject to those states' export controls, restrictions on foreign investment in domestic industries, or rules governing intellectual property rights. Therefore, defining national security merely (or even primarily) in military terms conveys a profoundly false image of reality. That false image is doubly misleading and therefore, doubly dangerous. First, it causes states to concentrate on military threats and to ignore other and perhaps even more harmful dangers. Thus it reduces their total security. And second, it contributes to a pervasive militarization of international relations that in the long run can only increase global insecurity.[9]

The Security Implications of New Trade Patterns

In the global economy, states compete not for territory so much as for capital and the development of technological innovation. The composition of domestic economies and their competing national development trajectories also affect the ability of states to compete and increase the potential for insecurity. As a result, the sharp distinction that realism identifies between the 'high' politics of war and military power and the 'low' politics of international trade is becoming less obvious. The power potential of low politics has increased in importance because of globalization, which is marked by 'the intensification of economic, political, social, and cultural relations across borders'.[10] The rise towards globalization has been aided by the integration of financial markets and capital mobility, the increasingly widespread adoption of information and communication technologies (such as the Internet and high-speed computers), the evolution of the multinational corporation (MNC), and increased competition over outward flows of foreign direct investment (FDI). Globalization has shifted the focus from the state as the primary actor responsible for national security to a new situation that increasingly suggests that non-state actors control the resources critical to maintaining military strength. Whereas military structures emphasize a hierarchical command structure and centralized control, information and communication technologies tend to decentralize control. This shift arises because,

> as the technology becomes cheaper and cheaper, it becomes less and less efficient to control information from a central authority. Indeed, one reason for the current increasing pressure in society to decentralize government, corporations, and other organizations is that low-cost information technology makes it affordable and feasible to decentralize. The demand and incentives for decentralization are following the technological opportunity.[11]

The sheer size of the economies of industrial nations provides a clear illustration of the power potential of low politics and the potential for technological diffusion. Note, for example, that 'If there is a single piece of knowledge that separates serious international economists from fashionable popularizers, it is a sense of how big the world economy is. [The] combined gross domestic products in 1990 [of industrialized nations] exceeded $19 trillion, and their combined domestic investment exceeded $14 trillion.'[12] As a percentage of total production of world goods and services, 'international trade amounts to about 15 percent. . . . Around $3.5 trillion worth of trade crosses international borders each year. This a very large number, several times larger than the world's military spending.'[13] While developing countries have an extremely high level of military spending relative to their poverty, the fiscal resources industrial countries of the world are expending on defence-unique development and procurement are decreasing. Future weapons systems are consciously designed to use state-of-the-art commercial parts and subsystems, except in cases where a technology or system is required in which no commercial source exists. This is because the unit production costs of defence-unique development lines have 'increased 5 to 7 percent each year, not counting inflation, since the end of World War II. At the component level, for example, the military is paying $10 for computer chips that are virtually the same as ones being sold commercially for $1; the $9 difference is due to contractor overhead and other costs of DOD's special but often unnecessary requirements.'[14]

One of the most significant non-state actors is found in the strategic alliances or coalignments between various high-technology firms. Such alliances are notable because they are a synthesis of multi-site, interfirm, and multi-partner networks; they are necessary for commercial technology development because of the escalating cost of R&D, the importance of economies of scale, and the dynamic nature of comparative advantage. Classical trade theory, such as Ricardo's nineteenth-century principle of comparative advantage, assumed that a country will specialize and export goods in which its productivity disadvantage is the smallest relative to its trade partners, and this will cause markets to arise spontaneously and encourage harmony between states. However, this equilibrium is increasingly threatened by the spread of oligopolistic corporations and strategic interaction. The trade environment, particularly in the realm of high technology, is one where a small number of powerful corporations can significantly influence market outcomes. Oligopolistic markets have profoundly affected the nature of competition between states because:

> there has been an important shift in economic priorities among industrialized nations from a focus on heavy industry to knowledge-based production. The foundation of a state's economic strength and ability to compete internationally is no longer sought in the promotion of heavy industries that depend on relatively simple technology and a large unskilled labor force. It is sought instead in knowledge-based production that relies on a cadre of highly trained engineers and a smaller, technologically sophisticated production workforce in all sectors of the economy.[15]

The changing production base of industrialized economies from heavy industry to knowledge-based industry has reduced the incentive for territorial aggression. This has been identified as a transition from Cold War era 'geopolitics' (the distribution of political and military power) to the present global system that stresses 'geoeconomics' (the distribution of wealth).

Despite the engaging debate between economic liberalism and neo-mercantilism, the significance of world trade on the international security regime is that the military domain of state autonomy is now increasingly enhanced by economic security rather than the acquisition of territory and resources or the conquest of peoples. That is, the role of the state in securing technological production and transaction has been replaced by international market forces. Incremental improvements on technology and shorter product cycles result in more reliable products and make goods more attractive to consumers. For the United States military, this has had significant consequences. The US Department of Defence 'pioneered a partnership policy by focusing on dual-use technology. The DOD moved to dual-use acquisition because it found that a captive defence industry cost too much, responded too slowly, and frequently failed to push technology as fast as market-driven firms.'[16] The demands for high-volume production for commercial goods allow one to make a 'plausible hypothesis that civilian developers who have mastered the new manufacturing can move complex systems from design to battlefield faster than traditional military suppliers.'[17] For example, the speed and reliability of Japanese commercial input units are often greater than those made in America and used for military applications. For example, the 'Westinghouse APQ 120 radar for the F-4 fighter lasts an average of eight hours before failure, whereas the Mitsubishi Electric equivalent for the F-4EJ lasts an average of forty hours.'[18]

The postwar system assumed a static hierarchy of world power. The international system was constructed on the assumption that the United States maintained the power resources necessary to act legitimately as hegemon. However, the relative position or ranking of states in the nineties is much more dynamic. In the postwar era it was 'assumed that the technical advantages that had accrued to the United States would never be lost, and all others would follow in its train.'[19] However, the United States is no longer the world's largest creditor nation, nor are its technological gains insulated from the process of technological diffusion and adoption by other states. On the contrary, other competing states are becoming more active in developing industrial policy rather than depending on a static notion of comparative advantage. For example, states increasingly adopt protectionist policies in the form of 'infant industry protection' where a strong state seeks to defend and promote its national industries in the early stage of industrialization through the use of government subsidies, the erection of entry barriers, or other methods. The strength of this arrangement is illustrated by the Japanese ability to develop technologies that become military or civilian in application. The dual-use capabilities of Japanese R&D were first formally acknowledged by a study team of the US Defense Science Board in 1984, which concluded that Japanese technology was at or ahead of the sixteen different dual-use technologies. These technologies were widely acknowledged as the 'key' or 'base' technologies for advanced manufacturing in the next century, including gallium arsenide devices [e.g., semiconductors].[20]

These technologies are of such significant scope and influence that the ability to develop, generate, and accumulate production knowledge will affect the relative position of states. For example, the development of militarily significant technologies, coupled with the decreasing competitiveness of the American military supply industry, has significant security implications. Increasingly, technological advancement of R&D—based on the improvement of current technology through incremental innovations, as well as the nurturing of radical innovations—leads to technological gains. The process of 'cyclical development' is important for high technology because firms that can produce new processes and designs before others gain an advantage in the marketplace. The turnover period for new developments is very rapid, and the shorter the product cycle is, the greater the market lead. Technology leadership is defined by IBM's former chief scientist, Ralph Gomory, as being 'the speed of the development and manufacturing cycle that appears as technical innovation or leadership. And it takes only a few turns of that cycle to build a commanding product lead.'[21] Given the importance for a state to obtain the latest military technology, defence organizations need to realize the importance of market structures on R&D capabilities. Advanced military technology now must be competitive within the product cycle. Those firms competing for defence contracts must be capable of 'producing a wide range of established military systems with equal or superior technology and capabilities, but faster, far more cost-effectively, and with greater reliability in the field.'[22] As foreign firms take steps to increase their interest in defence production, it must be questioned what impact such shifts present to American hegemony. Observers of these developments have begun to question how states will use 'expanding capabilities for producing items desired by military establishments, including dual-use components and military end products'.[23]

As the dominant military and economic state, the US has had the ability to exercise power through the mechanisms of influence it established during the postwar era. In exchange for the provision of key collective goods (security, open markets, and monetary stability) the United States maintained the power to exploit its own position and enforce rules aimed at preserving world order and its position within that system or regime. Given its sphere of influence, the US has employed its financial power to transform the economy in ways that maximize its influence and maintain its international hegemonic position. However, as wealth grows in other states and their relative position within the existing international system improves, so, too, does the potential for other states to alter the foundations of the international system, even if the desire to do so is yet unknown. Such a shift has profound effects on the global system because it encourages additional competition over resources and capital. Furthermore, when uneven growth occurs, states may employ policies to protect their declining industries. The acquisition of new growth sectors is promoted by the development of technical breakthroughs. As Robert Gilpin observes:

> States aspire to be the source of technological innovation and to acquire industrial superiority over other societies. The possession of a technological monopoly in the expanding sectors of the world economy enables a state to extract 'technological rents' from other economies in the system. . . . every state, rightly or wrongly, wants to be as close as possible to the innovative end of 'the product cycle' where, it is believed, the highest 'value added' is located.[24]

The rising frequency of trade conflicts over high-technology goods may become a model for future debates concerning different conceptions of security. If technological capabilities can alter national patterns of external dependence, then it should be questioned whether states can achieve greater influence through technological ascendency.

Albert O. Hirschman's classic (1945) study of the politics of foreign trade offers a useful point of departure for conceptual analysis. His seminal work explores how economic interdependence can result in a relationship of mutual dependence in which a state can exploit and manipulate the vulnerability of another state. Hirschman argues that 'the power to interrupt commercial or financial relations with any country . . . is the root cause of the influence or power position which a country acquires in other countries [through its trade relations].'[25] Hirschman's analysis of how nations can capture gains from trade provides additional insight into the current situation. A nation rich in natural resources has a vastly different potential for economic leverage than a nation wealthy in the production of dual-use technologies, such as semiconductors. Semiconductors are a strategic commodity because they are the essential electronic components of integrated circuit (IC) development. They are the intermediate inputs that allow numerous electrical functions to be placed on a single circuit. In short, they are the basic building blocks of a wide variety of commercial products, ranging from supercomputers to video games. Semiconductors are the critical components in advanced weapons systems, and the accuracy of intermediate-range and intercontinental ballistic missiles is dependent on semiconductor technology. Their importance cannot be overstated since 'the integrated circuit industry makes possible new products, transforms existing goods, and changes the ways that all products will be made. Those countries which most effectively apply the possibilities of microcircuitry in their national economies will grow in strength and wealth relative to the others.'[26]

The largest single user of semiconductor technology during the postwar era has been the Pentagon. During the Cold War, the size of the semiconductor market was dominated by military contracts. However, as technological advances grow out of commercial innovations, the military share of the semiconductor market is dwindling. A tension exists for defence planners because while the sources for semiconductors have changed, the military's demand for reliable technology is increasing. The Pentagon remains reliant on a global system of communication satellites, computers, and terrestrial telecommunication systems. Furthermore, it makes use of battlefield computers used primarily for remote sensing of enemy troop movements, precise targeting and firing, and damage assessment. Military computers are integrated into systems of command, control, communications, and intelligence (C3I). These systems 'combine computers, radars, information displays and communications gear to monitor hostile forces, process information for military commanders and transmit their orders.'[27] Semiconductor technology has become vital as computers have expanded the range, speed, and accuracy of weapons systems. One danger is that as the US obtains microchips from commercial vendors located in foreign countries, the ICs could be compromised due to a 'virus' that could cause the weapons to fail to perform when required. This is a unique vulnerability introduced by ICT since hostile actors cannot readily intercept or decipher signals, but they can jam civilian communications links and thereby disable the C3I system, knock out power grids, or engage a software program that 'detonates' at a set time and proceeds to destroy or rewrite data. As the real size of the battlefield has increased over the earth and into space, the control of semiconductor production grows more vital. A significant degree of uncertainty exists as to the security of Pentagon computers. Analysts from the investigative arm of the US Congress, the General Accounting Office, reported that 'computer hackers cruising the Internet posed a serious and growing threat to national security, with the Pentagon suffering as many as 250,000 "attacks" on its computers last year [1995].'[28] While the Pentagon denied knowledge of any instance where hackers obtained secret information, the vulnerability of states to new forms of terrorism extends beyond that of hackers. The changing nature of security allows not only rogue or hostile states to engage in information warfare, but also, for example, terrorists and criminal groups who seek access into government computers and destroy records of funds transfers.

Conclusion

How should states define what is 'critical' technology? Should this be defined according to each state's interests, or should external or international bodies govern the decision and standardize the procedurals and definition? Dual-use technologies are integral to both defence and commercial industrial bases, but their relationship with national security is increasingly blurred. For example, high-definition television (HDTV) was a technological development that was not included on the critical technologies list 'even though many defence officials say it is important to security-related weapon systems, medical technology, and many other products.'[29] The sophistication and adaptability of dual-use technology have developed beyond former definitions of strict utility or military-specific uses. The concern over dual-use technologies stems from the fear that relative gains in technological progress could lead to growing dependence on critical technology, and thereby grant a source of leverage over a state's behaviour. The difficulty in controlling technology is that, unlike traditional commodities, it can be transferred and transformed at different levels.

The globalization of production in an interdependent world heightens the potential of critical technologies to be transferred to other states, including hostile states and actors. When the supply of technology is concentrated and scarce, national and economic security can be endangered. Under such circumstances, foreign suppliers can place limits or conditions on the use of a product. The complex situation in which strategic control of critical goods can limit national autonomy raises a number of critical questions. For example, at what point is the concentration of foreign control considered dangerous? Does the oligopolistic behaviour of domestic firms present a similar threat to national autonomy? Are the so-called 'input' industries that other sectors depend on more vulnerable to economic statecraft? While the relationship between economic prosperity and technological capability influences a state's international economic position, the development of dual-use technology has extended the debate to include the security implications of innovation and technology. Technological capabilities can alter national patterns of external dependence, and therefore other states may be in the position to achieve greater influence through technological leadership.

During the postwar period, the technological strategy of allies has been fused to American initiatives and the American security arrangement. Will this remain so? The issue for relative gains theorists is to determine at what point 'cooperative ventures disproportionately benefit its allies'.[30] The question, then, is to what degree states will pursue their individual interests. Underlying the reshaping of international rules is the issue that the 'new world is not so much about disorder as it is about the absence of order and, especially, the absence of leadership (internationally, nationally, and locally).'[31] Technological ascendancy and economic gains may become sources of future tension in the international system. The shifting relative position of states has created an international system whereby the old postwar principles for order are of diminishing utility. In this light, analysts must consider whether states respond to external challenges by using economic, technological, or military capabilities as instruments of statecraft.

Notes

1   Eugene B. Skolnikoff, *The Elusive Transformation: Science, Technology and the Evolution of International Politics* (Princeton, NJ: Princeton University Press, 1993), 50. Emphasis added.

2   United States Department of Defence, 'Defense Science and Technology Strategy: Investment Priorities' (US Government Computer System Web Site last updated 13 May 1997) [http://www.dtic.mil/dstp/DSTP.index.html]. Site accessed 7 June 1997.

3   Michael Borrus, Wayne Sandholtz, Steve Weber, and John Zysman, 'Prologue', in Wayne Sandholtz, Michael Borrus, and John Zysman, eds, *The Highest Stakes: The Economic Foundations of the Next Security System* (New York: Oxford University Press, 1992), 3.

4   Cassandra Burrell, 'U.S. Commerce Official Calls Computer-Export Rules Unenforceable', *New York Times Online*, CyberTimes Section, 13 June 1997. [http://search.nytimes.com/search/daily/...]

5   Robert Gilpin, *The Political Economy of International Relations* (Princeton, NJ: Princeton University Press, 1987), 11.

6   Due to spacial constraints, for a full description of these various forms of information warfare, please refer to the original document from which this table was extracted: Martin Libicki, *What is Information Warfare?* ACIS paper 3 (Institute for Strategic Studies: National Defence University, Aug. 1995). [http://www.ndu.edu/ndu/inss/actpubs/act003/a003cont.html]. Accessed 7 May 1997.

7   Philip Shenon, 'Report Warns of Security Threats Posed by Computer Hackers', *New York Times Online*, CyberTimes, 23 May 1996.

8   Matt Richtel, 'The Left Side of the Web Seeds Global Grass Roots', *New York Times Online*, CyberTimes, 14 June 1997.

9   Richard H. Ullman, 'Redefining Security', *International Security* 8 (Summer 1983), as reprinted in Sean M. Lynn-Jones and Steven E. Miller, eds, *Global Dangers: Changing Dimensions of International Security* (Cambridge, Mass.: MIT Press, 1995), 15.

10 Charles W. Kegley, Jr, and Eugene R. Wittkope, *World Politics: Trend and Transformation*, 6th edn (New York: St Martin's Press, 1997), 249.

11 Bruce Berkowitz, 'Warfare in the Information Age', *Issues in Science and Technology* (Fall 1995): 60.

12 Paul Krugman, *Pop Internationalism* (Cambridge, Mass.: MIT Press, 1996), 194.

13 Joshua S. Goldstein, *International Relations* (New York: HarperCollins, 1994), 311.

14 National Economic Council, Office of Science and Technology Policy, 'America's Advantage Dual-Technology' (Feb. 1995). [http://www.dtic.dla.mil/techtransit/nec/nec_toc.html]. Accessed 7 Apr. 1997.

15 Beverly Crawford, 'The New Security Dilemma Under International Economic Interdependence', *Millennium: Journal of International Studies* 23 (Spring 1994): 32.

16 Lewis Branscomb et al., *Investing in Innovation: Toward a Consensus Strategy for Federal Technology Policy* (Boston: John F. Kennedy School of Government, Harvard University, 1997). [http://www.ksg.harvard.edu/iip/techproj/invest.html]

17 Steven Vogel, 'The Power Behind "Spin-Ons": The Military Implications of Japan's Commercial Technology', in Sandholtz et al., eds, *The Highest Stakes*, 33.

18 Ibid., 70.

19 Crawford, 'The New Security Dilemma', 29.

20   Richard J. Samuels, 'Reinventing Security: Japan Since Meiji', *Daedalus* 120 (Fall 1991): 56.

21   Ralph Gomory quoted in Vogel, 'The Power Behind "Spin-Ons"', 34.

22   Ibid.

23   Samuels, 'Reinventing Security', 61.

24   Gilpin, *Political Economy*, 99.

25   Albert O. Hirschman, *National Power and the Structure of Foreign Trade* (Berkeley: University of California Press, 1945), 16.

26   Michael Borrus, John Millstein, and John Zysman, *U.S.-Japanese Competition in the Semiconductor Industry* (Berkeley: Institute for International Studies, University of California, 1983), 118.

27   The Pentagon, Strategic Defence Initiative Organization, Multinational Programs Division, *A Guide to International Participation in the Strategic Defense Initiative* (Washington, Dec. 1990), 27.

28   Shenon, 'Report Warns of Security Threats'.

29   Vogel, 'The Power Behind "Spin-Ons"', 67.

30   Ibid., 80.

31   Michael Hawes, 'East is East: The Paradox of Japan in the New World', *Queen's Quarterly* 99 (Winter 1992): 1060.

—— □ ——

Chapter 4

TECHNOLOGIES OF ABSTRACTION: CYBERDEMOCRACY AND THE CHANGING COMMUNICATIONS LANDSCAPE

—— □ ——

Michael R. Ogden

————

tech•nol•o•gy (n.) Of or derived from technique; application of practical, mechanical sciences especially in industry or commerce; technical methods, skills, knowledge . . .

American Heritage Dictionary (1994, 3rd edition)

ab•strac•tion (n.) Considered apart from concrete existence; not applied or practical; without reference to a specific instance; difficult to understand; a preoccupation . . .

American Heritage Dictionary (1994, 3rd edition)

————

The above definitions bespeak an inherent contradiction reflected in the title of this chapter and, indeed, in society today. Specifically, the practical application of the 'mechanical sciences' that have made possible the explosive growth in both the scope and scale of human communications has also increased society's addiction to the gee-whiz products and shiny new toys of the next wave of 'electronic technology du jour' while simultaneously obfuscating important issues of human action and agency in the brave new 'virtual' world we are fast creating. Even now, the major media are promoting, advertising, and exciting people with talk of a digital information revolution and the concomitant network of networks called 'cyberspace'[1] that has become its popular manifestation. Indeed, it appears that no one is immune to the seemingly 'insistent slogans and claims that the latest technological advances in computer-mediated communication will bring knowledge, pleasure, community, economic development [and] personal liberation.'[2]

Due in part to the mesmerizing digital song of the computer pied pipers[3]—and despite the anxious remonstrations of the neo-Luddites[4]—the general public remains enamoured with the technology of our newly crowned 'Information Age'[5] even if only cautiously so. This anxious support of information technology, however, appears to be based more on faith than on understanding. After all, who but a few could possibly understand the esoteric realms of microelectronics, fibre optics, satellites, or the globe-spanning telecommunications networks? Little wonder few individuals feel they have any real control over the technologies that now impose with increasing urgency upon their lives. Thus, crucial decisions about the technologies that are making the dream of a National and/or Global Information Infrastructure (NII/GII) a reality appear—at least on the surface—to be made almost anonymously.

Still, the twenty-first century—the 'Age of Information'—fast approaches and much remains unsettled. Obviously, we can ill afford to continue pretending we are naïve about the consequences of computer-mediated communication technology. Neither can we afford to be ignorant of the 'power politics' invoked by information technology's application.[6] Ignorance, in this case, is not bliss. In today's fast-paced, interconnected, complex world—made all the more so by information technology-induced change and unrealistic or reckless demands—ignorance is downright dangerous! Our 'inability to understand technology and perceive its effects on our society and on ourselves is one of the greatest, if most subtle, problems of an age that has been so heavily influenced by technological change.'[7] Fortunately, ignorance need not be a permanent condition.

Roger Karraker's often quoted opening paragraph to his seminal article, 'Highways of the Mind' (1991), stated succinctly the issues that should still be of concern to every individual today:

A quiet but crucial debate now underway in [the US] Congress, in corporate board-
rooms, and in universities, has the potential to shape American life in the twenty-first
century and beyond. The outcome may determine where you live, how well your children are educated, who will blossom and who will wither in a society in which national
competitiveness and personal prosperity will likely depend on access to information.[8]

This statement continues to ring true, but now with an increased sense of
urgency. In a follow-up article Karraker further cautioned, 'If we create digital
networks that do not provide for open access, two-way switched systems,
affordable rates, privacy, and [freedom of speech], we will short-change the
public and harm the public interest for generations to come.'[9] It therefore
becomes a moral imperative that people learn about the intellectual, social,
commercial, and political leverage presented by participation in the communications revolution that is cyberspace—while the freedom to do so still exists.
David Johnston, chair of Canada's Information Highway Advisory Council
(IHAC), stressed this sentiment poignantly in an April 1997 press release when
he stated, 'the new communications and information technologies are already
creating a global information society. A world without borders is on the hori-
zon. There are enormous opportunities . . . in this new environment, but only
if we move quickly to seize them. . . . if we are to survive and flourish . . .
in the 21st century, [we must] get connected now and use the Information
Highway.'[10]

This chapter explores these issues, among others. Yet, its purpose is also
one of synthesis and of visioning. At one level, an attempt is made to make
sense of the trends and dynamic changes taking place in communication and
information technologies that have the potential to transform society dramatically. Yet at another level, if we specify the requirements for a future NII based
only on current services and the extension of existing application features, the
NII (and for that matter, the GII as well) will probably fall far short of our expectations and needs. As such, the NII/GII may not become a true, large-scale, networked information infrastructure without the joint effort of both the private
and public sectors. Nor would it likely provide universal or equitable access
across nations or across populations within nations—providing usefulness at
moderate costs for students, the elderly, minorities, non-professionals, and others—without a strong, guiding social contract to oversee public policy. Thus,
three alternative visions of where the telecommunications-computer convergence might possibly lead will be examined in order to understand better the
functional requirements of the future NII/GII: what it will look like, who stands
to gain, and who might lose out. Finally, as individuals become more aware of
the intellectual, social, commercial, and political leverage possible through participation in cyberspace, it becomes increasingly more important to ensure the
extension of democratic principles into this vital new sphere of human agency

before the political and economic big boys seize it, censor it, meter it, and sell it back to us.[11] There is obviously a clear and present danger in the continuation of our existing track record of *laissez-faire* or *post-hoc* policy-making, in allowing others (business leaders, military brass, technocrats, or even expert researchers) to direct and/or control the language and definition of this new communications landscape. 'Make no mistake about it: the metaphors we employ as we create these new digital networks will shape our society as significantly as the railroads shaped the late nineteenth century and interstate highways shaped the mid-twentieth century.'[12]

In the Furnace of the 'New'

The technologies used for self-expression, human intercourse, and recording of knowledge are in unprecedented flux.[13]

If there is one thing that Moore's Law[14] has taught us it is that the pace of technological advancement is no longer a simple linear projection. Propelling this march toward 'more, faster, smaller, cheaper' are unceasing advances in the core, enabling technologies of the information revolution. 'Each year, advances in microchips, optoelectronics, and other building blocks make possible new products and services that bring more people into the Information Age. These newly aware customers soon demand new features and the . . . cycle continues.'[15] By examining present advancements in computer technology, it is easy to believe the forecast that by early in the next century, today's supercomputing power will be on the desktop if not in the laptop! Likewise, predictions of microchips in cars to make them smarter and safer, virtual reality applications that assist medical students in learning anatomy, or software agents acting as information valets managing appointments and scanning the vast on-line storehouses of data to assemble personalized newspapers or television programs for us, are—we are told—all likely consequences of current advances in the new information technologies. One thing that is certain, however, is that many of today's technologies are in the process of converging to deliver the services of tomorrow. Furthermore, the potential importance and impact of this trend are just now being assessed.

At the focal point of this technological confluence is the powerful and all-encompassing network of communication and information services made possible by the potential unification of telephone, television, and computer systems. Frequently referred to as the National Information Infrastructure or even the Global Information Infrastructure, and popularized in the media as the 'Information Superhighway', the form this network finally takes will undoubtedly have an enormous impact on our individual lives, our businesses, and our society. Indeed, perhaps a shift in metaphor is in order. Recently initiated efforts to address the form and function of the NII/GII have taken a decidedly 'engineering approach' to what is essentially a social-political problem. Instead of regarding the NII/GII as a 'superhighway', which emphasizes the technical infrastructure—the route rather than the destination[16]—perhaps we should view it as a gathering place, an 'agora',[17] or 'virtual polis'[18] that focuses on the rich variety of human interaction possible. The question should not be 'if we build it, will they come'? Rather, is what is being built a 'needful thing'? This perspective would suggest a different framework for understanding and analysing public policy issues related to the NII/GII as well as some principles for addressing those issues. The 'Information Superhighway' is not just about wires, optical fibres, satellites, computers, and telephones; rather, it is about people and how they choose to interact with each other and the world at large. Manufactured need will not suffice to motivate 'real' people to connect, nor will it maintain a long-term information market—and let us face it, the NII/GII is not about information, but about 'communication' and trying to find a new basis for our global economy. Alas, just when public policy began to focus on the need, form, and function of the NII/GII,[19] forecasting and conceptualizing the hardware future of telecommunications usurped the debate and made the waters even murkier than ever due in large measure to what was happening with technology.

The assumptions of the 'old' communication network providers and their regulators, customers, and suppliers included fixed overhead, fixed bandwidth, physical analog connections, and segregated, hierarchical network architectures contained within national borders. This was largely predicated on the belief that each medium of communication, and the services associated with it, was fundamentally distinct from the others and that they therefore required different regulatory frameworks. In the US, this meant 'the telephone was operated as a common carrier; print media in accordance with the First Amendment; and [broadcast]-based media was defined by a "public interest standard".'[20]

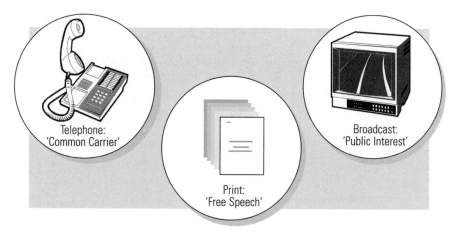

Figure 1: Assumptions of the 'Old'

Today, the information network beginning to take shape organizationally and technologically is increasingly a high-speed, high-bandwidth, all-digital network (although with a mix of analog/digital interfaces during the transition). Moreover, as a result of this digitization, high-capacity fibre optics and coaxial cable are being made even more efficient while satellite capacity and capability have also increased. Broadcasting and wireless communication networks are likewise moving towards all-digital systems, although somewhat slower than wire-line or satellite systems. Nevertheless, even with hybrid systems proposed for broadcast and wireless communications, much of the information carried will be in digital form—enough to change the way networks are controlled and telecommunication appliances are used.[21]

Thus, as the communication and information technologies converge and the service providers begin to merge accordingly, the 'new' computer-based technologies carry with them a new and different set of assumptions, including variable bandwidth allocations with logical, instead of physical, connections and a non-hierarchical network architecture based on interoperability, diversity, and open systems with distributed processing nodes and terminals. All of which means the evolving NII/GII is capable of carrying not just text, but audio, video, graphics, animation, and anything else that can be coded in digital form quickly and seamlessly.

This technology trend has tremendous possibilities. It most certainly is being used for entertainment, enhancing both the technical quality (e.g., better

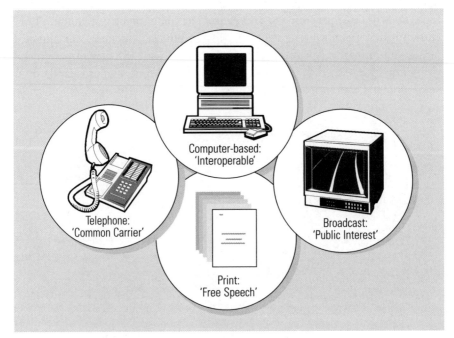

Figure 2: Furnace of the 'New'

resolution via digital high-definition television) and the channel capacity of television programming as well as providing video dial-tone for such services as movies on demand. The technological capabilities of the NII/GII also offer one-to-many and each-to-all multimedia communications while giving users access to all kinds of information services, including stock quotes, airline schedules, weather maps, calendars of events, libraries, government documents, and so on. It is used in education, not just for the remote delivery of lectures, but for interactive tutorials, for simulations, and for research. It carries an endless array of interest group discussions, where anyone can enter a discussion on just about any topic at any time providing a vehicle for free speech and civic action. And, of course, it will be used for a wide variety of commercial transactions, including shopping and banking from home.[22]

Overreaching in Cyberspace?—The NII/GII Policy Debate

Porush's Law: Participating in the newest communications technologies becomes compulsory if you want to remain part of the culture.[23]

It is obvious that the potential commercial and political value of the newly emerging information network has not gone unnoticed—numerous interest groups have been manoeuvring for influence over its design and ownership since its inception. However, the 'debate' ensuing over the form and function of the NII/GII has so far been a staged event. 'Mass-circulation magazines like *Newsweek* and *Time* have run cover stories about the coming "revolution" that are little more than regurgitations of industry public relations. Lifestyle magazines like *Wired* and *Mondo 2000* stimulate consumer demand for new gadgets and informed acquiescence to governmental and corporate policies—in the name of spurious "liberation" and "empowerment".'[24] Because information technology is a particularly important driver of productivity growth, governments are expected to play an important role with an eye to the larger national agenda, and thereby promote or enhance technological innovation through strategic investments in information technology. Canada's Information Highway Advisory Council took this a step further when it called for government to 'act as a persuasive model user of new communications technologies. . . . Governments at all levels should "re-engineer" themselves using integrated, government-wide information and communications systems [and provide their citizens] access to responsive, efficient and cost-effective public services . . . [because] new information technologies are [indeed] changing the relationship between . . . governments and citizens.'[25] However, the fact is, most governments find it difficult to define their proper role in fostering information technology primarily because 'computer and communications technologies have advanced so rapidly over a period of four decades that they are themselves agents of instability, insecurity, and change.'[26] For governments, this prospect of supporting what could easily derail the status quo and disrupt power hierarchies is unsettling.

Typically, the public policies guiding most governments in fostering an NII (let alone a GII) are usually discussed under two headings: telecommunications policy and information policy. The former deals primarily with the regulatory environments, standards, and international trade issues governing the provision of telecommunications services.[27] The latter deals with the government's interest and the public's rights in creating, storing, accessing, and disseminating information, as well as encompassing the protection of intellectual property rights and defining conditions of what constitutes fair use.[28] Such telecommunications and information policies generate a complex body of laws and legal principles that largely determine the structure of the information industry and the rules under which it competes. Within this complex environment, governments define their role and practise their telecommunications and information policies.[29]

For example, in the United States prior to 1996, the basic telecommunications law of the land was the Communications Act of 1934, which predated commercial television, transistors, computers, satellites, lasers, fibre optics, and cellular telephones. 'For years, national regulators . . . compartmentalized communication technologies, setting up separate ground rules for print, telephony, and broadcasting. Together, these three sets of rules were designed to achieve a broad range of communication-related goals.'[30] The 'compartmentalization' of communication technologies entrenched in the US by the Communications Act of 1934 is easily defended after the fact if we consider it was predicated on the following assumptions:

- a 'natural monopoly' existed in the telecommunications industry, warranting price as well as entry federal regulation;
- the broadcast spectrum was considered scarce and required federal 'rationing' and oversight; and
- the analog technologies of the day dictated the form and function of communications.

As the US communications infrastructure shifts from incompatible analog technologies to interoperable digital technologies—bringing about the convergence of computers, telecommunications, and broadcast media that will eventually form the foundation of the future NII/GII—the old 'three-pronged' approach loses its relevance and makes increasingly less sense. It has been proposed that the industry structure now emerging consists of three new and inextricably linked categories; namely, platform providers, conduit providers, and content providers. 'Platform providers include vendors of the hardware and software building blocks of personal and corporate computing. Conduit providers establish the electronic highways through which the information flows. Content providers develop and commercialize the software applications, information, and entertainment that flow through the highways to and from the platforms.'[31] This structure has emerged due in large measure to the 'inter-changeability' of the digital technology, allowing for the mixing and matching of hardware and services to create a variety of multipurpose networks. This new environment needed new legislation.

The Telecommunications Act of 1996,[32] signed into law by President Bill Clinton, went far in eliminating many inconsistencies brought about by tech-nological convergence, industry mergers, and sectoral shifts, and thereby attempted to address contemporary telecommunication and information policy concerns. The Act was crafted ostensibly to advance the public good by pro-moting competition and reducing regulation. 'By significantly deregulating all segments of the communications industry, lawmakers . . . sought to create a more level regulatory playing field while at the same time fostering competi-tion. They hope that, with competition, the government's role as regulator [could] be reduced considerably.'[33] However, in its present form it has been criticized as being in violation of rights protecting the freedom of speech through the banning of nebulously defined indecent or 'obscene' communica-tion.[34] Furthermore, certain provisions repealed price controls on cable and phone rates and permitted greater concentration of media ownership, thus worrying many consumer advocacy groups.

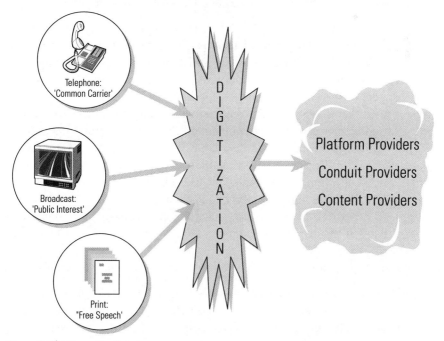

Figure 3: The Emerging Structure

Neither does there appear to be adequate public quid pro quo in the Act as it now stands. Many voice disappointment over a lost opportunity to formulate a truly visionary telecommunication and information policy foundation for the US:

> Although the Telecommunications Act of 1996 was generally welcomed as being long overdue, none of the parties to it were completely satisfied with the results. Arrived at through the course of intense Congressional lobbying, the law that was eventually adopted represented a carefully crafted compromise rather than a bold blueprint for the future. . . . One should not, therefore, expect the Telecommunications Act of 1996 to lead to [any] real reform. To the contrary, as things stand now, it will likely yield nothing more than a hyped-up, digital version of the past.[35]

Still, the conventional wisdom in Washington is that if all unnecessary legal and regulatory barriers are removed, then private interests will step in to build the NII/GII. Vice-President Al Gore first voiced this sentiment in a speech made before the National Press Club in December 1993 when he stated:

> This Administration intends to create an environment that stimulates a private system of free-flowing information conduits. . . . Our goal is not to design the market of the future. It is to provide the principles that shape that market. And it is to provide the rules governing this difficult transition to an open market for information. We are committed in that transition to protecting the availability, affordability, and diversity of information and information technology, as market forces replace regulations and judicial models that are no longer appropriate.[36]

Indeed, some argue that the debate over whether or not the government should be involved in building the NII/GII is meaningless because the simple fact is, government cannot afford the hundreds of billions of dollars it would cost to lay optical fibre to every home, office, school, factory, hospital, and library in the United States. 'Fiscal reality dictates that the creation of the [NII/GII] will be a joint effort between the government and the private sector.'[37] Within the US, the Clinton-Gore administration hopes that by establishing protocols, standards, and test-bed projects, private industry will be encouraged to do the rest.[38] The US also hopes that employing such efforts—while calling on every nation to establish an equally ambitious agenda—will serve as 'the basis for engaging other governments in a consultative, constructive, and cooperative process that will ensure the development of the GII for the mutual benefit of all countries.'[39]

Canada's IHAC took up the mantle of this effort in its final report, stating:

> With technologies that increasingly destroy distance, the challenge of seizing the opportunities of the new age is not merely national, but global in nature. The new technologies are truly creating an arena independent of jurisdictions and boundaries. With

> this new reality comes an ever more pressing need to align national strategies with the worldwide movement toward a global information society.[40]

However, before any government commits to any telecommunication and/or information policy, it must first arm itself with an understanding of the situation at hand and the commitment to seek intervention for redress of private enterprise's failures should such action be warranted. In the US, this means reaffirming the government's social contract and commitment to the public interest as it relates to cyberspace: 'the [Clinton-Gore] administration must make clear . . . that it will do whatever is necessary to ensure affordable access to the network. It must also help to educate Congress concerning the policy implications behind the network.'[41]

There is still much contention surrounding the respective roles government and business should play in the building of the NII/GII. The Canadian government's perspective is similar to that of the US, namely, that the success of the NII/GII will be determined by the marketplace, not by government—'hence, the primary role of the government should be to set the ground rules and act as model user . . . the private sector should build and operate the [NII/GII]. Those who make the investments should bear the risks and reap a fair reward.'[42] What appears likely, however, is that the NII/GII will probably be 'an extremely heterogeneous collection of [mostly privately owned and operated] local and regional information infrastructures and long-haul networks [whose] component parts will be [publicly accessible and] developed at different rates and organized in different ways . . . [In other words,] an array of computerized networks, intelligent appliances, applications, and services that people [will] use to interact with digital information.'[43] Interestingly, little is asked of the public's role—that of the user-citizenry—in the construction and conduct of the NII/GII. Whereas the on-line debates in cyberspace are polarizing over these issues, such discussions remain largely ignored by both the 'captains of industry' and Washington's bureaucrats.

What does appear certain, however, is that actions taken over the next few years will, in many ways, determine the political and economic structure of cyberspace for decades to come. Perhaps this is where the real challenges surrounding the building of the NII/GII exist—not in its physical hardware construction, but in its social construction. Within this realm the people's voice must and should be heard. This may come about not so much as a result of the mega-mergers taking place within the information sector as businesses jockey to be the new platform, conduit, and/or content providers of the future NII/GII. Nor would it be the result of the phenomenal progress in making computers faster, more powerful, and better able to augment the human mind. Rather, the most important resources on the world's networks are still people.[44]

Scenarios of the NII/GII

> [T]o find a technological fix for our dissolving communities is not new. Yet because we are increasingly afflicted with that particularly postmodern disability, acontextuality, we tend to forget failed dreams.[45]

The likelihood, for now anyway, is that the emerging NII/GII—the information superhighway—will not be a single entity, even though the name may suggest otherwise. As was suggested earlier, it will probably be an aggregation of many different networks—local, regional, national, multinational, one-way, two-way, point-to-point, point-to-multipoint, wire line transmissions, and wireless—each providing a variety of services. Initially, and perhaps for quite some time, most of these networks will likely be disconnected from each other, only allowing occasional cross-network exchanges.[46] None the less, certain components and services will predominate, each offering its image of the NII/GII as the 'one true vision' of the Information Age that we should all support. Of course, the officially stated US federal government position on the NII/GII is an important force, as are those of other national governments, intergovernmental organizations (e.g., the European Union, the International Telecommunications Union, the Organization for Economic Co-operation and Development, and the World Trade Organization), and the various non-governmental groups active in areas of education and computer advocacy (e.g., Electronic Frontier Foundation and Computer Professionals for Social Responsibility, among others).

The most vocal in offering their perspective to the public, however, have been the commercial interests, especially those that already control the technological base on which the NII/GII will likely be built. This includes the local, regional, and national operating companies of the telephone system and numerous cable and satellite television companies, many of whom already own wires into most homes and, in the case of the telephone companies, most businesses as well. Other potential players are the entertainment industry and news and information outlets, which aim to corner the market for providing much of the content on the NII/GII. Likewise, the computer, consumer electronics, and communications companies, which will build the switches, communication gear, and home terminals to make it all work, are equally preoccupied with carving out a market niche of their own. All of these have been trying to position themselves, through mergers, acquisitions, and strategic alliances, to guarantee that they will have a part in, or even ownership and control of, the NII/GII.[47]

Although this environment still remains very much in a state of perpetual motion, the following three alternative visions are 'snapshots' of a possible future NII/GII. As such, they may be a bit blurry or poorly framed, yet each is derived from a variety of sources with its own gallery of champions as well as detractors. Each, however, presumes capabilities that could be realized with available and emerging technologies not long after the turn of the century. Furthermore, new technical breakthroughs, regulatory framework changes, competitive initiatives, and, ultimately, market acceptance will inevitably affect and alter their respective outcomes. Each of these scenarios presents a vision of the NII/GII that alludes to who will have access, what it will cost, what services will be available, what equipment will be needed to access it, how it will be governed, and how it will work. These 'visions' have very different implications for society. The struggle unfolding now is over which vision will prevail.[48] The winner will probably be the one that best 'sells' its image of the network to the financial community, policy-makers, and the public. In the end, however, what can be said with reasonable certainty is that the actual outcome could conceivably contain aspects of each vision and yet be completely different from all three.

The Information Society[49]

If we are to believe the government hype, then life 'in cyberspace . . . will shape up exactly like Thomas Jefferson would have wanted: founded on the primacy of individual liberty and the commitment to pluralism, diversity, and community.'[50] In this vision of cyberspace, people can live (physically) almost anywhere they want without forgoing opportunities of association or useful and fulfilling employment by 'telecommuting' to their 'virtual offices' or gathering at 'Cyberspace Inns'[51] all within easy access via the information superhighway. The best 'schools' (such as they would exist in cyberspace), teachers, courses, and vast storehouses of information would be available to all students without regard to geography, distance, resources, or disability. This promotes a vision of education as a mechanism of encouraging individual student exploration, interaction, discovery, and growth with the instructor acting as mentor and guide.

Furthermore, in the new global economy, where knowledge is the key resource—and thus, the key to prosperity—the principle of lifelong learning becomes essential for ensuring competitiveness. Workers will begin to demand access to the widest possible variety of learning opportunities and tools, pushing the integration of computer-based technology and learning and creating business opportunities in course-ware development, course delivery, and software applications. Likewise, services that would improve health care and respond to other important social needs would all be available 'on-line' without having to wait 'in-line' whenever and wherever one needs them. Because of the free flow of information across local, state, regional, and national boundaries, access to government information at all levels becomes a 'right' of all citizens in the facilitation of their informed participation in the democratic process at whichever level they so choose. As well, businesses would use the network to develop new ideas and new modes of interactive use, or use the network as a way to restructure themselves, improve communications, share ideas more effectively, and get closer to their customers. Small manufacturers could get orders from all over the world electronically, and with detailed specifications in a form that the machines could use to produce the items.[52] Individuals would also have access to movies-on-demand and all the hottest video games, and could do their banking and shopping from the comfort of their own homes whenever they chose.

Couch Potatoes in Cyberspace

We have heard this one before. Remember the promise that television would bring us an educational and information cornucopia pouring forth from the end of an electrical wire? Now, the telecommunications and cable TV executives are seeking to marginalize alternative visions while simultaneously trying to allay concerns over their proposed mega-mergers, insisting that the melding of entertainment and communications giants presages the coming of an electronic superhighway that will connect students with learning resources, provide a forum for political discourse, increase economic competitiveness, and speed us into the multimedia information age.[53]

Big business, however, is not interested in free markets; rather, it wants captive markets, and it will design the NII/GII for its own benefit and to meet its own needs. This particular vision is one that sees the NII/GII as a huge conduit between the Fortune 500 companies and a whole world of potential consumers.[54] The popularized vision of the 500-channel, high-bandwidth information superhighway into the home offered up by the media will actually treat the users as customers to be targeted rather than as citizens to be connected. Consumer choice will be greatly limited by monopolies, both horizontal and vertical. The concept of 'common carriage' will have disappeared in most markets, while control of not only the network but also most of its services will be in the hands of the few, shutting out small businesses and individuals as information providers. Access equipment will be designed for obsolescence, requiring subscribers to replace or upgrade it frequently to remain on-line. The information superhighway of this vision will push product and 'infomercials' at customers while collecting and trading consumer data to fuel ubiquitous and 'in your face' advertising.[55] Despite mounting evidence to the contrary,

> buzzwords like 'interactive' and 'choice' [will] frequently [be] employed. 'Choice,' however, means no more than a consumer choosing a product offered by the seller of services or commodities. . . . 'Interactive' means the ability to punch in your credit card number and order products via screen commands from home. The very language of interactivity and the new data communications [will be] subverted by [an] emphasis on one-way flow and sales.[56]

Finally, privacy will be rare on the commercialized information superhighway while freedom of speech, freedom of assembly, and other constitutional rights will likewise be severely restricted. 'Instead of treating cyberspace as a new communications medium to which the U.S. Constitution extends, policy-makers will regard it as special territory in which the constitution has limited applicability.'[57]

Staged Transition

Thanks in part to the increasing popularity of the Internet—a network of computer networks that some see as the prototype of the way the NII/GII could and should operate—computer users have discovered that high-powered, state-of-the-art equipment such as that needed for full-motion video is nice, but not necessary, for serving the public good. Many people are using the widely available narrow-band technology and a computer with a modem and a CD-ROM drive for communication, information access and dissemination, transaction-oriented tasks, and various 'edutainment' activities.[58] Thus, individuals of all age groups, income levels, ethnic backgrounds, and educational attainment are able to use this equipment, if given proper training and support, in the context of activities that serve their needs and capture their interest.[59] One of the compelling aspects of this vision is 'interactivity'. If we see the NII/GII as a meeting place, then we will recognize that the purpose of the information superhighway is to bring people together, to foster community. Access would therefore be open to everyone and interaction would be encouraged. This type of connectivity will further allow users to participate actively in communities of interest, not in 'virtual' isolation from each other, but as an overlay to real-life communities. The important issues will be social, not technical: How do people interact? What kind of facilities are needed to support co-operation and group work? How can people with similar interests find one another? How are the benefits and costs of the system shared equitably? The communication landscape of this scenario is seen as always growing, adapting, and changing in response to new ideas and initiatives. Governance is not so much about imposing rigid control as building an environment that fosters co-operation and trust.[60]

These attributes, therefore, suggest that the development of the NII/GII might proceed in measured stages. We will develop and use information technology applications in layers, starting with basic network services. The evolution will be driven by applications that provide new levels of interactivity and connectivity rather than applications that are simple extrapolations of the passive models of the past. It would be pull-oriented rather than push-oriented. It would support forms of exchange other than product consumption. It would offer public services as well as private ones. It could allow us to preserve our privacy if we so desired. It would enhance communication within real-life neighbourhoods. It would connect rather than target us.[61] Instead of one or two individual 'killer applications' attracting users to the information superhighway, a large number of diverse applications that touch many different parts of our lives will drive the demand for incrementally higher and higher levels of bandwidth and services from the infrastructure.[62] In turn, as user demand increases, so will the technological capabilities to deliver such services at lower and lower costs enable the definition of 'basic services' to grow and expand as the network does—pulling the bottom up with it as it goes. Finally, infrastructure providers would make their money selling communications connectivity and bandwidth instead of zirconium jewellery, movies, and pizza. 'Such a system would generate more total value when summed across the entire economy, yielding a higher gross national product and a better standard of living.'[63]

Whither Cyberdemocracy?

The good news from Washington is that every single person in Congress supports the concept of an information superhighway. The bad news is that no one has any idea what that means.[64]

Whatever the origins of the technologies employed, or the policies eventually put in place to guide them, the fundamental questions about the design and use of the NII/GII remain. 'Will the information superhighway be decentralized, inexpensive, and open? Will it facilitate grassroots production and distribution? Or will it permit the media giants to establish a one-way flow of home shopping and movies-on-demand?'[65] Thus, what appears missing from the above three scenarios of the NII/GII is a clear articulation of the rights and responsibilities of the user-citizenry. In other words, how can we ensure the exercise of democratic principles in cyberspace beyond that of a 'yes/no' push-button on the remote? This has important ramifications on the outcome of the above scenarios, for cyberdemocracy implies the possibility that governance in the twenty-first century could include a great deal more 'activism' on the part of its citizens. In other words, informed participation in such activities as national advisory plebiscites, initiatives, and referenda that would impose the public's will directly on government policy, or at least on certain issues of national importance. If cable shopping channels can install 'high-speed, large-capacity computerized systems to process millions of viewers' telephone credit card orders', so the argument goes, '[t]he same or similar technology can be recruited to tabulate votes, process polls, and count the results of initiatives and referenda, dialed in from anywhere.'[66] Exactly how this will transpire on the NII/GII still needs to be worked out. The same technology that is able to identify and link citizens and political institutions to facilitate the conduct of direct democracy—as well as other forms of legitimate constituent participation in the democratic process—could also, if not formulated correctly, facilitate nationwide identification systems and increased governmental surveillance.[67] Likewise, the technology environment could institutionalize entry barriers where whole segments of society lacking the economic wherewithal to 'buy in' could be written off—if they are not already. Such issues need to be carefully monitored as governments undergo an inevitable re-engineering in their attempts to become more responsive to an increasingly more electronic society.

In the end, however, 'The question is not whether the transformation to instant public feedback through electronics is good or bad, or politically desirable or undesirable. Like a force of nature, it is simply the way our political system is heading. The people are [already] being asked to give their own judgment before major governmental decisions are made';[68] political parties and special interest groups employ a multitude of pollsters for just this purpose. Armed with this information, our politicians then massage their rhetoric (and public identities) in order to reinvent themselves as leaders in the public's latest image of what a leader should be and attempt to illustrate in mediated sound bites how they have always been this way. Still, the argument continues to stress that 'Since personal electronic media, the teleprocessors and computerized keypads that register public opinion, are inherently democratic . . . their effect will be to stretch our political system toward more sharing of power, at least by those citizens motivated to participate.'[69]

Herein lies the dark lining to the silver cloud of cyberdemocracy; direct democracy via sophisticated information technology could also bring with it the inevitable tendency to pressure political leaders to respond quickly—perhaps too quickly—to every impulsive ripple of public opinion and hold the nation hostage to the tyranny of the majority. Such a tendency could fundamentally alter the conduct of government and perhaps even threaten some of our most cherished constitutional protections.[70] Such protections were put into place by the framers of the Constitution, who were as wary of pure democracy as they were fearful of governmental authority. What makes this particularly pernicious is that, in the emerging cyberdemocracy where information is a source of social power, those who are typically the downtrodden (many minority groups as well as the poor) are not even aware that they are on the verge of being disenfranchised.[71] So far, the information revolution has been largely waged by highly educated and informed advocates, people who often have tremendous resources at their disposal. These advocates have spoken quite well on behalf of their own needs; some have even attempted to speak to the needs of the 'information-poor'. But the 'information-rich', however well-meaning, have largely determined and prioritized the issues of the information revolution and the emerging cyberdemocracy according to their own visions and realities. 'Public or low-cost access to computers, communications channels, and data bases should be sought in [all] schools, homes, libraries, and community organizations'[72] if the promise of cyberdemocracy is to be realized. But information access as a basic public service is broached only tentatively at the national level.

Whereas communities with 'freenets' can be lauded for their efforts in public computing,[73] the implementation of these projects invariably assumes an 'information-rich' public proactively seeking and demanding such services.

Interestingly, it is perhaps within the most conservative branch of the US government, the judiciary, that the protection of the rights of the 'information-poor' may find redress from the excesses of the majority will in our future cyberdemocracy. 'As the political system grows ever more responsive to majority impulses, and the legislative and executive branches feel increased pressure to bend to the public will, the judiciary . . . under the Constitution . . . is in the best position to blow the whistle on runaway majorities.'[74] In our emerging cyberdemocracy, the judiciary will have the increasingly difficult and sensitive role of protecting the rights of unpopular minorities and thwarting the popular will when it gets out of hand. If the present American constitutional system of checks and balances transits into the twenty-first century relatively intact, then future courts in the US will 'have the ultimate responsibility to stop any tyrannical exercise of power, even by impassioned majorities of sovereign citizens. In the absence of such court protection, it is unlikely that any barrier would remain to protect unpopular minorities from being trampled on by majorities who believe they are in the best position to know what is in their own best interest.'[75] Without such protections, it could be argued, direct democracy in cyberspace could degenerate into an 'electronic Bosnia'—albeit a less physically violent one—where a weak state presides over 'warring' factions backed by media conglomerates battling for control of the communications landscape.

Therefore, in our emerging Information Age, it is important to recognize and state outright the basic principles of civil rights and responsibilities that should be imputed to cyberspace. We should not, as Thomas Jefferson admonished over two centuries earlier, allow something of such importance to 'rest on inference'. In the US, at least, this means, the declaration of the applicability of the American Constitution and the Bill of Rights to the issues posed by the advent of new uses of communications and information technologies.[76]

Within the US, the problem of melding old but still valid concepts of constitutional rights with new and rapidly evolving technologies is, perhaps, one of the most profound challenges to the 'common good' yet faced by our society. The meaning of freedom, structures of self-government, definition of property, nature of competition, conditions for co-operation, sense of community, and nature of progress will each need to be redefined. How well the US can adapt such cherished rights as the First Amendment issues of freedom of speech, press, and association and Fourth Amendment guarantees of the right to privacy and protection from unwarranted governmental intrusion, as well as Fifth Amendment assurances of the right to procedural fairness and due process of law, will depend on the degree of wisdom that guides the courts, legislatures, and governmental agencies entrusted with authority in this area of its national life. After all, 'Information technology provides us with the key to restructuring our governing system, simultaneously permitting more distribution and new concentration of power. The result may be more equality and more inequality, more cohesion and more splintering, more cooperation and more competition, more democracy and less.'[77] To protect the invariability of constitutional principles, despite accidents of technology, policy-makers should look not at what technology makes possible, but at the core values the Constitution enshrines—its protection of people rather than places, and its regulation of the actions of government and perhaps of corporations as well, but not of private individuals. To guarantee this, some have advocated the addition of a twenty-seventh amendment to the US Constitution, which could read:

> This Constitution's protections for the freedoms of speech, press, petition and assembly, and its protections against unreasonable searches and seizures and the deprivation of life, liberty or property without due process of law, shall be construed as fully applicable without regard to the technological method or medium through which information content is generated, stored, altered, transmitted or controlled.[78]

Ultimately, however, the form and function of the emerging NII/GII as well as the protection of US constitutional principles in the future will depend on whether or not ordinary citizens are up to the task of making sound judgements about which vision they wish to pursue and are willing to monitor the day-to-day decisions of government in the emerging computer-mediated landscape of cyberspace. Otherwise, these decisions will be made for them. 'A key question is whether we should trust the wisdom of citizens to guide our [democracy] into the future. An important insight into this question emerged from George Gallup, who reviewed his experience in polling American public opinion over half a century and found the collective judgment of citizens to be "extraordinarily sound". Gallup discovered that citizens are often ahead of their elected leaders in accepting innovations.'[79] Thus, if citizens want to exercise greater civic responsibility in the future cyberdemocracy, they must also familiarize themselves with the new communications landscape to shape it in the image they desire, and they must seek to acquire greater civic competence in the conduct of democracy in cyberspace. If the NII/GII is the information superhighway to the twenty-first century and 'technology is driving the future', then we must remember that 'the steering is [still] up to us!'[80]

Notes

[1] 'Cyberspace', a term originated by William Gibson in his novel *Neuromancer* (1984), has slipped into popular parlance as the unofficial moniker for the Internet—or, more specifically, what the Internet could become. Thus, as a product of science fiction and as an 'artifact' of the future, cyberspace is a slippery word to define. For our purposes cyberspace will be used here to signify a conceptual 'spaceless place' where words, human relationships, data, wealth, status,

and power are made manifest by people using computer-mediated communications technology. See M. Ogden, 'Politics in a Parallel Universe: Is There a Future for Cyberdemocracy?', *Futures* 26 (1994): 713–29.

2   J. Brook and I. Boal, eds, *Resisting the Virtual Life: The Culture and Politics of Information* (San Francisco, Calif.: City Lights Books, 1995), viii.

3   See N. Negroponte, *Being Digital* (New York: Alfred A. Knopf, 1995); W. Mitchell, *City of Bits: Space, Place and the Infobahn* (Cambridge, Mass.: MIT Press, 1995).

4   See C. Stoll, *Silicon Snake Oil: Second Thoughts on the Information Highway* (New York: Doubleday, 1995); S. Talbott, *The Future Does Not Compute: Transcending the Machines in Our Midst* (Sebastopol, Calif.: O'Reilly & Associates, 1995).

5   See F. Machlup, *The Production and Distribution of Knowledge in the United States* (Princeton, NJ: Princeton University Press, 1962); D. Bell, *The Coming of Post-Industrial Society* (New York: Basic Books, 1973); W. Dizard, Jr, *The Coming Information Age: An Overview of Technology, Economics, and Politics* (New York: Longman, 1982); H. Dordick and G. Wang, *The Information Society: A Retrospective View* (Newbury Park, Calif.: Sage, 1993); M. Porat, *The Information Economy*, 9 vols, US Department of Commerce, Office of Telecommunications, Special Publication 77–12 (Washington: Government Printing Office, 1977).

6   M. Ogden, 'Electronic Power to the People: Who Is Technology's Keeper on the Cyberspace Frontier?', *Technological Forecasting & Social Change* (Special Issue, Technology and Law in the 21st Century) 52, 2 & 3 (June/July 1996): 119–33.

7   R. Volti, *Society and Technological Change*, 3rd edn (New York: St Martin's Press, 1995), 3.

8   R. Karraker, 'Highways of the Mind', *Whole Earth Review* 70 (Spring 1991): 4.

9   R. Karraker, 'Making Sense of the "Information Superhighway"', *Whole Earth Review*, 82 (1994): 19.

10   Information Highway Advisory Council [IHAC], 'Preparing for a Digital World is Canada's road to the Future', news release, 4 Apr. 1997. Internet document [http://strategis.ic.gc.ca/SSG/ih00156e.html].

11   Ogden, 'Politics in a Parallel Universe'.

12   Karraker, 'Making Sense of the "Information Superhighway"'.

13   Ithiel de Sola Pool, *Technologies of Freedom* (Cambridge, Mass.: The Belknap Press of Harvard University Press, 1983).

14   Simply stated, Moore's Law observes that the processing power of a microchip (as indicated by transistor density) doubles at least every 18 months. Thus, as more and more sophisticated circuits are packed ever more tightly into these small wafers of silicon, the chips themselves have become tiny but incredibly powerful computers, vastly outperforming the room-sized mainframes of years past and finding application in almost every facet of our lives.

15   P. Coy, 'Faster, Smaller, Cheaper', *Business Week*, 12 July 1994, 54–7.

16   D. Davis, 'Trading Land for Cyberland', *SEEDlinks* 15 (Aug. 1995): 13–14.

17   M. McFarland, 'Humanizing the Information Superhighway', *IEEE Technology and Society Magazine* 14 (Winter 1995–6): 11–18.

18   M. Ogden, 'Politics in a Parallel Universe'.

19   For a description of US government policy approach to the NII, see *The National Information Infrastructure: Agenda for Action* (1993). For a more current, in-depth examination, see United States Advisory Council on the National Information Infrastructure, *A Nation of Opportunity: Realizing the Promise of the Information Superhighway* (Washington, 1996). The GII concept was first introduced by US Vice-President Al Gore at an International Telecommunications

Union-sponsored conference in Buenos Aires in March 1994. The GII, as articulated by the US government in *The Global Information Infrastructure: Agenda for Cooperation* (1995) by the Information Infrastructure Task Force, is envisioned to be a planetary information network connecting large cities as well as small villages around the globe and is primarily based on private investment, competition, open access, universal service, and flexible regulation. These same sentiments were also incorporated in the ITU's *Buenos Aires Declaration on Global Telecommunications Development for the 21st Century.*

20   L. Garcia, 'The Failure of Telecom Reform', *Telecommunications* [Americas Edition] 30, 9 (Sept. 1996): 43.

21   R. Solomon, 'Telecommunications Technology for the Twenty-First Century', in W. Drake, ed., *The New Information Infrastructure: Strategies for U.S. Policy* (New York: Twentieth Century Fund Press, 1995), 93–111.

22   See McFarland, 'Humanizing the Information Superhighway'; Ogden, 'Politics in a Parallel Universe'; The White House, *America in the Age of Information* (Washington, 1994). Available via [http://www.hpcc.gov/cic/forum/CIC_Cover.html].

23   David Porush, 'Ubiquitous Computing vs. Radical Privacy: A Reconsideration of the Future', *Computer-Mediated Communication Magazine* 2 (Mar. 1995). Available via [http://sunsite.unc.edu/cmc/mag/march].

24   J. Drew, 'Media Activism and Radical Democracy', in Brook and Boal, eds, *Resisting the Virtual Life: The Culture and Politics of Information*, 75.

25   Industry Canada, *Connection, Community, Content: The Challenge of the Information Highway*, Final Report (Phase I) of the Information Highway Advisory Council (Ottawa, 1995), 4. Internet document [http://strategis.ic.gc.ca/SSG/ih01070e.sgml].

26   L. Branscomb, 'Information Infrastructure for the 90's: A Public Policy Perspective', in B. Kahin, ed., *Building Information Infrastructure: Issues in the Development of the National Research and Education Network* (New York: McGraw-Hill, 1992), 17.

27   T. McGarty, 'Alternative Networking Architectures: Pricing, Policy and Competition', in Kahin, ed., *Building Information Infrastructure*, 218–70.

28   B. Kahin, 'The NREN as Information Market: Dynamics of Publishing', in Kahin, ed., *Building Information Infrastructure*, 323–43.

29   Branscomb, 'Information Infrastructure for the 90's', 15–30.

30   Garcia, 'The Failure of Telecom Reform', 43.

31   R. Stearns, 'The Promise of the National Information Infrastructure', in National Academy of Engineering, *Revolution in the U.S. Information Infrastructure* (Washington: National Academy of Engineering, 1995), 27.

32   The full text of this landmark piece of legislation is accessible in hypertext form via [http://www.technologylaw.com/techlaw/act_index.html].

33   Garcia, 'The Failure of Telecom Reform', 43.

34   For additional information on the Communication Decency Act (Title V of the Telecom Act of 1996) as well as the court case challenging this piece of legislation, see the postings available via the Electronic Frontier Foundation's Action Alerts at [http://www.eff.org/pub/Alerts/].

35   Garcia, 'The Failure of Telecom Reform', 43–4.

36   A. Gore, 'Remarks by Vice President Al Gore at National Press Club', The White House: Office of the Vice-President, Washington, 21 Dec. 1993. Full text available from Almanac Information Server by e-mailing a document request to almanac@ace.esusda.gov.

37   A. Biesada, 'Paving the Digital Superhighway', *UnixWorld* 10 (Dec. 1993): 59.

38   Gore, 'Remarks by Vice President Al Gore at National Press Club'.

39   Information Infrastructure Task Force [IITF], *The Global Information Infrastructure: Agenda for Cooperation* (Washington: National Telecommunications and Information Administration, Department of Commerce, and Office of the Vice-President, Feb. 1995), Internet document [http://www.iitf.nist.gov/documents/docs/gii/giiagend.html].

40   Industry Canada, *Preparing Canada for a Digital World*, Final Report (Phase II) of the Information Highway Advisory Council (Ottawa, 1997), 2. Internet document [http://strategis.ic.gc.ca/SSG/ih01650e.html].

41   G. Cook, 'NSFnet "Privatization" and the Public Interest: Can Misguided Policy Be Corrected?', executive summary, COOK Report on Internet—NREN, 1 (10 & 11), Dec. 1992. Available via gopher://ietf.cnri.reston.va.us/

42   Industry Canada, *Connection, Community, Content: The Challenge of the Information Highway*, Final Report (Phase I) of the Information Highway Advisory Council (Ottawa, 1995), 3. Internet document [http://strategis.ic.gc.ca/SSG/ih01070e.sgml].

43   W. Drake, ed., *The New Information Infrastructure: Strategies for U.S. Policy* (New York: Twentieth Century Fund Press, 1995), 4–5.

44   R. Stapleton, 'Opening Doors in the Global Village', *Computer* 25 (July 1992): 94–6.

45   Stephen Doheny-Farina, *The Wired Neighborhood* (New Haven: Yale University Press, 1996).

46   J. Johnson, 'The Information Highway from Hell: A Worst-Case Scenario', *CPSR Newsletter* 14 (1996): 16–18.

47   McFarland, 'Humanizing the Information Superhighway'.

48   Ibid.

49   This description draws mainly from US and Canadian government sources. *Critical Connections: Communication for the Future* (1990) by the US Office of Technology Assessment attempts to provide a broad context for evaluating the impact of new communication technologies. *National Information Infrastructure: Agenda for Action* (Sept. 1993) paints a glowing picture of the US in the Information Age. *America in the Age of Information* (1994) presents the US federal government's strategic plan for information and communications technologies. The US government's *A Nation of Opportunity: Realizing the Promise of the Information Superhighway* (1996) sets forth recommendations for charting a course to meet the government's goals of the NII. The Canadian perspective has been articulated in three influential reports issued by Canada's Information Highway Advisory Council: *Connection, Community, Content: the Challenge of the Information Highway* (Sept. 1995); *Building the Information Society: Moving Canada into the 21st Century* (May 1996); and *Preparing Canada for a Digital World* (Sept. 1997). What differentiates the Canadian reports from their US equivalents is their expressed commitment to reflecting Canada's 'cultural expression' and 'linguistic duality' on the information highway, as well as a commitment to an accelerated national access strategy, the creation and promotion of Canadian content, and the need to build a lifelong learning culture.

50   M. Kapor, 'Where is the Digital Highway Really Heading: The Case for a Jeffersonian Information Policy', *Wired* 1 (1992). Available via [http://www.hotwired.com/wired/1.3/features/kapor.on.nii.html].

51   J. Coates, *Cyberspace Innkeeping: Building Online Community* (1992). Available via gopher://well.sf.ca.us, or by e-mailing John Coates at tex@well.sf.ca.us.

52 This is perhaps a reference to Alvin Toffler's idea of the 'prosumer'. See A. Toffler, *The Third Wave* (New York: William Morrow, 1981), 251–73, 366–8, for a more detailed description.

53 M. Kapor and J. Berman, 'A Superhighway Through the Wasteland?', *New York Times*, 24 Nov. 1993, op-ed page.

54 Johnson, 'The Information Highway from Hell', 16–18.

55 Ibid.

56 Drew, 'Media Activism and Radical Democracy', 75

57 Johnson, 'The Information Highway from Hell', 17.

58 R. Sterns, 'The Promise of the National Information Infrastructure', in National Academy of Engineering, *Revolution in the U.S. Information Infrastructure* (Washington: National Academy of Engineering, 1995), 25–38.

59 S. Miller, 'The Building Blocks of Electronic Democracy: Electronic Voting Is Not Electronic Democracy', *CPSR Newsletter* 14 (1996): 1–2, 18–19.

60 McFarland, 'Humanizing the Information Superhighway'.

61 Johnson, 'The Information Highway from Hell', 6–18.

62 Sterns, 'The Promise of the National Information Infrastructure'.

63 Johnson, 'The Information Highway from Hell', 17.

64 Quoted in J. Blake and L. Tiedrich, 'The National Information Infrastructure Initiative and the Emergence of the Electronic Superhighway', *Federal Communications Law Journal* 46 (1994): 398.

65 Congressman Edward Markey, quoted in Drew, 'Media Activism and Radical Democracy', 82.

66 L. Grossman, *The Electronic Republic: Reshaping Democracy in the Information Age* (New York: Viking, 1995), 153.

67 K. Phillip, 'Virtual Washington', *Time* (Special Issue, Spring) 145 (1995): 65–8.

68 Grossman, *The Electronic Republic*, 154.

69 Ibid.

70 Ibid.

71 Typically, these are the people who have never heard of the information superhighway, who will not purchase computers with modems, who have never touched keyboards, who do not know what the Internet is because their priorities are primarily focused on mere survival. For further discussion of this issue, particularly in the context of small developing countries, see M. Ogden, 'Pacific Islands, Information Technology and Universal Access: It's Not Just About Wires', *Development Bulletin* 35 (Oct. 1995): 19–22. Also available via [http://www2.hawaii.edu/~ogden/piir/pacific/NJAW.html].

72 I. Barbour, *Ethics in an Age of Technology*, The Gifford Lectures, vol. 2 (New York: Harper-Collins, 1993), 175.

73 See, for example, some of the efforts in creating a public electronic bulletin board and the placement of public terminals to encourage participation in Santa Monica, California. M. Wittig, 'Electronic City Hall', *Whole Earth Review* 71 (Summer 1991): 24–7; and J. Van Tassel, 'Yakety-Yak, Do Talk Back!', *Wired* 2 (Jan. 1994): 78–80; as well as other musings on experiments in direct democracy via electronic town meetings such as D. Elgin, 'Conscious Democracy Through Electronic Town Meetings', *Whole Earth Review* 71 (Summer 1991): 28–9; P. Varley, 'Electronic Democracy', *Technology Review* 94 (Nov.-Dec. 1991): 43–51; B. Kirschner, 'Electronic Democracy in the 21st Century', *National Civic Review* (Fall 1991): 406–12.

[74] Grossman, *The Electronic Republic*, 162–3.

[75] Ibid., 163–4.

[76] C. Firestone and J. Schement, eds, *Toward an Information Bill of Rights and Responsibilities* (Washington: The Aspen Institute, 1995).

[77] H. Linstone, 'Mediacracy, Mediocracy, or New Democracy: Where are the Information Age Jeffersons and Madisons When We Need Them?', *Technological Forecasting and Social Change* 36 (1989): 163.

[78] N. Levinston, 'Electrifying Speech: New Communications Technologies and Traditional Civil Liberties', *Human Rights Watch* 4 (July 1992). Available via [http://ftp.eff.org/].

[79] Elgin, 'Conscious Democracy Through Electronic Town Meetings', 29.

[80] Text of a bumper-sticker distributed by the Computer Professionals for Social Responsibility. Their homepage is accessible at [http://www.cpsr.org/home.html].

Chapter 5

WOMEN ON THE NET: IMPLICATIONS OF INFORMAL INTERNATIONAL NETWORKING SURROUNDING THE FOURTH WORLD CONFERENCE ON WOMEN

Dineh M. Davis

—

... it is not difference which immobilizes us, but silence. And there are so many silences to be broken.[1]

—

Introduction

Technologically assisted social movements have, by their inherent 'mass' qualities, enjoyed a long and well-documented public history. Few will argue the impact of written language or—many centuries later—the printing press in shaping new societies. The accelerated pace of advances in communication technologies coupled with recent shifts in national political structures act as further proof of technology's central role in educating the public, empowering the disenfranchised, and forming global communities. Comparatively speaking, the history of women's issues is less well known, given the private status of much of women's traditional work and their lack of access to mass communication media. Women's relationship with new communication technologies, however, is becoming well documented by feminists who find themselves at the forefront of this field.[2]

Aspiring to study the Internet-based communication patterns of thousands of women across the globe as they prepared for their largest international gathering requires attention to three separate developments: (1) the growing diversity in private and public concerns of women in the late twentieth century; (2) shifts in the global and local sociopolitical environments that continue to oppress women institutionally while presenting a growing potential for women's advancement through 'pockets' of organizational and individual support; and (3) growth of a global telecommunication infrastructure that stands ready to test a number of long-standing theories about the power of human interaction and communication. Each of these developments is a multifaceted phenomenon studied by scholars in disciplines such as political science, sociology, women's studies, international and mass communication, computer science, economics, and philosophy. Informed by this conjunction, the following synthesis will only attempt to highlight the intersection of interests in communication technologies, social movements, and women's interpretation and focus on human rights in preparation for a single collective action: the Fourth World Conference on Women and the NGO Forum on Women '95.

Given the widespread availability of background information on the women's movement in general[3] and on the Beijing conference and the NGO Forum in particular,[4] this study focuses more specifically on the manner in which electronic technologies helped or hindered women's efforts at global communication in 1995. Before proceeding with this case study, however, it is important to place such communication patterns in their existing political and technological framework. While many technophile futurists have offered Utopian models of cyberdemocracy,[5] other students of new social movements have begun to re-acknowledge the existence of entrenched sociopolitical structures that continue to influence and moderate the social impact of new communication technologies.[6]

Tarrow's review of recent social movement literature[7] points to the need for crossing a number of paradigmatic boundaries to find overarching theories robust enough to handle the complexities of global social action initiatives. Within the discipline, he supports Lichbach's 1994 recommendation to combine elements from market-based collective action theories with those based on the rational choice model. Outside the discipline, he sees merit in incorporating social, technological, and economic theories that help explain the success or failure of collective action efforts. Women's issues, however, cross even more boundaries. Not only are women affected by political and public decisions, but by civil and private power structures as well. Not only must they abide by local customs, but they feel the pressure of global images and expectations. Not only are they denied many of the human rights taken for granted by men, but they suffer gender-specific discrimination such as systematic wartime rape, genital mutilation, and other local practices such as dowry and widow burnings.

Once we acknowledge the depth and breadth of women's issues as 'human issues' it becomes easier to grasp the true proportions of such global concerns. In turn, it becomes more obvious that improving such conditions is beyond the scope of a single collective action group or a cohesive social movement. Still, the existing framework was partially identified by Berry[8] when he observed that the actual beneficiaries of public interest groups played only a minor role in the decision-making process of such organizations, while Zald and McCarthy[9] noted that advocacy decisions for the multitudes are more often than not enunciated by the organizational structure and staff of the 'conscience constituency'. In the case of the Fourth World Conference on Women, the United Nations provided the institutional infrastructure around which hundreds of national and international NGOs built their support systems. Many feminists, as exemplified by Gittler and Light,[10] and national and international pro-feminist organizations welcomed the potential of new communication technologies, around which informal electronic networks grew and prospered.

With the organizing theme of Action for Equality, Development, and Peace, the Fourth World Conference on Women (FWCW) held the following 'real world' distinctions—separate from its electronic aura and incarnation:

> It was the largest conference ever sponsored by the United Nations. Approximately 30,000 individuals were involved in the two overlapping conferences: the United Nations Fourth World Conference on Women held in Beijing (September 4–14, 1995) and the NonGovernmental Organizations (NGO) Forum on Women held fifty kilometers away in Huairou (August 30 through September 8, 1995).[11]

It was the single largest gathering of women from around the world. Actual numbers of attendees—even if available—would be meaningless because of the difficulties in separating 'participants' from the media, local guides, Chinese officials and representatives in various capacities, etc. However, most estimates would place approximately 20,000 women in one location for a 10-day period. It is safe to say that the majority of these women did not have daily access to internationally linked computers in their home communities. It was the single largest gathering of experts in most professions and disciplines who also happened to be women. Therefore, these women represented many of the best and brightest minds from around the world. It was this awesome physical phenomenon that provided the impetus for an equally fascinating electronic world that mushroomed in its anticipation.

The Electronic Impetus

The primary global telecommunication network for all of the World Conferences on Women has been provided by the Association for Progressive Communication (APC). The United States is a member of the APC through the Institute for Global Communications (IGC)—a division of the Tides Foundation—which also sponsors WomensNet. In addition to many Web sites sponsored by the United Nations and local non-profit and non-governmental organizations, the following Beijing-related Internet mailing lists were monitored for this report:

> BEIJING95-L (unmoderated for men and women)
> BEIJING95-WOMEN (moderated, women only)
> BEIJING-CONF (UN Development Program sponsored)
> NEWW-BEIJING (Network of East-West Women living or invested in East and Central Europe or the former Soviet Union) (see Appendix for a listing of additional Web sites related to women's issues that were available in 1995).

Gathering preliminary observations regarding the use of these lists, and comparing them to academic lists I was using in parallel, I found that certain gendered use patterns emerged. Though there were no discernible differences in the way formal documents are shared on the network, women's informal interactions followed patterns that differed from North American male behaviour already observed by other researchers.[12]

Telecommunication network activity surrounding the 1995 Fourth World Conference on Women was perhaps no different from any that would surround a similar gathering for men—except, perhaps, for a greater number of bytes representing question marks and exclamation points—patterns that have carried over from women's speech, as observed by Tannen.[13] In context, however, these interactions were likely to foster thoughts regarding the advantages and shortcomings of electronic networks as the ultimate means for global communication among women. Thousands of women from hundreds of globally disparate nodes sent tens of thousands of messages, debated critical issues related to the Platform for Action, uploaded and downloaded volumes of official documents, made travel arrangements, exchanged suggestions for reading materials and trip preparations, offered last-minute invitations and swaps on Huairou sites, and—post-conference—submitted summaries and opinions on the outcome. The fact that these network activities were spawned in the peripheries of a very physical and global gathering of humans gives us the opportunity to observe the strengths and weaknesses of electronic connectivity vis-à-vis its face-to-face counterpart. Before examining these specific issues, however, we must begin with a presupposition and a brief discussion of communication differences between men and women.

If we were to look at telecommunication interactions from a purely physical and rational perspective, there should be no barriers—and therefore no differences between men's and women's use of the networks: we have equally capable brains, 10 fingers (though even one finger is not technically required!), and equal command of a language that can be represented in binary form. Differences emerge, however, if we begin to debate whether males and females prefer to use the same technologies and language for the same reasons and whether their thought patterns and responses to their environment resemble one another. Although an in-depth look at these issues is beyond the scope of the present paper, we may depend on existing studies that confirm gender differences in use of technologies,[14] applications of language and communication patterns,[15] and cognitive abilities.[16] Such differences are not significant enough, however, to preclude anyone from effective use of information and communication technologies (ICT). It is generally agreed that the manifestation of our differences is a result of social circumstances solidly entrenched throughout the world's cultures. The remainder of this paper is based on this premise rather than a theoretical agreement on the equality of sexes under existing social and political forces.

Discussion: The Costs of Electronic Travel

During the FWCW's NGO gathering in Huairou, I met a business entrepreneur from a West African country. Grace (not her real name) told me that, given a chance, she would go to every international conference in which her voice could be heard. It had been her experience that only if people outside her country became aware of women's obstacles in operating a business could she receive the needed assistance. As with anywhere else, receiving funding assistance was the most difficult barrier to expanding her business. Grace had seen repeatedly that those in her country with access to foreign capital diverted the funds through certain predetermined channels that assisted their own relatives rather than accepting legitimate applications from all sources. Though she was always on the lookout for funding sources, her travels abroad served many other purposes. In her travels she was focused on learning in its broadest sense:

immersing herself in a new environment to seek new information, meeting new people, understanding new cultures, seeing new products and variations in the way people conducted business, sharing her story with others, and establishing new friendships and connections worldwide.

Although there are clearly individual variations on such a theme, the majority of those who travelled to Huairou in September of 1995 had similar stories to tell. Could they all have stayed at home and simply networked through telecommunication media to accomplish their goals? Surely any one of Grace's goals could be reached via electronic networking. So why would intelligent humans fight visa restrictions and transportation problems, increase their expenses in time and money, and risk catching a new disease or dying on the road for the chance of physically participating in such a gathering? McAdam and Rucht suggest:

> For women . . . in one country to identify with their counterparts in another, a nontrivial process of social construction must take place in which the adopters fashion an account of themselves as sufficiently similar to that of the transmitters to justify using them as a model for their own actions . . . direct relational ties—even if minimal in number—between adopters and transmitters increase dramatically the chances of this process taking place.[17]

Time and again, those who have participated in electronic networking for establishing social ties confirm this necessity for occasional face-to-face meetings to solidify and expand cyber-relationships.

Of course, many chose not to go to Huairou physically but to participate through mediated sources alone. While only approximately 20,000 people gathered in one place, millions more witnessed or participated in the proceedings through public and private media text, voice, and video offerings. The 'full bandwidth' of an enormous gathering with its hours in the pouring rain, moments in ankle-deep mud, days in intense proximity of thousands of brains beaming in synchrony, and its many nights of mournings and celebrations was condensed into soundbites, sequential text, and montages that transformed a larger-than-life event into a manageable keepsake for future generations. It was an often-heard saying in Huairou that, 'Oh, you can always pick up the text of Hilary's [or Gertrude's, or Betty's] speech on-line; it's more important to be mingling with the crowds outside who are demonstrating, exchanging ideas, and making personal histories.' This was a critical form of information-gathering for women in China that went far beyond a binary format representable through ICT or quantifiable in terms of its tangible benefits.

While we are aware of the costs and risks of physical travel, not everyone has assessed the full costs of electronic travel. Certain more obvious factors are suggested here.

Hidden Identities/Hidden Agendas

Prior to the conference, a suggestion was made on-line to form a coalition of women's groups to hand-deliver the Platform for Action recommendations from Huairou to Beijing for consideration by the UN conference. This hand-to-hand delivery would require many miles of women occupying the roadside between Huairou and Beijing. It would be considered a 'demonstration' by the Chinese government—even if the women remained peaceful and did not obstruct traffic in any way. When I saw this notice, I could not help but wonder whether this was a legitimate suggestion, or simply a 'plant' by those in charge of security in Beijing to find out who the potential troublemakers might be. It would then be an easy step to take the participants' names from the network and delay assignment of hotel rooms to these individuals, which would in turn delay issuing of visas—thus pre-empting a move to 'demonstrate' in the most judicious and least obvious or inflammatory manner. Were all the women using the network aware that their messages could be monitored? How did we know the real initiators of certain messages or of certain suggestions for action? In reality, women living under dictatorships were more likely to remain alert and concerned whereas most Americans had less reason to be paranoid about security and privacy issues in this context.

Higher Access Costs and Unfavourable Fee Structures

As long as men and women are working in remunerative jobs in the public sector, their information exchange needs and patterns of use may be comparable. Once we move into the private and domestic spheres, the cost of information exchange is not always offset by tangibly quantifiable, monetary-based benefits. It is therefore even more critical to look at the cost of access as well as the fee structure for traffic over the lines. Models in our telephone industry have already shown shifts in usage dictated by message-unit fees versus a flat rate for services. Having to pay for every e-mail message received (as is the case outside of the US) reduces the individual's proclivity to tolerate duplicate messages or 'junk' mail initiated by marketers. Americans have less reason to be annoyed about such junk mail not only because many of us do not feel that we are paying for the intrusion, but also because it is already a part of our cultural belief system that clever capitalism should be encouraged (. . . if only *we* had been clever enough to make the first million dollars by advertising on a free or publicly subsidized medium!). Most of the rest of the world does not have the luxury of a low, flat rate service fee.

Limited Access Time

Just as many villages or rural communities in developing countries may have a single 'community' television in a public area for use by the entire neighbourhood, we are beginning to see the same shared access points developing for computer-based telecommunication systems. It is therefore critical to keep in mind that 'free' access does not necessarily mean unlimited access to the medium. In many sites connected to the Internet via the APC network, telephone access is so limited and line costs are so prohibitive that downloading of e-mail messages and the subsequent uploading of responses take place in very short 'batched' spurts in the least expensive time-slots offered by the phone company. This might mean that international communication is absolutely limited to true asynchronous mode with, at best, international contact once every 24 hours.

Language Barrier

Recent improvements in communication technologies have made it possible for individuals from non-English-speaking environments to be able to interact in many languages. Yet, such translations are neither trivial nor transparent on a system that was primarily designed for use by English-speaking individuals. Though the written text—read at one's own leisurely pace—provides the option for better comprehension and communication, for those who choose to interact 'live', language differences are a real barrier.[18] Even without the direct impact of new ICT, many non-English-speaking individuals must contend with English as their primary mode of global communication. In the Platform for Action, for example, language nuances such as the use of 'gender' instead of 'sex' or 'equity' instead of 'equality' made a significant difference in the connotation of certain women's rights such as their ability to choose a sex partner or to achieve an economic status equal to men rather than 'equitable' in the context of their existing and lower social status in relation to men.[19] Such debates are unfortunately likely to disappear on-line in an inclusive environment that must contend with the lowest common denominator of both language and cultural understanding.

Literacy Barrier

United Nations surveys place the world's illiterate adult population at one billion, with two-thirds being women. Such rates exceed 70 per cent in Africa and Asia. In developing countries, nearly 50 per cent of women over the age of 45 are illiterate. Now consider the fact that the technology of books and mass publishing has been with us since the mid-1400s. That is over 500 years of access! Such access did not require availability of pertinent local utilities such as a power source and a telephone. Such access was to a product that is relatively inexpensive, durable, and portable. The fact that we are still faced with such inequities in literacy rates should give some sobering thoughts to the academic élite who see the networks as every person's salvation and the direct route to a democratic form of government. The reality is that an illiterate population is a manageable population. Knowledge brings power, and shared power is the key to shared control. There is no need for new technology to show women how to read from a book. The last time Americans delighted in their powers of telecommunication to rid the world of illiteracy, they introduced the world to the wonders of television. The UN illiteracy figures noted above postdate the introduction of television by at least 40 years. That technology was touted for its power of magnifying the reach of teachers: one-to-many. At least with television there was the theoretical possibility of reaching the illiterate. What now?

The women surveyed by the APC in 1996 represented 28 countries from Africa, Asia and the Pacific, Eastern Europe, Europe, Latin America, the Middle East, and North America. Overwhelmingly, they identified education and training as their top priority and major obstacle to the use of electronic networks. It would be wise to overlay this critical concern about training on top of the historical data on women's illiteracy and the general rate of literacy worldwide. Viewed from that perspective it becomes more obvious that access, especially as defined by American telecommunication corporations, is hardly the sole or most appropriate answer.

Conclusion: Equality, Differences, and the Real World

Political scientists, politicians, futurists, technophiles, capitalists, and their respective media representatives speak of political and social equality for women on-line and presume that if they preserve cyberspace from the blight of censorship, equality and democracy will prevail. What we tend to forget is that these are self-selected groups of individuals with spheres of influence in the public arena. They may be our 'best and brightest', but in many instances the very qualities that have led them to their positions of power have equally distanced them from those who do not share their language or brain chemistry. It is not enough for women to be equal to men on-line because life does not begin and end on-line. Equality must begin in real life before permeating cyberspace. Cyberspace is not inhabited by aliens. Earthlings take their culture and cultural biases with them wherever they go—including the world of electrons. If women have gained the opportunity to mingle with men on-line it is because prevailing human conditions on earth have made their trip—as tenuous as it might be—a possibility.

In 1995, the FWCW served as an impetus to increase women's presence on electronic networks. At the same time, organizations such as the UN, the APC, and the Institute for Global Communications provided resources in the form of funding, technical support, and human connectivity. If this type of human infrastructure did not exist, there would be no real gain by women in the international arena—regardless of how many satellites may be in space or how many miles of fibre-optic cable may be circling the earth. In 1993 Berry assessed the changing nature of interest group politics in the United States and concluded: 'Citizen groups have been particularly important in pushing policymakers to create new means of structuring negotiations between large numbers of interest group actors. The greater participation of citizen groups, the increased number of all kinds of interest groups, and change in the way policy is made may be making the policymaking process more democratic.'[20] One might note that Berry's interpretation of a more democratic participatory system leading to a positive shift in policy-making was not based on changing ICT, but on the phenomenal growth of liberal advocacy groups—a trend that began in the 1960s, long before new communication technologies had a chance to affect social structure. By triangulating the perceptions of scholars from different disciplines we are likely to find a more balanced—though decidedly more complex—answer to the puzzling shifts in our social and political power structure. Technological advances alone cannot begin to make a difference in human life.

This chapter began with a presupposition born of common sense as well as scientific inquiry: each human marks a given point in a continuum of personality characteristics and mental or emotional traits observed among both men and women. This continuum stretches between the two end points of 'prototypically female' and the 'prototypically male'. Therefore, the differences between men and women are a matter of distribution within the general population, with few individuals falling exclusively within the characteristics of their sexual or gender prototype. Given this presupposition, the chapter's discussion of traits can be applied equally to both men and women. The only difference may be that in some cases we will find a preponderance of men on one side of the continuum or women on another. When both men and women are observed for their mediated communication behaviour patterns, researchers focus on differences to the detriment of pointing out similarities and overlaps. By focusing on just one sex, and by providing interpretive rather than quantitative analysis, I have tried to focus attention on the realities of this applied technology in human life.

Cycles, Continua, and Context

Western, rational thought works best—and is admired at its zenith—in the abstract. Cycles are best recognized when they have ended, and continua are forced apart into bipolarities because that is when they are most amenable to quantification. Yet humans live within ongoing cycles, are far more likely to inhabit a spot along a continuum, and are absolutely always in context. While the information exchange cycle is currently viewed from a binary perspective in technologically mediated environments, the majority of the world's population is privileged to experience it within an all-encompassing organic cycle. While the organic cycle of information exchange is all-inclusive, it cannot be retrofitted into a purely binary pattern. By the same token, the Western-based reductionism of a binary exchange cycle may not be wholly appropriate to the task of global understanding. Choosing the path to internal as well as international understanding depends on our ability to apply appropriate technologies towards the delivery of appropriate messages in a given cultural context. Not all humans need or respond to ICT in the same manner. Women's use of ICT should be seen as a part of a human needs continuum with four dimensions: work and play, stability and change, volunteerism and conscription, connectivity and separation.

The Doer/Player Dimension

For many years researchers and observers of computer culture have often differentiated our approach to computers based on whether we are using this device strictly to a get a job done or whether we relish the fringe benefit of 'playing' with our work tools. Many have concluded that girls and women are more likely to be application-oriented (doers) than men. Of course, if we remove men from our equation, we find that the continuum of work/play exists among women as well. It is possible, however, that the ratio of players to doers leans more heavily towards female doers rather than players. Is this a biological phenomenon or simply a matter of cultural necessity? Would women play more if they had less work to do? Or, if women had time to play, would they be more likely to choose communal games that involved other humans rather than machines? Much of the answer may depend on the cultural value placed on each type of human association. Unless we are to consider American culture as the de facto world model, it would be presumptuous to assume that every existing world culture is aspiring to 'play' with technology rather than simply use it as a tool for accomplishing necessary tasks. Women around the world continue to have much serious work ahead and there is no reason to believe that they will be any less accomplished than men in harnessing the powers of ICT to achieve their goals. The continuously increasing number of World Wide Web sites that are produced and used by women attests to their capabilities in this arena.

The Grasper/Griper Dimension

Inability to come to grips with new technology and the need for stability plague most men and women. In their haste to show gender differences in computer use, many researchers use women's willingness to profess their unease with new technology to mask the fact that many men also experience the same anxieties. However, because in most cultures men are 'expected' to be able to deal with any new technology, they are far more reticent to share such a shortcoming publicly. Women, on the other hand, are more at ease in seeking help and admitting their lack of knowledge. Again, when the gender domains are separated, it is easy to detect both graspers and gripers among men as well as women. Graspers are more likely to be ahead in the race to obtain, implement, and use new communication technologies. The cultural implications of following this impulse are entirely dependent on the individual's country of residence and its government's policy on following the lead of First World nations. A recent survey indicates that over 100 network users from 28 countries had taken the initiative to respond to 'Women's Networking' questions posed by the APC (1996). The respondents were uniformly positive about their ability to use this international network to further their goals of educating women about the technology as well as the flow of information across national boundaries. If we were to locate these women along our continuum, though they may have much to complain about, they are more likely to be graspers than gripers and, as such, they are appropriately the first volunteers as well. By definition, they are also a self-selected group of respondents who can tell us nothing about those who have chosen not to participate in this electronic forum.

The Volunteer/Conscript Dimension

Access is not enough! Affinity and choice may be just as critical in determining the individual's ultimate acceptance of the technology. Many futurists and proponents of cyberdemocracy believe that access is the key to equality. However, that can only be true if access is defined in the broadest possible manner, including not just the free and continuous physical connectivity, but also a barrier-free interface that causes no hesitation on the part of the individual to use the system. Ideally, such an interface should require nothing beyond an individual's desire to interact with another human—as one might in a face-to-face conversation. Although this may well be within the theoretical grasp of scientists and technologists, we are not likely to implement such systems universally anytime soon.

Many individuals use ICT not because these are their preferred modes of communication, but because they are the only option. It is not every individual's free choice to use such technologies; rather, they are conscripts in the legion of users. This pattern should become even more apparent when ICT reach saturation levels, as the initial stages of implementation are likely to attract personally motivated volunteers. At this point in the development of international telecommunication networks, we see a preponderance of volunteer women who are technophiles as well as well-balanced doers and players. Early volunteers must be proficient enough with the technology—to tinker with or play with the technology—to operate these primitive systems.

The Buffer/Connector Dimension

One of the major advantages of asynchronous (one-way at a time) communication is that individuals may choose when and whether to respond to a message. Many individuals choose this 'buffering' mechanism to avoid interaction with others, while others will gladly welcome the opportunity to 'connect' by adding yet another mode of communication to their existing repertoire of options: face-to-face, postal service, telephone, and fax, to name the most common. Researchers such as Tannen[21] have observed that men and women communicate for different primary purposes: men primarily to exchange information; women primarily to build relationships. While asynchronous communication is generally adequate for information exchange or sustaining relationships, it is less commonly used as the preferred method for beginning and building long-term relationships. In the context of the FWCW, women were equally interested in information exchange and relationship-building. Despite obvious information overload—especially for system operators and NGO staff—personal (relationship-type) messages were exchanged routinely. Not only were women actively involved in the facilitation process of telecommunicated messages along the network, but they were also creating new paths outside the network by using fax and telephone trees, postal service, and even radio broadcasts to relay messages that originated on the Internet.[22]

One of the innovative uses of the Internet during the Beijing conference was Internet voice mail to relay full on-site interviews to destinations outside of China for immediate radio broadcast. This method was totally informal and independent of the official media path. It bypassed the long and tedious process to which major news media adhered in clearing the material with government officials before relaying the news through satellite channels. An even more informal and personal use of the mediated network was based on the expedient of sending messages to one's own e-mail account outside China. This included reporting summaries of daily activities, program notes, etc. via e-mail, thus avoiding the use and transport of paper on a daily basis or upon leaving China.[23] Patterns of communication unique to women were most apparent in the informal interactions that took place on-line, with primary distinguishing characteristics being flexibility and tolerance. In nearly 10 months of monitoring the Beijing conference lines (May 1995 through February 1996) I was able to distinguish the following three manifestations of tolerance.

1. *Tolerance for opinions.* Every imaginable subject within the general bounds of 'human rights' was posted. These topics ranged from the legal rights of prostitutes to the Vatican's stand on the rights of the fetus; from domestic concerns in an African, European, or Asian country to international policies and politics; from lesbian and gay rights to domestic violence, rape as a war crime, and the plight of the girl child. Every topic related to the Platform for Action, and every suggestion for its change or improvement received bandwidth and time. Even tangential concerns (such as Harry Wu's plight in China) received a fair share of transmission time. Though opposing views were aired, very few met with overtly intolerant responses. Even then, the reprimands were 'gentle' compared to other professional list interactions I have monitored.

2. *Tolerance for procedural variations and violations.* Even at the height of message loads just preceding the conference, very few objected to being inundated with irrelevant or duplicate messages. On one occasion when a member complained about consistently receiving multiple copies of certain documents because of the overlap in the two Beijing conference lines, the list owner reminded everyone about the ground rules for each list and the fact that the owner was simply transmitting messages and not censoring or filtering the material. The immediate reaction from many quarters was in the form of full support for the system operator and a small flood of thank-you notes for a job well done. As well, there were always newcomers (to networking as well as to the list) who committed 'newbie' *faux pas* without causing the typical avalanche of hate mail by the already-initiated. This atmosphere of tolerance is a welcome requisite to building international connections that can survive the often inhospitable nature of the infrastructure and its software systems.

3. *Minimal flaming.* Except for a set of interactions between an American national based in Hong Kong and a Chinese woman there was little else that could be classified as 'flaming'. In this particular set of interactions, there were ideological and cultural differences as well as their potential second-order effect related to English language use. Even in this instance, others stepped in to moderate the misunderstanding rather than fuelling the fire or 'taking sides', which is the typical outcome of many male flame wars. On the occasion of a male participant using condescending language to admonish some women for their lack of understanding of an international issue, the basic reaction was to ignore the comments. Here is one example of direct mediation by a woman, addressed (though consciously indirectly) to the male participant:

> I am offended by the tone of several of the messages I have been reading—I will not name names; and I feel it is affecting the quality of the communication. If you disagree with someone's comments or opinions, please do so in a thoughtful manner without attacking or criticizing. I do not feel that this conference should be restricted to 'facts', 'science' and only information that can be substantiated by a textbook; we are also sharing ideas, opinions, in an attempt to understand each other and how our attitudes and own experiences affect the world around us. I do not wish to generalize here—but why is it that a number of men recently have been criticizing women's posts in particular? This is creating a very hostile environment for those participating. Can we please return to a more positive and supportive way of communicating?[24]

Before and during the conference most interactions were goal-oriented—focusing on the plans for the conference—but messages that followed the conference were intended to keep the process alive and operational for the long run. Although many reports were posted after the conference that shared the outcome of specific projects as well as the final Platform for Action, there were as many calls for continuing the interaction and expanding the electronic community through the initiation and upkeep of new Web sites. Interactive networks provided a format that turned information recipients into active participants. This empowering mechanism can and does help create a balance of power among the various members of the Net. APC (1996) survey respondents confirm this feeling of empowerment experienced by those who were able to share their knowledge with others on the network rather than simply receive information from an authoritative source.

Cultural differences were manifested in the form of language and technological barriers. In the context of language, it was apparent that native and non-native speakers of English could not always separate language from culture. For example, a Chinese woman reprimanded an American by saying:

> Your message sound [sic] very bossy to me since you always demand full attention from others like a single child. . . . You don't have to attack and challenge all the time to show your capabilities. . . . Probably nobody has tried to teach you how to behavor [sic] and care about your manner. . . . Try to learn some basic principles of democracy and learn how to communicate with others on an equal base [sic].[25]

This was one of the very few incidences that might be classified as 'flaming' on-line. Unlike the male habit of fanning the flames or standing by to watch the show, members of the conference line tried to mediate and mend fences. Many saw the problem not in the context of personal affront, but rather as a lack of cultural understanding.

Manifestation of culture through the technological infrastructure is a far more insidious problem. In many cultures 'being visible' means drawing unnecessary attention to oneself. This can in turn be equated with self-promotion. Under this precept, once women stop 'lurking' on the network and start speaking, they become visible, draw attention to themselves, and are thus subjects of self-promotion. Although we have spent at least two generations in the US promoting this behaviour as not only acceptable but necessary to women in professional settings, it is still against the fundamental values of many individuals (both men and women). Mediated technologies in the US have taken the edge off the individual's reticence to remain private. We are routinely subjected to the private affairs of individuals on television and radio talk shows. We see the parody of public figures in private situations on soap operas, talk television, and sit-coms. Still, even American women are more reluctant than men to participate in electronic public fora.[26] Such hesitance is accentuated in cultures that have not received the same 'push' from the business sector and the media.

Another ICT imperative is the World Wide Web's homepage phenomenon. This overtly self-promoting, open display of personal information is unlike any other culturally sanctioned form of public disclosure (especially for women), given that the page owner has no control over who views the page and for what purpose. In addition, it is a static information source masquerading as an active—if not always interactive—information phenomenon. Who among us is truly capable of updating homepage information as often as necessary? In addition, a presence on the Web presumes access to high-end computing and telecommunication facilities, neither of which is a given in most developing countries. In fact, the US is likely to dominate the netwaves for the foreseeable future because of its relatively large population base with a technological advantage.

The coincidence of the FWCW taking place in the mid-1990s (which also saw a major growth spurt in international networking based on a combination of hype and availability of the telecommunication infrastructure) makes it difficult to assess the independent effects of these factors on women's use of electronic networks. Although academicians in developed countries have the luxury to focus on emerging technology and view it as a panacea to entrenched social problems, those in less fortunate circumstances seem to remain entrenched in the status quo. By taking a long-range view we can absolve ourselves of the difficulties that surround us or are about to approach in a not-too-distant future. Looking back over the last 100 years, however, we can have a fair perception that providing the technology of communication does not necessarily equate with providing an educational content through those media.

Ultimately, no matter how technologically gifted they are, most women and men will need to step back from their terminals and computers into a world that provides nourishment for their souls, comfort for their families, and—if they are lucky—a soft pillow to rest upon at the end of a long day. If, by then, this world has not caught up with the full value of women in their own communities, the most die-hard among them will fail to make an electronic shelter that will alone provide women with continued sustenance.

Appendix: Web Sites

Dozens of World Wide Web sites were created in response to the FWCW by a variety of NGOs and governmental and private agencies. The most relevant among them:

http://www.igc.apc.org/womensnet/beijing/beijing.html
http://www.undp.org/fwcw/daw1.htm
http://www.igc.apc.org/gfw
http://www.whitehouse.gov/WH/EOP/Women/IACW
http://www.ifias.ca/gsd/gsdinfo.html
http://www.interaction.org/caw.html

For a complete listing of APC conferences related to women's issues one may contact: womensdesk@igc.apc.org or see the Womensnet site at: http://www.igc.apc.org/womensnet/wom-conf.html

Some regional sites advertised through the Beijing conference line included:

Women for Women in Bosnia: http://embassy.org/wwbosnia.html
Japan Women's On-Line Media Project: http://tsuru.suehiro.nakano.tokyo.jp/WOM
Area Mujeres-Agencia Latinoamerica de Informacion: http://www.ecuanex.apc.org/alai/comgen.html
Network on East-West Women: http://www.igc.apc.org/neww/
China: http://www.ihep.ac.cn/china_www.html
Chinese Organizing Committee for the Beijing conferences: http://www.ihep.ac.cn/women/main.html
Regional co-ordination unit for Latin America: http://www.nando.net/prof/beijing/in.html
Basecamp Seattle: http://www.scn.org/scripts/menus/w/WC/international.menu
Native American Indian Health Service: http://www.tucson.ihs.gov

Notes

1 Audre Lorde, *Sister Outsider* (Trumansburg, NY: Crossing Press, 1984), 42.

2 For excellent additional sources, see Alice Mastrangelo Gittler, 'Taking Hold of Electronic Communications: Women Making a Difference', *Journal of International Communications* 3 (1996): 85–101; Alice Mastrangelo Gittler, 'Building Effective Electronic Information Strategies For Beijing Follow-Up', paper read at Global Information through Computer Networking Technology in the Follow-up to the Fourth World Conference on Women, New York; S.C. Herring, 'Gender and Democracy in Computer-Mediated Communication', in Rob Kling, ed., *Computerization and Controversy: Value Conflicts and Social Choices* (San Francisco: Academic Press, 1996), 476–89; Jennifer S. Light, 'Not the Old Boys' Network: Women's Groups and Global Computer Networking', Philosophy dissertation (University of Cambridge, 1994); Dale Spender, *Nattering on the Net: Women, Power and Cyberspace* (Toronto: Garamond, 1995).

3 See, for example, Sara Evans, *Personal Politics* (New York: Vantage Books, 1980); Jo Freeman, 'The Origins of the Women's Liberation Movement', *American Journal of Sociology* 78 (1973): 792–811; Betty Friedan, *The Feminine Mystique* (New York: Norton, 1963); Julia T. Wood, *Gendered Lives: Communication, Gender, Culture* (Belmont, Calif.: Wadsworth, 1997).

4 Examples include Beatrice Dierks, 'The UN Fourth World Conference on Women', *National Women's Studies Association Journal* 8 (1996): 84–90; Dorothy O. Helly, 'Beijing '95: The Fourth World Conference on Women', *National Women's Studies Association Journal* 8 (1996): 171–8; NGO Forum on Women, *Final Report* (1995); Priscilla Sears, 'What Is Difficult Can Be Done at Once. What Is Impossible Takes a Little Longer: The Beijing Conference', *National Women's Studies Association Journal* 8 (1996):179–85.

5 See Ogden's review in this volume.

6 Doug McAdam and Dieter Rucht, 'The Cross-National Diffusion of Movement Ideas', *Annals of the American Academy of Political and Social Science* 528 (July 1993): 56–74; Sidney Tarrow, 'Social Movements in Contentious Politics: A Review Article', *American Political Science Review* 90 (1996): 874–83.

7 Tarrow, 'Social Movements in Contentious Politics'.

8   Jeffrey M. Berry, *Lobbying for the People: The Political Behavior of Public Interest Groups* (Princeton, NJ: Princeton University Press, 1977).

9   John D. McCarthy and Mayer N. Zald, eds, *Social Movements in an Organizational Society: Collected Essays* (New Brunswick, NJ: Transaction Books, 1987).

10 See note 2 above.

11 For the purposes of this study, my references to the FWCW include the NGO Forum on Women.

12 Herring, 'Gender and Democracy in Computer-Mediated Communication'.

13 D. Tannen, *Gender and Discourse* (New York: Oxford University Press, 1994).

14 Rob Kling, 'Social Relationships in Electronic Forums: Hangouts, Salons, Workplaces, and Communities', in Kling, ed., *Computerization and Controversy*, 426–54; Roger Silverstone and Eric Hirsch, eds, *Consuming Technologies: Media and Information in Domestic Spaces* (London: Routledge, 1992).

15 Tannen, *Gender and Discourse*; Wood, *Gendered Lives*.

16 D.F. Halpern, *Sex Differences in Cognitive Abilities*, 2nd edn (Hillsdale, NJ: L. Erlbaum, 1992).

17 McAdam and Rucht, 'The Cross-National Diffusion of Movement Ideas', 73.

18 Association for Progressive Communication, APC Women's Networking Survey—Initial Findings (Sept. 1996): (private e-mail, Maureen James).

19 Helly, 'Beijing '95'.

20 Jeffrey M. Berry, 'Citizen Groups and the Changing Nature of Interest Group Politics in America', *Annals of the American Academy of Political and Social Science* 528 (July 1993): 30.

21 Tannen, *Gender and Discourse*.

22 Association for Progressive Communication, APC Women's Networking Survey—Initial Findings.

23 Ruth P. Dawson, 'When Women Gather: The NGO Forum of the Fourth World Conference on Women, Beijing, 1995', *International Journal of Politics, Culture and Society* 10 (1996): 7–27.

24 Catherine Poole. Recent posts: beijing-conf.Poole 1995.

25 Xiaolin Li, 1995. Xiaolin's response: beijing95-I.

26 Herring, 'Gender and Democracy in Computer-Mediated Communication'.

Chapter 6

A THOUSAND POINTS OF DARKNESS: ELECTRONIC MOBILIZATION AND THE CASE OF THE COMMUNICATIONS DECENCY ACT

Leslie A. Pal

At its core, democracy is a specific form of communication between rulers and ruled, and therefore how we communicate should have some effect on the quality and nature of democracy itself.[1] If we assume that some technologies of information—at least fundamental and epoch-making ones such as the printing press and television—are forms of communication, then we could also expect that they will bring in their train new forms of democracy. This syllogism is at the heart of debates about the impact of new information and communication technologies (ICT) on contemporary governance. The new ICT (described in the Introduction to this volume) correlate with completely new means of communication, and thus may dramatically affect our political institutions and practices.

A key question is what the nature of this impact will be, particularly in reference to the newest ICT such as the Internet and in particular the World Wide Web. To date, most of the analyses of the impact of modern communications technologies have focused on fax technology, telephones, computers, and some aspects of the digital revolution. The Web—as a broad public phenomenon—is only about four years old, and so there has been little analysis of how political dynamics might evolve in these new electronic networks.[2] This chapter breaks some new ground in exploring mobilization networks and strategies on the Web around a prominent public policy issue, the US Communications Decency Act (CDA) of 1996. Though the CDA story is far from over (the US Supreme Court upheld a lower court's decision that sections of the Act were unconstitutional constraints on free speech, but new legislation will likely be introduced), the cyber-furore around the Act aroused the on-line community and provided an intriguing window into mobilization on the Net, about the Net, and for the Net. The CDA contained clauses that made 'indecent' communications on the Internet a crime, and immediately mobilized 'netizens'[3] to fight what they saw as unjustified censorship. Electronic mobilization around the issue complemented rallies across the country, as well as litigation sponsored by dozens of groups. The *New York Times* noted that the law's passage 'galvanized the chaotic cyberspace community as nothing had before.'[4] An on-line pundit called the CDA the

> Stamp Act of the Net. It forced the digital culture to see itself as a separate entity, and to defend the freedoms, privileges, and traditions it has patched together in recent years.
>
> It made clear that the values characterizing the Net are profoundly different than those governing much of the country. It united a fractious, fragmented, diverse collection of individuals, businesses, and communities in a way that had never occurred before, and might not have been possible without the dunderheaded political posturing of our elected leaders.[5]

Although this characterization is typically dramatic, it may capture an important aspect of the issue: it brought together hundreds of individuals and organizations in a medium that is noted for its fractiousness and fragmentation. In a gesture of solidarity, hundreds of Web pages had their backgrounds darkened on 8 February 1996, or 'Black Thursday', when the bill was passed, uniting the Internet in what one protester called 'a thousand points of darkness'.[6]

Images like these give the Net-politics around the CDA a populist, almost revolutionary, flavour, but the literature on the political impacts of these new ICT has been divided on whether they will enhance or corrupt democratic practices. At one extreme, there are writers like Alvin Toffler[7] and John Naisbitt who have no doubts at all about the radical and beneficial effect ICT will have on democracy and governance institutions. Naisbitt sees ICT providing individuals with unparalleled access to information, to connectivity, to interaction, and ultimately to decision-making through electronic communications networks that will realize the full promise of democracy—people ruling themselves without the need for intermediaries such as political representatives. This radical deinstitutionalization will lead to a world of 'governance without government'.[8] Analysts like Lawrence Grossman echo, with only slightly muted tones, this optimism about electronic democracy. Grossman writes that the 'big losers in the present-day reshuffling and resurgence of public influence are the traditional institutions that have served as the main intermediaries between government and its citizens—the political parties, labor unions, civic associations, even the commentators and correspondents in the mainstream press.'[9] The more quickly 'information flows, the less people feel the need to rely on proxies to make decisions for them and the more they want to decide for themselves.'[10] Other writers have noted the empowering consequences of ICT for the mobilization of interest groups,[11] global social movements,[12] and local democratic practices.[13]

The contrary position—though it tends to focus more on pre-Internet technologies—is much more pessimistic about the democratizing potential. For some analysts, the key point is that these technologies do not exist in a vacuum, and that they will be used by existing political and economic élites to further consolidate their power. Selnow's study of high-tech election campaigns, for example, shows how modern polling techniques, databases, and computer-assisted analysis strengthen candidates against voters.[14] Alexander[15] and Preyra[16] have both highlighted similar concerns about the capacities of political parties to access and manipulate huge quantities of personal information in order to win campaigns. Critics in this vein emphasize the ways in which ICT are used by political authorities to simplify issues and to appeal less to the informational needs of the electorate than to their entertainment or sensory tastes. Most of these critiques have a greater validity for television than for the

Internet and the Web, where it does appear that information is the *raison d'être* of the medium.[17] However, the same feature that ICT proponents see as beneficial—the capacity to reach a wide variety of interests—can be viewed as a political liability for a stable democracy. At least until recent developments in the cable industry, television and radio were mass media that could arguably be seen to forge mass publics. The Internet and associated ICT potentially fragment that public into an almost infinite array of interests and groups, unbounded by the limits of technology or geography. The most arresting version of this thesis is that of Sherry Turkle, who argues that the 'Internet carries a political message about the importance of direct, immediate action and interest-group mobilization. It is the symbol and tool of a postmodern politics.'[18] While she does not see this development in an entirely negative light, she does express some worries about what it means about community. Others have expressed similar concerns about the fragmenting potential of ICT on the political community—their very potential to facilitate mobilization may encourage people to generate more and more narrowly focused interest groups.[19]

This is obviously too rich a mine of hypotheses to explore in one chapter. However, the key fault line between the interpretations seems to be the degree to which ICT, and the Internet in particular, facilitate political mobilization by citizens and networks of groups. Just as important, given the lack of empirical research on the nature of such mobilization, is a careful assessment of its dynamics and characteristics. This is the more modest goal of this chapter. It focuses on political mobilization around the CDA on the World Wide Web.[20] It does not review UseNet[21] or chat groups, the conventional print media, or 'real world' rallies and lobbying. All of these would have to be studied to capture the full dynamics of political mobilization around the CDA issue and the Internet's place and impact in that mobilization. Rather, my focus is exclusively on the Web, and consists of an analysis of some 100 sites linked to the CDA issue (see Appendix). The anarchy of the Web makes 'site lists' of this sort difficult to compile, and underscores the important methodological issue of 'issue construction' in a space where the conventional clues on political visibility and impact are missing. The methodology adopted was to begin with some 'central sites', such as the Electronic Frontier Foundation (EFF) and the American Civil Liberties Union (ACLU), and work out from those links until that electronic trail began to either fade or fold back self-referentially. Subsequently, a search was conducted on the CDA using WebCompass,[22] which corroborated the importance of the key sites we uncovered but did not itself reveal any major omissions.

The chapter focuses on two broad sets of questions. Firstly, who was mobilizing around this issue? Were all sides of the issue equally represented? Of the organizations, how many were Net-based as opposed to extensions of real-world organizations onto the Internet? What was the balance between individuals and organizations? Answers to these questions should help cast some light on the issue of ease of mobilization. Whether viewed as empowerment or as fragmentation, most theory argues that the ease and speed of ICT (especially the Internet) encourage groups (often with very scattered 'membership') to be formed around more specific issues, as well as in wider and more flexible coalitions or networks. Secondly, what mobilization strategies were used in this campaign? Were there unique strategies that flow from the nature of the medium? How were more conventional strategies adapted, enhanced, or limited as a result of the medium? Answers to these questions should help us sort out what in fact is new about this medium and further clarify its potential as a tool for political mobilization.

Background

Table 1 provides a brief chronology of the tangled CDA legislative saga from February 1995 to July 1996. The CDA is Title V of the Telecommunications Act of 1996, which was signed into law by President Clinton on 8 February 1996. Its chief architect was Senator James Exon, and while the original amendment he proposed was tempered through the legislative process, it still aimed at controlling the transmission of obscene materials over the telecommunications system. The CDA addresses abuses both in telephony and in telecommunications, but the key provisions were obviously aimed at the Internet. The legislation targeted interstate as well as foreign telecommunications that involved the creation, solicitation, and transmission of 'any comment, request, suggestion, proposal, image, or other communication which is obscene, lewd, lascivious, filthy, or indecent, with intent to annoy, abuse, threaten, or harass another person.' The provision of 'obscene or indecent' material to those under 18 years of age, even those underaged persons who initiate the contact, was prohibited. Internet service providers were to be responsible for content as well, since they, too, were liable for knowingly permitting the transmission of objectionable material. Finally, there were provisions explicitly targeted at interactive computer services that made the following available to persons under 18 years of age: 'any comment, request, suggestion, proposal, image, or other communication that, in context, depicts or describes, in terms patently offensive as measured by contemporary community standards, sexual or excretory activities or organs, regardless of whether the user of such service placed the call or initiated the communication.' Those found guilty under these provisions were liable to a fine or up to two years in jail. (Various defences were allowed under the Act, most importantly good faith efforts undertaken to restrict access to adult sites.[23])

The ACLU filed for a temporary restraining order against the CDA on 8 February 1996. It had several objections to the legislation.[24] The CDA con-

☐ **Table 1:   Chronology of the CDA, 1 February 1995 to June 1997**

Date	Action
1 Feb. '95	S314 referred to the Senate Commerce committee.
1 Feb. '95	S314 introduced by Sens Exon (D-Nevada) and Gorton (R-Washington).
21 Feb. '95	HR1004 referred to the House Commerce and Judiciary committees.
21 Feb. '95	HR1004 introduced by Rep. Johnson (D-South Dakota).
23 Mar. '95	S314 amended and attached to the Telecommunications Reform bill by Sen. Gorton. Language provides some provider protection, but continues to infringe on e-mail privacy and free speech.
7 Apr. '95	Sen. Leahy (D-Vermont) introduces S714, an alternative to the Exon/Gorton bill, which commissions the Department of Justice to study the problem to see if additional legislation (such as the CDA) is necessary.
24 May '95	The House Telecommunications Reform bill (HR1555) leaves committee in the House with the Leahy alternative attached to it, thanks to Rep. Ron Klink (D-Pennsylvania). The Communications Decency Act is not attached to it.
14 June '95	Communications Decency Amendment passed by the US Senate.
14 June '95	The Senate passes the CDA as attached to the Telecommunications Reform bill (S652) by a vote of 84-16. The Leahy bill (S714) is not passed, but is supported by 16 Senators who understand the Internet.
21 June '95	Several prominent House members publicly announce their opposition to the CDA, including Rep. Newt Gingrich (R-Georgia), Rep. Chris Cox (R-California), and Rep. Ron Wyden (D-Oregon).
30 June '95	Cox and Wyden introduce the Internet Freedom and Family Empowerment Act (HR1978) as an alternative to the CDA.
4 Aug. '95	House passes HR1555, which goes into conference with S652.
4 Aug. '95	House votes to attach Managers Amendment (which contains new criminal penalties for speech on-line) to Telecommunications Reform bill (HR1555).
4 Aug. '95	House votes 421–4 to attach HR1978 to Telecommunications Reform bill (HR1555).
26 Sept. '95	Sen. Russ Feingold urges committee members to drop Managers Amendment and the CDA from the Telecommunications bill.
7 Dec. '95	The House half of the telecommunications conference committee votes the 'indecency' standard for on-line speech into the Telecommunications bill.
31 Jan. '96	The House and Senate prepare to sign off on the conference report for the Telecommunications bill and rush a vote to the floor.
1 Feb. '96	The House and Senate pass the Telecommunications bill (S652/HR1555, 414–16 and 91–5.
8 Feb. '96	Plaintiff's [ACLU] Memorandum of Law in support of a motion for a temporary restraining order and preliminary injunction.
8 Feb. '96	CDA signed into law.
26 Feb. '96	Citizens Internet Empowerment Coalition complaint against the CDA, filed in Philadelphia.
10 May '96	Closing arguments.
12 June '96	US District Court of Eastern Pennsylvania grants injunction against CDA on First Amendment free speech grounds.
26 June '96	US government announces it will appeal court decision.
1 July '96	US Department of Justice files official appeal.
6 Dec. '96	US Supreme Court agrees to hear appeal.
28 June '97	US Supreme Court declares CDA unconstitutional.

travened First Amendment rights of free speech, hinged on undefined terms such as 'indecency' and 'patently offensive', interfered with the privacy rights of minors, and treated on-line communications differently from print communications (which have stronger First Amendment protections than broadcasting). The ACLU was joined by 18 other plaintiffs in its action.[25] On 15 February a temporary restraining order was issued by the court on the grounds that the provisions on 'indecency' were constitutionally vague. On 26 February a coalition led by the ACLU, the Citizens Internet Empowerment Coalition, the American Library Association, and several major commercial enterprises, such as America On-Line, Compuserve, Prodigy, and Microsoft, filed suit as plaintiffs in federal court in Philadelphia. A panel of three judges from the United States Court of Appeals (Third Circuit) agreed to hear the case, and handed down its decision on 12 June 1996. The panel unanimously agreed to grant the injunction, principally on the grounds that the provisions on decency were constitutionally vague and contravened the First Amendment protection on free speech. The decision also concluded that the Internet is an entirely new medium, and moreover that it is a profoundly democratic one that outstrips even the print media's capacity to be a vehicle for the free exchange of ideas.[26] On 1 July 1996 the Department of Justice announced an appeal to the Supreme Court. The court rendered its decision in late 1997, upholding the earlier verdict.

Free speech and obscenity issues are intrinsically explosive, and so the uproar around the CDA should not be surprising. For netizens, however, this case had several special features. Firstly, it was a direct challenge to the communitarian self-image of a good deal of the on-line community because it implied that the Internet is little more than a storehouse of pornographic and offensive material. Secondly, it united corporate interests such as Microsoft and America On-Line—interests often reviled in the on-line community—with small-scale organizations and individuals dedicated to the Internet. Free speech and censorship are powerful rallying cries, and they served to neutralize often very strong differences among the players. Thirdly, the CDA sought to treat the Internet like broadcasting, which traditionally has had stronger government regulation than print. To netizens this was the ultimate 'newbie' outrage—a complete lack of understanding of a medium and a world that netizens know intimately but which is opaque to outsiders. More importantly, for netizens the Internet is not merely a new way of communicating; it is a completely different mode of social and communicative action. The CDA was an attempt by the 'old order' to constrain and tame the new.

Battling the CDA: Sites and Actors

A total of 104 sites were analysed for this paper. The raw list is provided in the Appendix to this chapter, and represents only a fraction of the total number of sites that would have been involved in free speech and censorship issues. However, these sites did more than sport a logo: they were engaged in a more direct way with the initiative by disseminating information, providing links, or helping to organize rallies or court action. These sites were sponsored by 66 individuals and organizations, with some sponsors maintaining more than one site. In terms of 'advocacy sites' (not just information), six organizations accounted for 26 sites (Electronic Frontier Foundation[27]—six; *Hot Wired Magazine*—six; Sleeping Beauty[28]—five; ACLU—three; Center for Democracy and Technology—three; Voters' Telecommunications Watch—three). All of these organizations were opposed to the CDA, as indeed the majority of sites were.

This raises the first interesting observation about the CDA players: they were almost exclusively anti-CDA. Only six sites could be construed to be clearly pro-CDA, and five of those were individuals. The Christian Coalition, which was often cited as a force behind the efforts to censor adult materials, in fact made no mention of the CDA on its homepage during the period of analysis, though it was prominently mentioned in conventional media as a leading organization in support of the bill.[29] While information about the government's legislation, appeals, and court arguments was freely available, engaged cyber-interlocutors were not. There might be several explanations for this. The Internet is likely to be somewhat self-selecting, and people who are disinterested in on-line communications will not be found there. Netizens are likely to be partisans in favour of the medium. Another explanation is that conservative forces supporting the CDA may have thought that going on-line would take them deep into enemy territory and would effectively validate the Internet's importance for speech and debate rather than its significance as an electronic sewer. Although this is more a matter of strategy, it is none the less interesting that the electronic debate on the CDA was so heavily skewed towards one side. In the CDA case, a preliminary analysis suggests that it was a conversation among the converted.

Another issue is the degree to which the organizations were primarily 'Internet-oriented' as opposed to dealing primarily with non-Internet agendas that they then extend into cyberspace. This is an important issue from the point of view of gauging the degree to which the Internet is indeed a new 'political space' rather than simply the extension of the traditional public square with all its actors into an electronic format. Two models might be conceived to capture the extremes of this phenomenon. The first is the 'Internet as extension' model, where 'real-world' actors simply begin to do all the things they did before but through the new medium. Greenpeace or a political party, for example, might simply go on-line in pursuing its political or fund-raising agendas. Being on-line is not an end in itself, and the group's or party's agenda has relatively little to say about the Internet itself. The other model is the 'Internet as *sui generis*', where organizational agendas and strategies are exclusively devoted to the

Internet. The Electronic Frontier Foundation (EFF) is a good example, as is the Internet Society.[30] These organizations were formed to deal with Internet and telecommunications issues, they have developed practices unique to the Internet, and their real-world presence, while unavoidable, is largely in service to their virtual presence on the Net.

The Internet is far too complex to fit either model, and will obviously be a mix. But it is still an empirical question as to what that mix is, and the degree to which the Internet is evolving into a distinct political space, with distinct actors and distinct practices. The CDA fight could not be pursued exclusively through the Internet—the court injunction required participation in conventional decision-making institutions. The on-line community might have railed to no avail on the Net without actually pursuing the injunction. Interestingly, the first move to acquire a temporary injunction was undertaken by the ACLU, not a netizen.[31] The Philadelphia case was launched by the Citizens Internet Empowerment Coalition (CIEC), a collection of libraries and publishers rather than Internet organizations *per se*.[32] However, the CIEC was itself formed through the Center for Democracy and Technology,[33] along with the American Library Association and others. Plaintiffs in the Philadelphia suit included a strong contingent of Internet service provider and software companies, as well as groups worried about censorship.[34] However, the anti-CDA fight was clearly a mix of Internet and conventional organizations. It is difficult to gauge, but the success of the CDA lobby may have been due in part to the formidable alliance of groups such as the ACLU and Microsoft, along with netizens. It is worth commenting on the structure of this network, however.

Any free speech campaign brings together organizations and groups that might otherwise have little in common—from civil libertarians to publishers of adult materials. In the case of the CDA fight, the coalition was both very diverse and 'loosely coupled' across some disparate sectors, including major software companies, libraries, journalists, prisoners' groups, AIDS awareness groups, gay and lesbian organizations, international social movements, and so on. In this case, the breadth of the coalition had something to do with the nature of communications over the Internet in at least two senses. Firstly, so many different groups are linked to the Web and through the Internet that any proposed regulatory framework will automatically affect a wide range of organizations in both the public and private sectors. This would not be as true, for example, of radio and television broadcasting. So there is something intrinsic to the medium that encourages wider coalition-building, and that is the nature of interconnectivity itself. The other important feature of the Net is that it permitted, through the electronic organizations, a much wider scope of mobilization than would have been possible, for example, had only the ACLU through its conventional communications been working on the case. It was possible, with astonishing rapidity, to weave together a coalition of over 40,000 members in a matter of weeks or months, so that by April 1996 the EFF's Blue Ribbon Page was listed by WebCrawler as the sixth most linked page on the Web.

A final question concerns the balance of individuals and organizations in the CDA case. The Internet is often lauded as a sphere within which individuals are dramatically empowered in their ability to communicate and participate. The topography of 'sites' in cyberspace lends credibility to this perception, since any site is equal to any other in terms of accessibility, and committed individuals can sometimes put themselves in the centre of a network through links and the provision of valued information. This is clearly distinct from mobilization in a conventional context, where organizational resources are usually considered to be critical in determining success.

The data show that 30 of 104 sites were 'individuals' in the sense that they did not appear to be formally connected to any larger organization (journalists were not considered individuals because of their media affiliation). This is a substantial proportion of the total. However, it is also important to try to gauge their role in the network around the CDA issue. Most of the individual pages were diatribes or exhortations, sometimes with links to 'anchor' organizations such as the ACLU, the EFF, the CIEC, or to documents that had been put up on the Web by media or research organizations. While the 'central nodes' of the network consisted of organizations linking to each other's pages, individuals' pages tended to have links only to the organizations and not to each other. Thus, while they were wired, they were wired only to the edges of the network. Figure 1 provides a schematic example of this network pattern.

Network patterns are crucial to understanding the nature of political mobilization on the Net, since the network is virtually the only artefact of the mobilization in the first place. Friedland has commented on the distinctive characteristics of electronic networks in using the term 'distributed responsibility' to describe a system 'which makes widely decentralized nodes of the network primary information gatherers.'[35] Several characteristics of the CDA network of Web sites deserve to be highlighted. Firstly, as noted in the previous paragraph, it was a network consisting of both 'real' and 'virtual' organizations. Groups that would not exist except for the Internet itself are suddenly important players in political mobilization. Secondly, the network was 'loosely coupled' in the sense that while it retained a strong core of self-referential organizations and groups, that core was supported and supplemented through live hyperlinks to both organizations and individuals that widened the potential scope of mobilization quite dramatically. Participation was received from all around the United States, without any complications of distance or space. Thirdly, the role of individuals, while 'peripheral' in one sense, can also be seen to be more strategic in another—the Net provided them with the capacity and opportunity to be information brokers on the network itself. Finally, while the network had a core, the

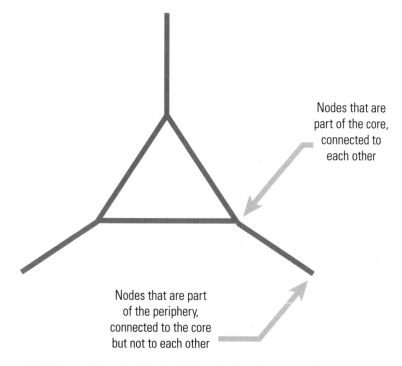

Nodes that are
part of the core,
connected to
each other

Nodes that are part
of the periphery,
connected to the core
but not to each other

Figure 1: A Schematic Network of 'Core' and 'Peripheral' Nodes

informational resources were distributed and exchanged throughout the network as a result of the distributed nodes of which it consisted. Unlike the more
conventional model of political mobilization that has some pre-eminent group
or institutionalized entity at the centre, the network was a system of multiple
linkages and exchanges in all directions.

Strategies

Once we have some idea of who is out there, what is it that they do? The
interesting question here is whether an issue like the CDA generates lobbying
and other political strategies that are distinct to the Internet, and to what
degree conventional strategies, tactics, and techniques are adapted to the Net.
We list these strategies in a rough order from the more conventional to the
more distinctive.

Court Case

The filing of a suit, of course, was almost emblematic of American politics, and
in this sense a very conventional political strategy. However, it had several
twists that made it distinctive and may also be harbingers of litigations to come.

Firstly, the Philadelphia courtroom was itself wired so that proceedings could be broadcast over the Net. According to the CIEC:

> In order to demonstrate the nature of the Internet and the effectiveness of user empowerment technologies, CIEC arranged to wire the court room directly to the Internet. The Center for Democracy and Technology, with the help of Bell Atlantic and Philadelphia law firm Schnader, Harrison, Segal & Lewis (an amicus counsel in the case), has installed a T-1 circuit and a small local area network in the Ceremonial Room of the Philadelphia court. To the best of our knowledge, this was the first time in history that a Federal Courtroom has been wired to the Net for the purposes of a Trial.[36]

Secondly, it was possible for supporters to register as plaintiffs simply by filling out an on-line registration form. The CIEC page of 14 June 1996 noted that one could 'still become a named plaintiff—and sue the Federal government along with 45,000 other netizens and a score of Internet businesses.' By December 1996 the appeal had generated 55,000 members. The actual list of formal plaintiffs was 27. However, the potential ease with which a citizen might join with others in a court challenge suggests that the scepticism about the efficacy of legalized politics might be misplaced in the electronic age.[37] That scepticism hinges on the high barriers to entry in legal proceedings—the costs, the knowledge of legal proceedings, the difficulty in accessing legal materials and decisions. The Net lowers these barriers substantially by permitting on-line registration, organizational recruitment, and easy monitoring of legal decisions, as well as instant access to the text of those decisions themselves. Thirdly, the sheer amount of primary material available for anyone interested in the case is a significant adaptation of information strategies typically used by interest groups and social movements. In the past, it would have been prohibitively expensive for a group to mail out full texts of court decisions, and they would typically have relied more on summaries and their own newsletters and communications. The Web allowed full text of both the CDA appeals and the eventual legal decisions to be immediately available to anyone with a modem. In addition, on-line chats were available through the CIEC with lead counsel Bruce Ennis and key officials from the CDT, America On-Line, and the American Library Association. This is an Internet version of call-in radio, but has the distinctive feature of not having to rely on major broadcasters for air time or scheduling. The Net allowed the CIEC to put its people on-line immediately after the decision at a time that suited it, not ABC or PBS.

All of these characteristics echo the point made by many observers of the new ICT: by allowing citizens direct access to information, they undermine those intermediary institutions that acted as information brokers, translators, and broadcasters in the past. The anti-CDA coalition had no need of mainstream media—they could put their material on-line directly. Indeed, they had their own electronic media allies in organizations like *Hot Wired*. While they ultimately had to work through legal institutions, the Net made those institutions much more transparent by permitting real-time Net broadcasts of proceedings, conversations with lawyers, and access to mountains of legal documentation.

Rallies

No political movement can exist entirely in cyberspace. It obviously has to connect with the political system in some fashion. The Internet in theory permits the rapid mobilization of large numbers of people around a political issue through the dissemination of information. One of the questions about digital democracy is the degree to which it actually mobilizes real constituencies, as opposed to merely creating a wave that momentarily unites bands of surfers into a mob of enflamed dilettantes that quickly evaporates once the next wave arrives. The anti-CDA forces did encourage 'real' rallies. In June 1996 the CDA page referred to rallies planned for the night of the Philadelphia decision in New York, Pittsburgh, and San Francisco. No data have been uncovered at this point on how successful these rallies were. In one sense, the Internet makes them superfluous—as noted earlier, the CDA fight brought netizens together who already shared a common view and were prepared to be 'modem-ilized' around the issue. Rallies and other manifestations of collective action in part serve to frighten authorities with the sheer physical mass of the opposition but also to weld solidarity within that opposition. It is not clear how 'rallies' serve either of these purposes for a constituency that is spatially scattered and (at least on censorship issues) of one mind.

Letter-Writing Campaigns

Another conventional strategy in political mobilization is letter-writing campaigns to incumbent politicians. The CDA case was no different, with several Web pages urging netizens to write to their congressional representatives as well as the President. One thing that is different about cyberspace campaigns is their ease. Web pages that urged letters typically contained e-mail addresses for key legislative actors,[38] and netizens were sometimes directed to on-line listings of contact numbers and addresses for politicians across the country.[39] Drop-down menus made the traditional 'protest form letter' as easy as selecting items from a menu and then pressing the 'send' button.[40] A particularly effective example of this was the campaign co-ordinated in mid-December 1995 when the CDA was under consideration. 'On Tuesday December 12 1995, over 20,000 concerned net.citizens flooded key members of Congress with phone calls, faxes, and email messages urging them to oppose legislation which would prohibit the transmission of "indecent" material online. This was the largest demonstration of the strength of the Internet Community to date.'[41]

There are other distinctive characteristics to electronic epistolary campaigns. Firstly, even if they do not involve e-mail, the use of computers and faxes can help co-ordinate widely dispersed groups that might otherwise have difficulty banding together to deal with government policy. Grossman cites the case of how home-schooling parents in February 1994 flooded Congress with thousands of letters, faxes, and phone calls to the extent that they shut down the switchboard. They defeated an amendment that would have detrimentally affected them.[42] E-mail campaigns have the same character—they can mobilize large constituencies of widely dispersed individuals. Of course, the very ease of e-mail may cause politicians to discount it in comparison with original letters, but a large number of protests remains impressive, whatever its ease to organize.[43] Another feature, though this is conjectural, is that e-mail campaigns weaken the grip of local politics. When letters come from everywhere and are aimed at a host of political representatives, those representatives will experience what appears to be a national campaign, not a regional or local one.

Black Thursday

The Center for Democracy and Technology and the Voters' Telecommunications Watch together organized a 'Black Thursday' campaign. For 48 hours, participating Web sites were 'blackened' so that only their typeface and some icons were legible.[44] Major Internet entities such as Yahoo and Netscape participated, and Yahoo estimated that about 1,500 sites in all were involved, making it the 'single largest demonstration from the Internet community in history'. There are similarities between this strategy and ones used by other media in the past. Newspapers, for example, sometimes use watermarks to indicate some subliminal message, or highlight the masthead in some way. Television and radio sometimes have deliberate 'blackouts' on some stories or during some periods. In both instances, the medium is signalling to readers/viewers/listeners not through a direct message but through the altered texture of the medium itself.

Although this is certainly arguable, the impact of blackened Web pages is greater because of that medium's dependency on colour and graphics. In a sense, a Web page is both foreground and background simultaneously—in fact, technologically, the wallpaper and images for a site, which are in separate files in the 'background', are brought in as the site is accessed. Blackening a Web site has considerable visual impact, and it is impossible to miss in the same sense that it might be possible to overlook a watermark on a printed page, a highlighted masthead, or a missing program. The background of a Web page in an important sense *is* the page.

Icons and Images

The Web exploded into popularity in 1994 in large part because it combined both graphics and print, and more recently audio and video. CDA protesters were urged to download and post an image/icon of an AIDS-like ribbon (in blue) to show their concern. Later, a freely available javascript icon declaring victory and on to the Supreme Court was found on many sites. The two images, and one variant of the blue ribbon, are reproduced in Figure 2.

TO THE SUPREME COURT!

 Support Free Speech Online

Figure 2: Icons and Image

Objectionable Site Pointers

An intriguing feature of the CDA battle was the use of the Net to actually point people to sites containing material that might potentially be deemed 'offensive' under the CDA. The 'Banned Books' site,[45] for example, offered the following links, with brief annotations:

- Rick Dees's Ass
  From a Los Angeles Billboard.
- Playboy
  Playboy Magazine. Perfectly legal in print form, even available in Braille, but won't be on the Internet much longer.
- FCC v. Pacifica Foundation
  The case that defined indecency, complete with a number of examples of words that are 'patently indecent'.
- Roe v. Wade, 410 US 113 (1973)
  The Supreme Court's decision, and related papers.
- Water Birth Information
- Stop Prisoner Rape
  Sexually explicit material that would be banned includes accounts written by rape survivors and advice for prisoners on how to avoid gang rape and AIDS. The operators of this site have signed with the ACLU in a lawsuit to overturn the CDA.
- Coalition for Positive Sexuality
  A frank, honest site discussing issues of sexuality and reproductive health.

- Archive of the MindVox Fuck-You forum
A forum whose charter says, 'This is a forum for serious discussion and study of offensive ideas, speech, and behavior.'
- The Holy Bible, King James Version
Remember the part about Sodom and Gomorrah? How about Solomon 4:5?
- The Safer Sex Page
. . . Includes the Lesbian Safer Sex Guidelines cut-and-fold display to stand up on your nightstand!
- Lesbian.org
An online resource for lesbians.
- Christianity and Homosexuality Home Page
One of my favorites, if only for the irony. This is a Christian Right page offering alternatives and cures for homosexuality. They have a bunch of words (some of which are included in the BIG 7) designed to trigger hits from search engines.
- Cybernet Art Gallery
Ooh, art that features nude female forms.
- Problems Faced by Homosexual Youth
A paper on the trials and tribulations of growing up gay. As it is a paper about teenagers, one of its audiences is obviously those under 18.
- Aryan Crusader's Library
A page that isn't by definition 'indecent', and thus will not be affected by this law. However, unpopular speech is next, and some people would definitely feel that this page is more destructive than most of the others in this list, which will be affected.
- Bruno, an Internet comic strip
This is a strip that was printed in several college newspapers, and is now available on the Internet. For now.
- Internet Underground Music Archive
THE site for music on the net. Many of the songs featured here have lyrics that would violate the decency standards. So, instead of downloading the songs, you'll just have to wait until an all-ages show, or buy the album.
- The STD Homepage
Clearinghouse of information about Sexually Transmitted Diseases.
- Genital Warts Page
Information (from above page) about Genital Warts. Includes pictures. Definitely indecent (even a bit disgusting). However, definitely a public service.
- Dirty Words . . .
This is an overseas site. It is a translation guide from New York City slang to German, for all of the 'dirty' phrases used in the movie Kids (which, if I remember correctly, was bankrolled by Disney).
- Breastfeeding Articles and Resources
Just what it says it is.

- How to Use a Condom
  Cartoon Guide to condom use. A similar pamphlet can be found at all public health centers in the US, and probably somewhere in most high schools, but not for much longer on the Internet.
- gopher://gopher.cc.columbia.edu:71/00/publications/women/wh14
  A section on self-care from the Barnard/Columbia Women's Handbook.

In a similar vein, another site listed links to classic works of art and the 'seven dirty words' that would be banned under the CDA.[46] While vivid examples and even civil disobedience are conventional tactics, the Internet makes it both more difficult for government authorities to control and police this practice and easier for citizens to access such materials. Interestingly, the key organizations involved in the CDA fight did not provide these links themselves, relying instead on simpler examples or exhortations. It was usually the individually sponsored sites that took this step.

Civil Disobedience

The Internet is often characterized as an uncontrollable frontier that attracts extreme individualists and non-conformists. We noted earlier that a significant proportion of the sites in our sample were contributed by individuals, and at least a few of these expressed extreme frustration with the CDA to the point of counselling civil disobedience. The most vivid example was the page entitled Lizard's All-Purpose, Multi-Functional, Free Speech: Civil Disobedience, Enemies List, and Survival Guide.[47] Its author wrote:

> The government still hasn't gotten it. They still think the masses are all in favor of censorship, government snooping on innocent citizens, and giving up essential liberty for temporary security. They still think they are controlling the feed of information, that the American populace is still brainwashed. They are wrong, and the sooner they learn that, the easier it will be for them to adjust to a world where their power and influence is simply not what it was.
>
> Note to any government types who might be reading this: You're losing. Hell, you've lost, you just don't know it. Give up now, and you can preserve at least some dignity, some illusion of power. Keep fighting, uselessly, and the illusion will be gone totally. Your choice.

The page contains advice on civil disobedience on the Net (principally dealing with service providers that have discontinued some sites), a 'free speech survival guide', and various diatribes against Christian supporters of the CDA, fascists, and the Simon Wiesenthal Centre. The good news is that pages like this were rare—only one other in our sample came close, with a 'rant of the week' against the CDA.[48]

Conclusion

As we noted at the beginning of this chapter, there is a consensus that new ICT dramatically lower the barriers to entry into the political marketplace. Mobilization is in principle easier because larger numbers of people can be contacted and politically aroused through electronic means. Networks can be established more easily without regard for distance, and because interests can be targeted so specifically that people can be mobilized around what really and immediately matters to them, not some abstract political ideology that then will serve as the springboard for subsequent political action. Some observers see in these possibilities the emergence of a new and more fundamental democratic politics, as citizens get directly engaged in the process. Others worry about the fragmenting effect of this brave new world of 'virtual interest groups'. This chapter was a preliminary probe of this question of mobilization in the context of the CDA and with specific attention to the Web as a means of political communication.

At one level, the scope of electronic mobilization was not large, especially given the salience of the issue for netizens. We surveyed just over 100 sites, but even if for some reason our sampling was flawed, doubling that number would still not amount to anything close to a 'social movement' in terms of the number of organizations or individuals. The other way to see this, however, is to understand that many of the organizations (like the CIEC and the EFF) are themselves either coalitions of organizations or of other membership groups. When these are added to the 55,000 members that signed up with the CIEC, it amounts to an impressive degree of mobilization in a relatively short time (approximately one year). The other dimension of mobilization is not mere scope but the range of groups drawn into the network. As we noted above, the Net facilitated a distinctive type of coalition of 'real' and 'virtual' groups, corporations and small non-governmental organizations, individuals and supplementary networks.

It is precisely the type of network—the distributed connections and exchanges—that is most distinctive about what emerges through electronic mobilization. The network around the CDA was not completely non-hierarchical—there were special nodes such as the EFF and the ACLU—but it was looser than the types of coalitions one typically sees in conventional politics. The geographic dispersion, the variety, and the integration of individuals as well as organizations—all exchanging information and creating a field of political knowledge and opinion to which everyone had contributed in some way—are distinctive. The amount of information and the speed with which it could be distributed were also unique.

As for tactics and strategies, our review of Web sites showed some strong borrowings from conventional political strategies, leavened, however, by distinctive features that mark electronic campaigns. The court case was a conventional strategy, but was supplemented by on-line information, interviews, and live feeds. Rallies were mounted across the United States, co-ordinated through e-mail and Web page announcements. Letters were sent electronically, but much more easily and frequently. Given the hypermedia context of the Web, icons, images, and the 'thousand points of darkness' campaign were central to mobilization. Finally, the sheer capacity to point people to both informational and objectionable sites is a distinct feature of electronic mobilization.

While this case study suggests some caution in our assessments of both the scope of electronic lobbying and mobilization as well as it uniqueness, it also raises several questions. Firstly, would Internet dynamics be different for an issue not so tightly bound to the judicial process? Might a policy issue still in the legislative phase, or in the pre-legislative phase, call forth different dynamics from the Web? We must also remember that the CDA battle was a defining moment for many netizens, and that their political capacities may grow as they develop more robust policy networks. Secondly, there were virtually no appeals for funds or financial support of any kind. Political mobilization in modern democracies is very much about money, and so the absence of appeals by major organizations is puzzling. It may be that even as late as June 1996 the weak security of financial transactions over the Internet prevented these types of appeals, but in that case people could have been asked to mail their donations. Even the invitation to join the CIEC did not involve a request for funding. Thirdly, and most importantly, what was the impact of all this activity on both public policy and the cohesion of netizens as a political constituency?

It would appear that the mobilization efforts around the CDA were both distinctive for their electronic character and markedly successful. The CIEC's claim of almost 55,000 adherents and the broad national coalition of companies, non-governmental organizations, and individuals was impressive and quickly formed. Ultimately, of course, their lobbying efforts to deflect the Senate's harsher version of the CDA were unsuccessful, even though the litigation strategy was. The CDA therefore provides some conflicting evidence about the nature of electronic mobilization. It is true, as much of the theoretical literature has hypothesized, that networks and strategies are indeed different in cyberspace from conventional politics. What remains unclear, however, is the wider impact of these new players and their practices on the rest of the political system.

Appendix: Site List, CDA Campaign (compiled July–August 1996)

Alchemy Mindworks
http://www.mindworkshop.com/alchemy/indcnt.html

Brock N. Meeks
http://cyberwerks.com:70/0h/cyberwire/cwd/cwd.96.02.06.html

David G. Menter
http://carbon.concom.com/dmenter/Netiquette/paint_pages_black.html

Eric Kidd
http://coos.dartmouth.edu/~emk/speech/

Henry Huang
http://www.cs.virginia.edu/~hwh6k/public/S314_stuff.html

J. Richard Wilson
http://pages.prodigy.com/freeside/protest.html

Jonah Seiger at CDT and Shabbir Safdar at VTW
http://www.cdt.org/petition.html

kathh@holli.com
http://user.holli.com/~kathh//anti.htm

Scott Banister
http://www.libertarian.org/

Scott Barton
http://www.isc.rit.edu/~sab0276/stv/cda.html#dates

Sleeping Beauty Publications, Ltd.
http://sleepingbeauty.com/world/liberty/fuckcda.htm

Sleeping Beauty Publications, Ltd.
http://sleepingbeauty.com/world/liberty/us_v_thomas.htm

Sonoma County Online
http://www.socool.com/socool/news/protest.html

'Lizard'
http://www.dnai.com/~lizard/civdis.htm

'Steel'
http://www.vic.com/~steel/distress/

???
http://mud.bsd.uchicago.edu/~mohanraj/prop.html

76612,3244@cserve.com
http://ourworld.compuserve.com/homepages/ermac_7/

ACLU
http://sleepingbeauty.com/world/liberty/aclubrief.htm

ACLU
http://www.aclu.org/

ACLU
http://www.aclu.org/court/pacifica.html

Adam Moore?
http://pathfinder.com/@@jzDISwYAxPashUnW/Netly/CDA/museum.html

American Family Association
http://www.gocin.com/afa/home.htm

Brad Lumley
http://chattanooga.net/~mlumley/censor/censor.htm

Brock N. Meeks
http://www.hotwired.com/Lib/Privacy/exon.privacy.html

Center for Democracy and Technology
http://www.cdt.org/cda.html

Center for Democracy and Technology
http://www.cdt.org/index.html

Center for Democracy and Technology
http://www.cdt.org/ciec/SC_appeal/DOJ_notice.html

Christian Coalition
http://www.cc.org/main page.html

Christian Coalition
http://www.cc.org/cc/speech/contract.html

Christian Interactive Network
http://www.gocin.com/

CIEC
http://www.cdt.org/ciec/index.html

ClariNet
http://www.clari.net/suitpage.html

Claudine Langan
http://www.public.asu.edu/~langcl/

CNN Interactive
http://allpolitics.com/

Daniel Weinstein
http://www.geocities.com/SiliconValley/3039/rights.htm

Electronic Frontier Canada
http://insight.mcmaster.ca/org/efc/efc.html

Electronic Frontier Foundation
http://www.eff.org/

Electronic Frontier Foundation
http://www.eff.org/Alerts/HTML/960612_aclu_v_reno_decision.html

Electronic Frontier Foundation
http://www.eff.org/pub/Censorship/Exon_bill/

Electronic Frontier Foundation
http://www.eff.org/pub/Legal/Cases/EFF_ACLU_v_DoJ/

Electronic Frontier Foundation
http://www.eff.org/pub/Alerts/960612_eff_cda_decision.statement

Electronic Privacy Information Centre
http://www.epic.org/free_speech/censorship/lawsuit/

Elliot Smith
http://minot.com/~smithe/comm.html

erifoley@indiana.edu
http://ezinfo.ucs.indiana.edu/~erifoley/rep.html

Flux
http://www.meat.com/upyours/

Gary Damschen
http://www.pageturners.com/CDA/index.htm

Gary Damschen?
http://user.holli.com/~jaelb//antiporn.html

Gerald Damschen
http://pageturners.com/CDA/rs_fma.htm

Global Image, Inc.
http://www.global-image.com/cgi-bin/exonizer/censored.cgi?document+cum

hawthorn@zelacom.com (Tom Rue)
http://www.zelacom.com/~hawthorn/liberty.htm

Hot Wired
http://box.hotwired.net/banned.html

Hot Wired
http://www.hotwired.com/frontdoor/96/24/index3a.html

Hot Wired
http://www.hotwired.com/frontdoor/

HotWired/Jon Katz
http://www.hotwired.com/netizen/96/24/katz3a.html

HotWired/Louis Rosetto
http://www.hotwired.com/netizen/96/24/index3a.html

HotWired/Todd Lappin
http://www.hotwired.com/netizen/96/24/index4a.html

Jesse S. Williams
http://www.oakland.edu/~jswillia/america/freedom.html

John Schwartz for the Washington Post
http://www.politicsnow.com/cgi-bin/displaySearch?WP+1765+%28decency%29%3Aall

John Schwartz for the Washington Post
http://www.politicsnow.com/cgi-bin/displaySearch?WP+1789+%28%22communi cations %26decency%26act%22%29%3Aall

Libertarian Party
http://www.afn.org/~libparty/960613.htm

Library of Congress
http://thomas.loc.gov/cgi-bin/bdquery/L?d104:./list/d104sh.lst:79[79-79]
(Communications_Decency_Act_of_1995)

Library of Congress
http://thomas.loc.gov/cgi-bin/bdquery/L?d104:./list/d104sh.lst:80[80-80]
(Communications_Decency_Act_of_1996)

Library of Congress
http://thomas.loc.gov/cgi-bin/query/z?c104:s.652.enr:

Marty Bruce
http://pegasus.cc.ucf.edu/~mab17431/ip.htm

Matthieu Navarro
http://web.club-internet.fr/navarro/index.html

n/a
http://www.xmission.com/~netrage/blow/blow.html

n/a
http://www.misha.net/~elfi/dec.html

n/a
http://157.242.97.98/t10/brian/t10cda.html

Neil Carolan and Andrew Krend
http://www.luhsd.k12.ca.us/~ak659819/anticda.html

Panix
gopher://gopher.panix.com:70/0/vtw/exon/media/doj-leahy

People for the American Way
http://www.pfaw.org/

People for the American Way
http://www.pfaw.org/alert/complain.txt

People for the American Way
http://www.pfaw.org/abtrr/afa.htm

pfenning@fast.net
http://www.users.fast.net/~pfenning/

PoliticsNow
http://www.politicsnow.com/

Progressive Networks
http://www.prognet.com/contentp/rabest/thebill.html

regebro@stacken.kth.se
http://www.stacken.kth.se/~regebro/cda.html

Republican National Committee
http://www.rnc.org/news/talking/tp-960201.html

Republican National Committee
http://www.rnc.org/news/release/rel960208.html

Republican National Committee
http://www.rnc.org/school/contract.html

Republican National Committee
http://www.rnc.org/

SenseMedia
http://sensemedia.net/CENSORED

Sleeping Beauty Publications, Ltd.
http://sleepingbeauty.com/world/liberty/butler.htm

Sleeping Beauty Publications, Ltd.
http://sleepingbeauty.com/world/liberty/pacifica.htm

Sleeping Beauy Publications Ltd.
http://sleepingbeauty.com/world/liberty/cohen.htm

Steve 'Stev0' Berlin
http://www.chaco.com/~stev0/oldrants/rant19.html

Steve Silberman
http://www.hotwired.com/special/lawsuit/index.html

Synergy HyperMail
http://entrepreneurs.net/solutions/emaildem/ed
pub.htm#17

The Washington Post
http://www.politicsnow.com/cgi-
bin/displaySearch?WP+1793+%28%22
communications%26decency%26act%22%29%
3Aall

US Library of Congress
http://thomas.loc.gov/

Voters Telecommunications Watch
http://www.vtw.org/speech/

Voters Telecommunications Watch
http://www.vtw.org/exon/

Voters Telecommunications Watch
http://www.vtw.org/

www.townhall.com
http://www.townhall.com/townhall/FRC/press/0
61296.html

Yahoo!
http://mirrors.yahoo.com/eff/speech.html

Yahoo!
http://www.yahoo.com/Government/Politics/Par
ties/Republican_Party/

Yahoo!
http://www.yahoo.com/Society_and_Culture/Ci
vil_Rights/Censorship/

Censorship_and_the_Net/Communications_Dec
ency_Act/Anti_CDA/

Yahoo!
http://www.yahoo.com/Society_and_Culture/Ci
vil_Rights/Censorship/
Censorship_and_the_Net/Communications_Dec
ency_Act/Internet_Indecency_Act_Ruled
_Unconstitutional/

Yahoo!
http://www.yahoo.com/Society_and_Culture/Ci
vil_Rights/Censorship/
Censorship_and_the_Net/Communications_Dec
ency_Act/Pro_CDA/

???
http://cyberweb.cybertoons.com/~bogstad/free
_the_net

Politics Now
http://www.politicsnow.com/cgi-
bin/displaySearch?APO+2337+%28decency%29
%3Aall

Politics Now
http://www.politicsnow.com/cgi-
bin/displaySearch?APO+2338+%28decency%29
%3Aall

Politics Now
http://www.politicsnow.com/cgi-
bin/displaySearch?APO+2215+%28decency%29
%3Aall

Notes

[1] Research for this chapter was supported by a grant (#410–96–0075) from the Canadian Social Sciences and Humanities Research Council. I would like to thank Daniel Hosseus for gathering the initial data on Web sites, and Alia Tayyeb for subsequent research assistance. This work was conducted primarily in July and August 1996.

[2] John E. Newhagen and Sheizaf Rafaeli, 'Why Communication Researchers Should Study the Internet: A Dialogue', *Journal of Communication* 46 (Winter 1996): 4–13.

[3] Despite its drawbacks, the term 'netizen' will be used as a convenience throughout to describe both individuals and organizations politically active in cyberspace.

4   Peter H. Lewis, 'Judges Turn Back Law to Regulate Internet Decency', *New York Times*, 13 June 1996, B10.

5   Jon Katz, 'Birth of a New Nation', *The Netizen*, 13 June 1996. http://www.netizen.com/netizen/96/24/katz3a.html (Last accessed 18 Dec. 1996.)

6   Peter H. Lewis, 'Protest, Cyberspace-Style, for New Law', *New York Times*, 8 Feb. 1996, A16.

7   Alvin Toffler, *Creating a New Civilization: The Politics of the Third Wave* (Atlanta: Turner Publications, 1995); Alvin Toffler, *Powershift: Knowledge, Wealth, and Violence at the Edge of the 21st Century* (New York: Bantam, 1990).

8   John Naisbitt, *Global Paradox* (New York: William Morrow, 1994), 48.

9   Lawrence K. Grossman, *The Electronic Republic: Reshaping Democracy in the Information Age* (New York: Viking, 1995), 16.

10 Ibid., 161.

11 Lewis A. Friedland, 'Electronic Democracy and the New Citizenship', *Media, Culture and Society* 18 (1996): 185–212; W.T. Stanbury and Ilan B. Vertinsky, 'Assessing the Impact of New Information Technologies on Interest Group Behaviour and Policymaking', in Thomas J. Courchene, ed., *Technology, Information and Public Policy*, The Bell Canada Papers on Economic and Public Policy (Kingston: John Deutsch Institute for the Study of Economic Policy, 1995), 293–379; Walter B. Wriston, *The Twilight of Sovereignty: How the Information Revolution is Transforming Our World* (New York: Charles Scribner's Sons, 1992), ch. 8.

12 Harlan Cleveland, 'The Twilight of Hierarchy: Speculations on the Global Information Society', *International Journal of Technology Management* 2 (1987): 45–66; Peter J. Spiro, 'New Global Communities: Nongovernmental Organizations in International Decision-Making Institutions', *The Washington Quarterly* 18, 1 (1994): 45–56, esp. 47–8.

13 Kees Brants, Martine Huizenga, and Reineke van Meeten, 'The New Canals of Amsterdam: An Exercise in Local Electronic Democracy', *Media, Culture and Society* 18 (1996): 233–47.

14 Gary W. Selnow, *High-Tech Campaigns: Computer Technology in Political Communication* (Westport, Conn.: Praeger, 1994). Though he notes in passing that 'So far, technology has worked on behalf of political campaigns, but computer equipment in the hands of citizens will further alter the relationship between candidates and voters' (p. 160).

15 C.J. Alexander, 'Plugging into New Currents: The Use of New Information and Communication Technologies in Party Politics', in Hugh G. Thorburn, ed., *Party Politics in Canada*, 7th edn (Scarborough, Ont.: Prentice-Hall, 1996), 594–610.

16 Leonard Preyra, 'Changing Conventions: Plebiscitarian Democracy and Party Leadership Selection in Canada', in Thorburn, ed., *Party Politics in Canada*, 7th edn, 213–24.

17 However, see Robert W. McChesney, 'The Internet and U.S. Communication Policy-Making in Historical and Critical Perspective', *Journal of Communication* 46 (Winter 1996): 98–124, for a view that 'the new communication technologies are, in fact, a product and a defining feature of a global capitalism that greatly enhances social inequality' (p. 99).

18 Sherry Turkle, *Life on the Screen: Identity in the Age of the Internet* (New York: Simon and Schuster, 1995), 243.

19 J.B. Abramson, C. Atherton, and G.R. Orren, *The Electronic Commonwealth: The Impact of New Media Technologies on Democratic Politics* (New York: Basic Books, 1988), 137. Also Julian Stallabrass, 'Empowering Technology: The Exploration of Cyberspace', *New Left Review* 211 (May/June 1995): 3–32. For a balanced view of both positive and negative potentials of ICT, see David Ronfeldt, 'Cyberocracy is Coming', *The Information Society* 8 (Oct.-Dec. 1992): 243–96.

20   The Internet is a generic term for the emergent network formed from the interconnections of
      all other electronic networks, both private and public. The Internet has distinct 'sectors', each
      with its own characteristics and implications for research. The World Wide Web can be
      defined as that sector consisting primarily of hypermedia communications using the TCP/IP pro-
      tocols. See John December, 'Units of Analysis for Internet Communication', *Journal of Commu-
      nication* 46 (1996): 14–38.

21   The key UseNet groups were alt.censorship and alt.society.civil-disob.

22   A product of Quarterdeck, WebCompass allows simultaneous, multiple searches on different
      search engines (e.g., Lycos, Alta Vista), and then returns its findings in a collated, indexed list
      with summaries of texts and links.

23   The full text of the CDA is available at the Library of Congress. http://thomas.loc.gov/cgi-
      bin/query/l?c104:/temp/~c104AoDu:e253573 (Last accessed 18 Dec. 1996.)

24   ACLU Brief in *ACLU v. Reno.* http://sleepingbeauty.com/world/liberty/aclubrief.htm (Last
      accessed 18 Dec. 1996.)

25   Human Rights Watch, Electronic Privacy Information Center, Electronic Frontier Foundation,
      Journalism Education Association, Computer Professionals for Social Responsibility, National
      Writers Union, ClariNet, Institute for Global Communications, Stop Prisoner Rape, AIDS Educa-
      tion Global Information System, Safer Sex Page, BiblioBytes, Wildcat Press, Queer Resources
      Directory, Justice On Campus, Cyberwire, Dispatch, The Ethical Spectacle, and Planned Parent-
      hood Foundation of America.

26   The full text of the decision is available at: http://www.cdt.org/ciec/decision_PA/
      decision_text.html (Last accessed 18 Dec. 1996.)

27   As it describes itself: 'The Electronic Frontier Foundation is a non-profit civil liberties organiza-
      tion working in the public interest to protect privacy, free expression, and access to public
      resources and information online, as well as to promote responsibility in new media.'
      http://www.eff.org/ (Last accessed 18 Dec. 1996.)

28   Sleeping Beauty is an adult-oriented site. http://www.sleepingbeauty.com (Last accessed 18
      Dec. 1996.)

29   For example, Steve Lohr, 'Conservatives Split on How to Regulate the Internet', *New York
      Times,* 9 Nov. 1995, D4. The Christian Coalition was and is a traditional Republican supporter,
      but in the CDA case it favoured government censorship, whereas Newt Gingrich (House
      Speaker) led House Republicans to propose a version of the legislation that would rely on self-
      censorship through techniques such as special blocking software or adult site registration
      schemes.

30   As the Internet Society (ISOC) describes itself: 'The Internet Society is a non-governmental
      international organization for global cooperation and coordination for the Internet and its inter-
      networking technologies and applications. The Society's individual and organizational members
      are bound by a common stake in maintaining the viability and global scaling of the Internet.
      They comprise the companies, government agencies, and foundations that have created the
      Internet and its technologies as well as innovative new entrepreneurial organizations contribut-
      ing to maintain that dynamic.' http://info.isoc.org/whatis/index.html (Last accessed 19 Dec.
      1996.)

31   Though a separate injunction was granted by federal judges in New York on 29 July 1996 in
      response to a request by an electronic newspaper entitled *The American Reporter.* See Peter

H. Lewis, 'Opponents of Indecency Rules on Internet Win Another Case', *New York Times*, 30 July 1996.

[32] Organizational membership: Association of American University Presses, Association of National Advertisers, Association of Research Libraries, Center for Democracy and Technology, Coalition for Networked Information, Media Access Project, Media Institute, Microsystems Software, National Association of State Universities & Land Grant Colleges, National Newspaper Association, People for the American Way, Recording Industry Association of America, Software Publishers Association, Special Libraries Association, Surfwatch Software, University of California Santa Barbara Library. The CIEC also claims over 55,000 members as of December 1996.

[33] Center for Democracy and Technology. http://www.cdt.org/index.html (Last accessed 18 Dec. 1996.)

[34] The 27 plaintiffs in the case included: American Library Association, America On-Line, American Booksellers Association, American Booksellers Foundation for Free Expression, American Society of Newspaper Editors, Apple Computer, Association of American Publishers, Association of Publishers, Editors and Writers, Citizens Internet Empowerment Coalition, Commercial Internet eXchange, CompuServe Incorporated, Families Against Internet Censorship, Freedom to Read Foundation, Health Sciences Libraries Consortium, HotWired, Interactive Digital Software Association, Interactive Services Association, Magazine Publishers of America, Microsoft Corporation, Microsoft Network, National Press Photographers Association, NETCOM On-Line Communication Services, Newspaper Association of America, Opnet, Prodigy Services Company, Wired Ventures, and the Society of Professional Journalists.

[35] Friedland, 'Electronic Democracy and the New Citizenship', 191.

[36] Citizens Internet Empowerment Coalition. http://www.cdt.org/ciec/index.html (Last accessed 18 Dec. 1996.)

[37] See Gerald Rosenberg, *The Hollow Hope: Can Courts Bring about Social Change* (Chicago: University of Chicago Press, 1991).

[38] See Mr. Bill's Bill . . . the CDA. http://www.vic.com/~steel/distress/ (Last accessed 18 Dec. 1996.)

[39] The Electronic Activist. http://www.berkshire.net/~ifas/activist (Last accessed 18 Dec. 1996.)

[40] The Exonizer. http://www.global-image.com/cgi-bin/exonizer/censored.cgi?document+cum (Last accessed 18 Dec. 1996.)

[41] http://www.cdt.org/net_protest.html (Last accessed 18 Dec. 1996.)

[42] Grossman, *The Electronic Republic*, 145.

[43] Krista Spurr (Acadia University) has also suggested another feature of e-mail campaigns: 'e-mail bombing', where so many messages are sent that they cause a collapse in the receiving system.

[44] Black Thursday (Yahoo). http://mirrors.yahoo.com/eff/speech.html (Last accessed 18 Dec. 1996.)

[45] Banned Books. http://box.hotwired.net/banned.html (Last accessed 18 Dec. 1996.)

[46] Free Speech. http://coos.dartmouth.edu/~emk/speech (Last accessed 18 Dec. 1996. Dead link as of 19 Dec. 1996.)

[47] http://www.dnai.com/~lizard/civdis.htm (Last accessed 18 Dec. 1996.)

[48] Steve Berlin's 'Rant of the Week'. http://www.chaco.com/~stev0/oldrants/rant19.html (Last accessed 18 Dec. 1996.) There was relatively little evidence of the extremism that some worry

might be encouraged through the Internet (though see the kathh@holli.com's page for allegations of death threats and aggression because of her/his stand favouring the CDA. See http://user.holli.com/~kathh//anti.htm (Last accessed 18 Dec. 1996.)

Chapter 7

TELEDEMOCRACY: CANADIAN POLITICAL PARTIES LISTENING TO THEIR CONSTITUENTS

Bill Cross

Introduction

Responding to demands for effective citizen participation in public decision-making, Canadian political parties in the 1990s are using advances in communication technology to facilitate the more widespread participation of their supporters.[1] Specifically, parties have used telephone technology both to facilitate the selection of their leaders and to gather the opinions of constituents on policy matters. Cable television and the Internet are also being used to facilitate communication between constituents and their representatives. This chapter examines specific uses of these devices by the parties, considers the success of these applications in increasing effective, widespread participation, and identifies their principal shortcomings.

In the aftermath of Canadians' rejection of élite-brokered constitutional deals in the 1980s and 1990s, many students of Canadian politics have identified a strong desire by voters to be active, ongoing participants in public affairs.[2] Political parties, because they have traditionally been viewed as primary vehicles for conveying grassroots policy concerns and preferences to elected representatives,[3] and because they are the only political organizations accessible in each local community, have been one of the targets of these efforts for increased citizen participation. The parties, some eager to capitalize on this voter sentiment and others fearful of being outmanoeuvred by their opponents, have turned to communication technology for assistance in making their internal processes more accessible to their constituents. Both this voter sentiment and the efforts by the parties to be more receptive to grassroots participation are not unique in Canadian history. The Progressives of the 1920s, the CCF in the 1950s and the Liberals in the 1960s and 1970s all made efforts to increase the opportunities for effective participation among their supporters.[4] What is different about the current activity is its reliance on technological developments to facilitate voter participation.

The literature on uses of communication technology for public decision-making suggests that there are three primary benefits of teledemocracy: (1) overcoming the obstacles of size and population dispersion that otherwise make direct democracy impossible in the modern state;[5] (2) permitting a greater number of citizens to participate by reducing the burdens to participation;[6] and (3) increasing equity in public decision-making by reducing inequalities in availability of participatory opportunities.[7] Advocates of the application of these technologies to Canadian parties, while largely concurring with this academic literature, have focused on the ability of technology to provide citizens with more opportunities for effective participation in public decision-making. Specifically, they have argued that teledemocracy offers the possibility of: (1) increasing the number of voters participating in public decision-making;[8] (2) providing citizens with additional information on issues of public policy;[9] and (3) facilitating the ability of policy-makers to be aware of voters' opinions on policy matters.[10]

This chapter evaluates the success of the parties' uses of teledemocracy according to how well they achieve the parties' stated objectives and advance the democratic norm of increased, effective citizen participation.[11] It reaches four conclusions. Firstly, the number of voters participating in the teledemocracy projects has been relatively low. Secondly, teledemocracy does provide more voters with more information on public policy issues than do traditional methods of political communication. Thirdly, teledemocracy is not particularly well suited to assisting elected officials in determining public opinion on policy issues, but is better able to determine intensity of conviction on a particular issue because the citizens most concerned with the issue are likely to be overrepresented among participants. Finally, teledemocracy tends to atomize voters and is therefore not well suited for collective decision-making and consensus-building. The first three of these conclusions address technology's success at enhancing the identified democratic norms. The fourth, while clearly an unintended consequence of the technology, concerns the necessity of accommodation in Canadian politics. We have long ago learned that technological advances often bring about important unintended consequences and their application to the political world is no different.

Experiments with Teledemocracy

Four types of teledemocracy experiments were examined: (1) the Reform Party's use of cable television and telephone technology to communicate with voters about, and determine their views on, particular issues of public policy; (2) individual MPs' use of telephone technology to conduct 'polls' of their constituents on policy questions; (3) use of the Internet by parties and MPs to communicate with voters; and (4) provincial parties' use of telephone technology to select their leaders. While this chapter considers only the parties' use of technology prior to the 1997 federal election, it is important to note that the campaign brought a significant increase in the parties' use of communications technology. All five major parties, and several minor ones, had campaign pages on the World Wide Web. These sites typically included the leaders' itineraries, updates from the leaders' tours, texts of campaign speeches, and policy positions. The parties also made increased use of sophisticated voter software packages for tracking supporters.

Cable Television and Telephones

The Reform Party has used a method that combines television with telephone polls to determine voters' views on several issues, including the federal budget, federalism, and physician-assisted suicide. On the latter issue, for example, in

April 1994 Preston Manning and four other Calgary area Reform MPs organized a telephone vote of their constituents in conjunction with a television program broadcast via a Calgary cable channel. In front of a studio audience of approximately 200, a panel of experts representing both sides of the issue discussed its merits. Manning appeared only briefly on the program to present his position. An estimated audience of 20,000 viewed the program, and 1,533 voted by phoning in their opinions.[12]

While the television show allowed interested voters to learn more about the issue, this was clearly a secondary objective. The primary objective, as stated by Manning, was for the MPs to learn the views of their constituents. While all five sponsoring MPs had previously expressed their opposition to physician-assisted suicide, they declared their willingness to consider the views of their constituents before making a final decision. MP Diane Ablonczy stated that this issue was particularly suitable to an MP voting the wishes of her constituents: 'This is an issue that wasn't discussed during the last election but which people care very deeply about.'[13] While Manning pledged to support the view of a majority of his constituents, 'Doug Kemp, an aide to MP Jim Silye, said only an unquestionable, clear majority would prompt Mr. Silye to vote against his conscience.'[14]

Several mechanisms were used to determine voters' views. Viewers were invited to phone a central number to vote, but since personal identification numbers (PINs) were not provided there was no mechanism to restrict each voter to one phone call. Sixty per cent of callers supported physician-assisted suicide.[15] As a control measure aimed at preventing one side of the issue from dominating the phone-in poll, 1,195 viewers were randomly selected and called after the program; 72 per cent of these viewers voted in favour of physician-assisted suicide while 19 per cent were opposed. Finally, a randomly selected sample of 602 constituents was polled on the issue, with 82 per cent voting in favour and 16 per cent opposed. Manning concluded from this exercise that 'The initial interpretation indicates a strong constituent support for physician-assisted suicide under specific conditions.' He reported that 'If a government bill was presented to Parliament tomorrow permitting physician-assisted suicide under those conditions, the participating MPs would vote for it in accordance with the expression of those constituents.'[16]

The Reform Party used this same technology nationally in its 'Canada Speaks' project aimed at determining voters' views on Canadian federalism. Manning announced in September 1994 that the party would be opening up phone lines from 26 September to 3 October for voters to phone in and express their views on three questions relating to Canadian federalism.[17] On 3 October, the party sponsored a television program, broadcast throughout most of Canada on cable television, providing a discussion of the relevant issues by a panel of experts, members of the studio audience, and taped comments from prominent Canadians. The program was broadcast in both English and French. The phone lines, available with both English and French instructions, were open through to the end of the television broadcast. The panel included ardent federalists, economists, and the well-known Quebec separatist, Josée Legault. Manning travelled extensively during the period leading up to the television broadcast seeking publicity for the project and encouraging Canadians to participate in it.[18] Voters wishing to telephone in their views were charged a fee of $1 per minute, with the average call lasting two minutes. Again, no PINs were distributed and voters could phone as often as they wished. Voters were asked three questions and approximately 10,000 answers to the individual questions were received.[19] It is impossible to know how many Canadians actually participated because some may have voted more than once.[20]

A similar process was used in February 1995 to determine Canadians' views on issues concerning the federal budget. The Reform Party sponsored a 90-minute program entitled 'You Be the Finance Minister' broadcast across Canada by more than 80 cable television companies. The program was hosted by Manning and included a panel discussing various perspectives on public finance. The panelists included Michael Walker of the Fraser Institute; Duncan Cameron, president of the Canadian Centre for Policy Alternatives; Diane Francis, editor of the *Financial Post*; and John Richards, an economist at Simon Fraser University and member of the NDP.[21] Three possible budget scenarios were discussed and evaluated.[22] Approximately 10,000 calls were received at a 1-900 number registering which of the three budget scenarios callers preferred. Ninety-three per cent of callers supported the first option, the position advocated by the Reform Party leadership.[23]

Telephone 'Polls'

Perhaps the largest effort at using teledemocracy to determine the views of constituents on a particular issue was Reform MP Ted White's project concerning amendments to the Young Offenders Act. The objectives of this project were to inform voters of the issues relevant to reform of the Young Offenders Act and to gauge opinion of constituents on possible reforms. The first objective was achieved through advertisements in the community newspaper, the *North Shore News*, and through the mailing of a 'householder' pamphlet to all residents. Both the advertisements and the pamphlet included what appear to be a balanced discussion of the opposing positions concerning reform of the legislation.[24] White also provided his constituents with a telephone help-line they could call for information on both the substance of the issue and the method of voting.

The second objective was met by an elaborate telephone poll. All registered voters in the riding were eligible to vote and were mailed a PIN between 1 June and 9 June 1994.[25] Voters could then telephone a 1-900 number between 15

June and 20 June to cast their vote. Voters needed to punch in their PIN to have their vote count, and the system limited each constituent to one vote. Callers to the 1-900 number were billed $1.95 per call. White anticipated a participation rate of 60 per cent.[26]

Callers were asked three questions to which they could punch in numbers on their telephone key pad indicating a yes or no answer—approximately 4,600 voters participated out of more than 70,000 potential voters.[27] White was very disappointed with the low participation rate, which he attributed to three principal factors: the three-day media campaign clashed with the Stanley Cup playoffs and the Vancouver hockey riot; the PIN numbers were sent out too long before the vote; and people knew that the Justice Minister's proposals would be pushed through Parliament with little or no input and felt that their votes would not count.[28]

Reform MP Bob Ringma has conducted several telephone polls of his constituents. Since 1993, Ringma has operated a system allowing constituents on the voting list to register with his office as potential televoters and receive a PIN. Such registered voters are then eligible to participate in occasional 'polls' that Ringma conducts on issues of public policy. Approximately 1,500 of Ringma's constituents have registered to participate in these votes out of a potential 90,000 voters.[29] To vote on an issue, a registered constituent need only dial a 1-800 number and enter his or her PIN and then additional numbers reflecting the preferred option. Almost 1,200 of Ringma's constituents participated in a vote concerning reforms to the Young Offenders Act, while 1,000 voted on whether the government should hold a binding referendum on capital punishment, and just under 600 voted on what English Canada's position should be in the event of a Quebec vote to leave Confederation.

Computer Technology
Another technology increasingly used by elected officials to communicate with their constituents is the home computer. A growing number of office-holders have established sites on the Internet that allow them to provide information to interested constituents and for constituents to communicate their views. In early 1997, for example, only a minority of MPs had homepages. By mid-1998, all of them did. However, the early ones were often individual efforts. Now, the pages are maintained by the parties.[30]

Alberta Premier Ralph Klein posted his government's January 1995 Throne Speech on the Internet and received more than 3,200 responses. When the province's budget was also made available, Treasury spokesperson Gord Rosko said: 'It's just another way to get information out to the public.'[31] Prime Minister Chrétien and several premiers, such as Ontario's Bob Rae and Mike Harris and New Brunswick's Frank McKenna, have also been available on the Internet.

All five of the federal parties, and many provincial parties, have Web sites offering various information.[32] These sites typically include the parties' most recent policy positions, recent press releases, and leaders' speeches, along with an invitation to respond to the party with any views the browser may have. Many also ask for voters' opinions on particular issues of public policy. For example, the Ontario Liberals' homepage asks browsers to respond to periodically changing questions. In October 1996 the party was asking for opinions on the following question: 'How have the Tory cuts to hospitals affected you?' In January 1997 the party was seeking voter opinion on the following question: 'How do you rate the Tory record on child poverty?'[33] Many party constituent groups, such as university clubs and constituency associations, also have their own sites. Some leadership candidates and general election candidates have also established homepages. The Reform candidate in the federal by-election in the Ontario riding of Ottawa-Vanier set up a freenet address that allowed him to communicate directly with interested constituents. Said candidate Kevin Gaudet: 'The move into the Internet, officially launched this week, is an attempt to bypass the media and talk directly to voters.'[34] All six Reform candidates for the 25 March 1996 federal by-elections also had homepages on the World Wide Web.[35]

Telephone Leadership Selection

The Nova Scotia Liberals (1992), British Columbia Liberals (1993), Alberta Liberals (1994), and Saskatchewan PCs (1994) have all selected their current leaders through a telephone vote of their membership.[36] While the details of each process vary somewhat, generally speaking the televotes work as follows. During a set window of several hours, party members telephone a central number and receive automated instructions to punch in their PIN on their telephone key pad. Once identified, voters are asked to punch in additional numbers identifying the candidate of their choice. After the voting period, a computer program tabulates the number of votes received by each leadership candidate. The technology is owned and operated by Maritime Telephone and Telegraph (MT&T). The parties are charged a substantial fee by MT&T for the service, and three of the four parties have off-loaded the costs onto voters. The Nova Scotia Liberals charged a voting fee of $25, the BC Liberals charged $20, and the Alberta Liberals charged $10.

In two of the votes, major technological difficulties created substantial problems. The entire voting system crashed during the voting period in Nova Scotia. Many party members were not able to get through on the telephone and the party was forced to cancel the vote and try again. The technological problems were solved and the party successfully held the vote two weeks later. The Alberta Liberals suffered similar though less severe glitches during their contest. Many party members complained that the telephone lines were continuously busy and that they were not able to vote. The party extended the voting hours, but did not reschedule the vote.

Participation rates have been below 50 per cent in each of these contests. The BC Liberals had the highest percentage of members vote in their contest with 49 per cent, compared with 42 per cent for the Nova Scotia Liberals, 36 per cent for the Saskatchewan PCs, and 28 per cent for the Alberta Liberals.

Discussion: Technology and Democracy

Each of the teledemocracy processes reviewed achieves different results. Accordingly, it is necessary to consider individually how each process measures up to the various democratic norms.

Participation

Participation rates have not been particularly strong in any of these projects. The leadership votes have had the largest number of participants of any of the teledemocracy experiments, yet even these have had an average participation rate of 39 per cent with not a single one reaching 50 per cent. Leadership selection processes making no use of modern technology have had both a higher percentage of members participating and a larger number of participants. Parties relying on members to mail in their ballots have realized a 41 per cent participation rate, parties with open conventions at which all interested members may attend and vote have achieved a 44 per cent participation rate, and parties using paper ballot voting in the ridings, the least sophisticated form of voting, have enjoyed the highest participation rate—57 per cent.[37] There is no evidence that the use of teledemocracy has increased the number of participants in leadership selection contests.

Telephone surveys conducted by individual MPs have also had relatively low participation rates. Despite the extensive efforts undertaken by White, less than 7 per cent of his constituents participated in his survey on the Young Offenders Act. Ringma's surveys of his constituents have had only a third or fewer of the number of participants received by White. The Reform Party's projects using both television and telephone technology have also not resulted in large participation rates. Less than 2,000 Calgarians participated in the vote on physician-assisted suicide. While these results are not overly impressive, it is worth remembering, however, that we have little information regarding the number of voters' participating in conventional methods of communication on policy issues. Indeed, it is unlikely that 2,000 Calgary voters would have communicated their opinion on physician-assisted suicide to their MPs had Reform not offered the teledemocracy option.

In considering why participation rates have been relatively low we need to examine the level of public awareness concerning these votes. In several of the televotes the participatory group was limited to those who closely follow public affairs and who are thus aware of the existence of the experiment. While notice of forthcoming televotes may be given once or twice in a local newspaper, and perhaps on a local radio and television broadcast, cost usually prevents significant mainstream advertising. As a result, many of these projects likely pass by with many citizens not even knowing of their existence.

The use of cable television broadcasts and the Internet is also problematic in this regard. Many citizens rarely watch local cable channels, and the range of television programming available makes it likely that only a small percentage will be attracted by a political discussion on a cable channel. Some of the Internet votes rely on voters' browsing on the member's or party's homepage to become aware that a 'survey' of constituents' opinions is under way.

Participation is also made more difficult by the lack of universal access to the required technology. In most of the undertakings examined, the method of active participation for voters was restricted to the telephone. While the vast majority of Canadians have telephones, the technology requires a touch-tone telephone, which a significant minority, estimated at more than 5 per cent, do not possess.[38] These citizens are effectively prevented from participating and having their opinions count. Rotary-dial telephones are likely most common among the poor, who cannot afford the extra monthly charge of a touch-tone line, and among the elderly, who do not see any need to adopt the new technology.

Those projects in which participants are invited to record their opinions via the Internet or some other computer service present even more significant questions of access. Many voters do not have home computers, and many who do are not connected to modems that would allow participation in these projects. Recent estimates are that more than two-thirds of Canadians never use the Internet.[39] In those projects that couple a cable television show with a telephone 'poll', citizens without cable television are effectively eliminated from participation. While a majority of Canadians have cable television, a quarter of them do not.[40] Again, the poor are overrepresented among those without cable television.

The project run by White in Vancouver North addressed many of these concerns. White ensured that all citizens would be made aware of the project's existence by taking several steps: (1) advertising the project in the local newspaper; (2) receiving substantial free coverage in the local media; (3) using his MP 'householder' mailing to announce the project; and, most importantly, (4) mailing a voter information sheet personally addressed to each registered voter in the riding. White even made efforts to update the voter registration list from the previous federal election so as not to exclude new residents or those who had recently moved from the pool of eligible participants. Interestingly, none of these efforts to inform voters of the public opinion survey or of the substance of the issue relied on any technology. Even though White's project was the most 'user-friendly' and most accessible of any of the teledemocracy projects reviewed, the participation rate remained low.

A further factor reducing voter interest in these contests likely results from voters' perceptions of how consequential their participation is. The Reform Party and its MPs have been clear that they would be guided by the results of these votes. However, voters are well aware of Canadian parliamentary practices providing little real opportunity for a third party to have substantial impact on public policy. White alluded to this when he suggested that one of the causes of low voter turnout was voters' belief that the Justice Minister's proposals would be pushed through Parliament with little or no public input, and thus that their opinions would have no impact.[41] Parties engaging in telephone leadership selection have all been opposition parties. Government parties using other forms of direct leadership selection have enjoyed a higher turnout of party members. Costs of participation may also keep participation rates down—particularly in the leadership selection contests. Telephone leadership votes have charged relatively large voting fees to offset the costs of the technology. For all direct-vote leadership selection processes, the participation rate for those charging a fee is only 39 per cent, while parties charging no fee have enjoyed an average participation rate of 55 per cent.[42] Many of the other teledemocracy projects using voter phone-in also charge a $2-$3 voting fee. While this may be a modest amount, it may discourage many from participating—particularly considering how remote the likelihood is of the participation effecting a policy outcome.

Representativeness

Consideration of the success of teledemocracy at conveying voters' policy preferences to political parties largely depends on how representative the participating group is of the entire electorate. It is often suggested that the results received through teledemocracy efforts are not representative of general public opinion but reflect the views of a small group of activists who follow public events closely and thus are aware of and participate in these events. Those most interested in the issue being debated, partisans of the party sponsoring the project, and those generally more politically active are likely overrepresented among participants. Factors such as the cost of participation and the necessity to have a home computer or cable television likely also skew the socio-economic status of participants.

There are some indicators, however, that those who participate may be more representative than many suggest. The results that White received in his telephone survey and the responses received by the Reform Party to their program on the budget are similar to those received by public opinion pollsters on these issues.[43] On the physician-assisted suicide issue the results received from the telephone program and from the scientific poll subsequently commissioned by the party also did not vary significantly. In leadership selection contests, studies of the Alberta and Nova Scotia Liberal contests indicate that the voters participating in the telephone votes were actually more representative of the provincial population on socio-economic characteristics than were delegates to recent leadership conventions.[44] Nevertheless, all participants in the teledemocracy projects have been self-selected. There is therefore no guarantee that the results received will be representative of anything more than the views of those participating. This is especially important because users of teledemocracy often portray the results received as being representative of public opinion. For example, White said of his project:

> Voter participation was lower than we predicted it would be when we announced the referendum about seven weeks ago. . . . Even so the total was many times greater than any opinion poll conducted in the area. People with polling experience will tell you that voting patterns are established within a few hundred calls so referendum '94 represents a very significant result.[45]

Of course, there is no statistical validity to this claim. No matter how many citizens participate in teledemocracy projects, as long as participation remains substantially below 100 per cent, the raw number of participants provides no evidence that the participatory group is representative of voters at large.

Teledemocracy methods, however, are likely good measures of intensity of opinion. Those generally politically active and those concerned with the specific issue being addressed are much more likely to participate than citizens at large. This is not necessarily a bad thing. Since these projects are typically advisory and not determinative of public policy, knowledge of intensity of feelings can aid politicians in their decision-making.

Informing Voters

Some of the televote projects have succeeded in providing voters with more information on public policy issues. The parties' Web pages are useful in providing their positions on many topical issues. Voters with Internet access can browse through the various Web pages and make comparisons. The television programs sponsored by the Reform Party have offered some balance of differing opinions and were likely informative to viewers. White's project largely succeeded in providing voters with balanced information concerning reforms to the Young Offenders Act. Other projects, however, have not provided much information to voters. For instance, many of the Web sites ask for constituents' policy views without offering any discussion of the issue.

The use of technology also raises the issue of the type of information it provides voters and whether it makes voters more atomistic. Voters stay in their own homes and form their opinions with no need to interact with others. Technology has not yet been successfully employed in widespread collective decision-making. The problem of size, particularly, is not easily overcome by technology. While technology is able to overcome the problem of distance—a small group of dispersed decision-makers can be brought together through such means as teleconferencing to participate in deliberation similar to face-to-face decision-making—it does not provide a means through which large numbers of voters can participate in a decision-making process that is deliberative and lends itself to the seeking of consensus. As Arterton concluded from a study of 13 US experiments with teledemocracy: 'As a medium of dialogue, each of these vehicles may be conveniently used by modest numbers of communicators; the emerging technologies do not promise that everyone can have his or her individual say in a national dialogue.'[46] Elshtain, too, has criticized teledemocracy on the grounds that it does not provide for deliberation, discourse with other citizens, or a sense of community—all of which, she argues, are vital in a successful participatory democracy.[47]

This is of particular concern in the case of leadership selection. Voters in direct election campaigns appear dependent on the media for most of their information. Not only do most voters not meet the candidates, but they have little opportunity to communicate with voters with different experiences from their own. By contrast, leadership convention delegates mingle in the same hotels and convention halls for several days, sharing opinions concerning the leadership candidates in both formal and informal meetings. Delegates have the opportunity to hear and consider the concerns of others from different socio-economic backgrounds and from different regions of the province. When voting day arrives, all delegates are assembled in one hall and a true sense of collective decision-making exists.

Unlike convention delegates, televoters do not have the opportunity to benefit from informal discussions with other members. In rejecting a proposal to replace the leadership convention, the Ontario Liberal Party's Leadership Procedures Review Committee suggested that:

> A convention allows delegates from northern Ontario and southern Ontario to get together and share their views and concerns; it allows delegates from rural ridings to try to convince delegates from urban ridings, and vice versa. Delegates can share their impressions of the candidates with each other—with their views unfiltered by the media.[48]

In parties with deep regional, linguistic, or rural/urban cleavages, the loss of collective decision-making opportunities may cause great difficulty in attempts to build consensus.

Conclusion

Teledemocracy is not a panacea for all that ails Canadian politics. The number of participants in teledemocracy projects has been relatively small and the connection between their participation and public policy outcomes has been virtually non-existent. These are not solely the result of inherent shortcomings in teledemocracy, but likely also result because such projects have been undertaken largely by opposition parties with limited opportunity to influence government policy.

Teledemocracy does allow activists to participate in the political process in an unmediated fashion. Telephone leadership selection allows party members to vote directly for the candidate of their choice without having their preferences filtered through convention delegates. However, considering that parties have adopted other methods of leadership selection that facilitate the direct choice of the party leader by the rank-and-file membership without the use of technology, it is difficult to see what teledemocracy adds to the practice. In fact, telephone votes have a lower participation rate than all other forms of direct party leadership selection. This is likely the result of the parties charging a substantial voting fee, as well as the disenfranchisement of those without touchtone telephones.

Cable television and the Internet do offer the potential to educate voters on public policy issues. That 20,000 citizens in the Calgary area watched an informative and balanced television program concerning physician-assisted suicide is clearly of value to the Canadian political system. The Reform Party has effectively used cable television to this end, and all of the federal parties have World Wide Web sites offering valuable information to voters on their policy positions. Of course, only a small portion of the electorate are Internet 'surfers' and the cable television audiences for the policy programs have not been particularly large.

The information received by the parties through teledemocracy is of limited value. Because participants are self-selected and participation rates are relatively low, there is no assurance that the information received is reflective of voter preferences. The opinions expressed, however, may assist parties in determining the intensity of opinion on an issue.

Finally, teledemocracy does not easily lend itself to collective decision-making. While technology may potentially allow for the collection of each voter's opinion on most issues, it does not yet offer the possibility for large groups of diverse citizens to communicate with one another and exchange ideas and information. The closest it comes in this regard is chat groups on the Internet or policy discussions on television that include representatives of different perspectives on the relevant issue.

All of the shortcomings of teledemocracy notwithstanding, it is important not to devalue the efforts of those attempting to increase public awareness on policy issues and the responsiveness of public officials to public opinion. This chapter began with the assertion that Canadians desire a more direct say in their public decision-making processes. The careful use of teledemocracy, particularly if adopted by those in government, may provide a vehicle to address these concerns.

Notes

[1] The author thanks S.J.R. Noel and A. Paul Pross for helpful comments on an earlier draft of this chapter.

[2] See, for example, Citizens' Forum on Canada's Future, *Report to the People and Government of Canada* (Ottawa: Ministry of Supply and Services Canada, 1991); *Report of the Royal Commission on Electoral Reform and Party Financing* (Ottawa: Ministry of Supply and Services Canada, 1991); Peter Dobell and Byron Berry, 'Anger at the System: What Canadians Think About Their Political System', *Parliamentary Government* 39 (1992): 5; F. Leslie Seidle, 'The Angry Citizenry: Examining Representation and Responsiveness in Government', *Policy Options* 15 (1994): 75; André Blais and Elisabeth Gidengil, *Making Representative Democracy Work: The Views of Canadians*, research studies of the Royal Commission on Electoral Reform and Party Financing, vol.17 (Toronto: Dundurn Press, 1991); Alan C. Cairns, 'An Election to be Remembered: Canada 1993', *Canadian Public Policy* 20 (1994): 229.

[3] See Giovani Sartori, *Parties and Party Systems: A Framework for Analysis* (Cambridge: Cambridge University Press, 1976); William M. Chandler and Allen Siaroff, 'Parties and Party Government in Advanced Democracies', in Herman Bakvis, ed., *Canadian Political Parties: Leaders, Candidates and Organization* (Toronto: Dundurn Press, 1991); Anthony King, 'Political Parties in Western Democracies', *Polity* 2 (1969): 111–41.

[4] See, for example, W.L. Morton, *The Progressive Party in Canada* (Toronto: University of Toronto Press, 1950); Evelyn Eager, 'The Paradox of Power in the Saskatchewan C.C.F., 1944–1961', in J.H. Aitchison, ed., *The Political Process in Canada* (Toronto: University of Toronto Press, 1963); Stephen Clarkson, 'Democracy in the Liberal Party: The Experiment with Citizen Participation under Pierre Trudeau', in Hugh G. Thorburn, ed., *Party Politics in Canada*, 4th edn (Scarborough, Ont.: Prentice-Hall), 154–60.

[5] See Iain McLean, *Democracy and the New Technology* (Cambridge: Polity Press, 1989), 108–10.

[6] See F. Christopher Arterton, *Can Technology Protect Democracy?* (Newbury Park, Calif.: Sage, 1987), 189. Arterton concludes that 'The principal observed impact of the use of technology for democratic politics is to reduce the costs and burdens of participation for citizens. These costs may be financial or they may be associated with time, travel and information necessary to participate politically.'

[7] Ibid., 50–1; Benjamin Barber, *Strong Democracy: Participatory Politics for a New Age* (Berkeley: University of California Press, 1984).

[8] This motivation has been particularly strong in decisions to use teledemocracy to choose party leaders. See 'Members Can Vote for Leader Over Phone', *Vancouver Sun*, 6 Mar. 1993, G3, reporting that the BC Liberal Party president, Floyd Sully, envisioned a large increase in party

membership corresponding to increased voter participation in the telephone selection of the party's new leader.

9   See, for example, 'Reform Will Seek High-tech Input on New-Look Country', *Calgary Herald*, 13 June 1994, A7.

10   See, for example, 'Press One for Touch of Teledemocracy', *Vancouver Sun*, 26 May 1994, A7. Certainly the parties' objectives go beyond these altruistic ones. It is unclear to what extent the parties are driven by concern that they 'appear' democratic or at least as democratic as their opponents. Also, some of the identified benefits, such as a better educated electorate, accrue to the political system as a whole and not solely to the political parties.

11   Efforts to increase effective citizen participation, specifically participation with a reasonable opportunity of influencing public decision-making, raise several issues concerning the appropriateness of this kind of widespread citizen involvement in Canadian politics. A compelling argument has been made that the compromises necessary to govern a country with the deep cleavages found in Canadian society can only be achieved through methods of élite accommodation and that these are jeopardized by increased direct citizen participation. See S.J.R. Noel, 'Political Parties and Elite Accommodation: Interpretations of Canadian Federalism', in J. Peter Meekison, ed., *Canadian Federalism: Myth or Reality*, 3rd edn (Toronto: Methuen, 1977). These questions, while fundamental to issues of Canadian democracy, are none the less beyond the scope of this chapter. This chapter does not consider the advisability of increased citizen participation in Canadian politics but rather focuses on the specific attributes of technological advances as vehicles for offering this participation.

12   'I'll Support Suicide: Manning', *Toronto Star*, 23 Apr. 1994, A12.

13   'Reform Taking Suicide Issue to Air in Major Experiment', *Globe and Mail*, 16 Apr. 1994, A7.

14   Ibid.

15   'I'll Support Suicide: Manning', *Toronto Star*, 23 Apr. 1994, A12.

16   Ibid.

17   'Reform Party Dials Up 1–900 Referendum', *Winnipeg Free Press*, 21 Sept. 1994, A10.

18   See 'Manning Peddles Reform, TV Show', *Halifax Chronicle Herald*, 26 Sept. 1994, A1.

19   The questions were: (A) Has Canada reached a point in its history when the issue of national unity must be resolved once and for all? 1, Yes; or 2, No; (B) Which course of action do you think is best for Canada? 1, Complete separation of Quebec from Canada; 2, Special association between Canada and an independent Quebec; 3, Changing the federal system for the entire country; or 4, Continuing the present system; (C) Who should set the framework for Canada's future? 1, The Canadian people through a bottom-up process; or 2, Governments and political leaders. Ninety-two per cent of callers agreed that the national unity question should be resolved 'once and for all'; 57 per cent believed that the federal system needed to be changed; and 92 per cent felt the issue should be resolved by a 'bottom-up process'. 'End Unity Debate, Reform TV Show Told', *Globe and Mail*, 4 Oct. 1994, A3.

20   Darin David Barney, 'Pushbutton Populism: The Reform Party and the Real World of Teledemocracy', paper presented at the annual meetings of the Canadian Political Science Association, Montreal, 6 June 1995.

21   'Callers Back Massive Cuts in Spending', *Calgary Herald*, 20 Feb. 1995, A1.

22   The three options were: 1, 'hold the line on taxes while reducing spending substantially'; 2, 'slight increase in taxes with modest spending reductions'; and 3, 'more spending on social programs and job-creation projects and reduced subsidies to business'. 'Hold Tax Line, Reform Listeners Urge', *Globe and Mail*, 20 Feb. 1995, A3.

23 'Callers Back Massive Cuts in Spending', *Calgary Herald*, 20 Feb. 1995, A1.

24 *North Shore News* (Vancouver), 18 May 1994. See also May/June 1994 householder from MP Ted White, 'Referendum '94: Teledemocracy, the Future Now'.

25 Ted White press release, 27 May 1994.

26 Ted White, 'Letter to the Editor', 23 May 1994; abbreviated version published in *Vancouver Sun*, 26 May 1994, A14.

27 The questions, and the number of respondents giving each answer, were: (1) Should the age be reduced to ten for charges to be laid under the Young Offenders Act? Results: Yes—3,067; No—1,539; (2) Should there be automatic transfer to adult court for serious crimes such as murder? Results: Yes—4,474; No—125; (3) Should there be a special category in the Young Offenders Act for repeat and dangerous offenders? Results: Yes—4,539; No—53.

28 Ted White 'Advertorial', *North Shore News* (Vancouver), 'The Post Mortem', 29 June 1994.

29 For full details of Ringma's televote project see his World Wide Web homepage at: http://www.reform.ca/ringma/televote.html.

30 Even so, formats vary. Liberal MPS' pages, for example, have identical formats, whereas Reform MPS seem to design their own as they see fit.

31 'Premier Attracts Internet Attention', *Calgary Herald*, 28 Jan. 1995, A2.

32 The World Wide Web sites of the five federal parties are located at the following addresses: http://www.pcparty.ca; http://www.liberal.ca; http://fed.ndp.ca/fndp; http://www.reform.ca; and http://www.blocquebecois.parl.gc.ca.

33 See the party's homepage at http:www.interlog.com/~liberal/q-period/question.html.

34 'Reform Party Drives on to Internet', *Calgary Herald*, 28 Jan. 1995, A1.

35 Douglas Derabbie, 'The Use of New Electronic Technology by Canadian Political Parties', paper presented at the annual meetings of the Atlantic Provinces Political Studies Association, Wolfville, Nova Scotia, Oct. 1996.

36 The Nova Scotia PCS also elected their current leader through a telephone vote of their membership. However, this process did not use any advanced technology as the phones were answered by party officials who manually recorded each member's vote. A fair amount of academic literature exists on these contests. See, for example, Agar Adamson et al., 'Pressing the Right Button: The Nova Scotia Liberals and Tele-Democracy', paper presented at the annual meetings of the Canadian Political Science Association, Ottawa, May 1993; Leonard Preyra, 'The 1992 Nova Scotia Liberal Leadership Convention', *Canadian Parliamentary Review* 16 (1993–4), 2–11; Donald E. Blake and R. Kenneth Carty, 'Televoting for the Leader of the British Columbia Liberal Party: The Leadership Contest of 1993', paper presented at the annual meetings of the Canadian Political Science Association, Calgary, June 1994.

37 For a full discussion of the various forms of direct leadership selection, see William Cross, 'Direct Election of Provincial Party Leaders in Canada, 1985–1995: The End of the Leadership Convention', *Canadian Journal of Political Science* 29 (1996): 295–315.

38 The most recent available numbers, from 1993, indicate that '8 percent of Bell Canada's customers still use rotary dial sets'. See 'Small Firm Battles Bell to Save Rotary Phones', *Globe and Mail*, 7 Sept. 1993, B1.

39 A 1996 study found that only 29 per cent of Canadians used the Internet at least once in the past year. See 'Internet Users Double in One Year, Survey Says', *Toronto Star*, 23 July 1996, B2.

40 Seventy-four per cent of Canadian households have cable television. Statistics Canada, 'Household Facility and Equipment Survey', 1996.

41 White, 'Advertorial'.

42 Cross, 'Direct Election of Provincial Party Leaders', 305. While the costs of televoting are less to the voter than travelling to a leadership convention, they may be higher than attendance at a leadership delegate selection meeting.

43 On the budget issue, for example, Gallup's finding that reducing government expenditures was a more popular option for reducing the deficit than raising taxes is consistent with the result of Reform's teledemocracy project. The Gallup Poll, 20 Mar. 1995.

44 Adamson et al., 'Pushing the Right Buttons'; Keith Archer and David Stewart, 'Electronic Fiasco? An Examination of the 1994 Liberal Leadership Selection in Alberta', paper presented at the annual meetings of the Canadian Political Science Association, St Catharines, Ont., May 1996.

45 Referendum '94 Results Released', press release from MP Ted White, 21 June 1994.

46 Arterton, *Can Technology Protect Democracy?*, 188–9.

47 Jean B. Elshtain, 'Democracy and the Qube Tube', *The Nation*, 7–14 Aug. 1982, 108–10.

48 Report of the Leadership Procedures Review Committee, 20 Mar. 1991, Ontario Liberal Party, 7.

Chapter 8

TAMING THE 'ELECTRONIC WILD WEST': CAN INFORMATION BE PROPERTY?

Julie Thorburn

Introduction

A number of different legislative and judicial concepts have been used to protect confidential information. They range from the law of contract, confidence, equity, criminal law, and, in limited circumstances, property, to legislative protection through statutes such as the Patent and Copyright Acts. Just as the old West had uneven law enforcement, so the new 'electronic Wild West' is marked by confusing legal regimes. This chapter explores the confused tangle of laws and regulations, and looks at two ways to deal with the problem. The first approach is to treat confidential information as property. Confidential business information constitutes property inasmuch as it generates income to its owner, has value, and is therefore not available to all.[1] Viewing such business information as property would make it easier to fit within existing legal concepts. The second approach is to use a new and independent concept that would give legislators or courts the flexibility to deal with the rights of parties without the necessity of complying with precedents established in property, contract, and equity, which are not necessarily best suited to deal with the specific and continuing problems and policy concerns governing confidential business information. The selection of the best method of protecting confidential information is increasingly important: information has become the greatest source of wealth at the end of the twentieth century.

The Growth in the Importance of Information and Technology

Most commercial legal disputes involve a dispute over wealth. In Roman times the central source of wealth was labour; in feudal times it was land; in the Commercial Age it was commerce and trade. During the Industrial Age wealth meant machinery. The large corporations of the Industrial Age created the need for communication over long distances, storage of information, and increased competition, which in turned fuelled the Information Age. In post-industrial society, information, more than labour, land, or concrete inventions, has become the basis of wealth. In 1956 white-collar workers, that is, those in technical, managerial, and clerical positions, outnumbered blue-collar workers for the first time in modern history. In 1982, more than 60 per cent of American jobs were information-handling jobs compared to only 13 per cent manufacturing jobs.[2]

Information is a combination of equipment, techniques, and the creative efforts of those who use it. New information is created at ever-increasing speeds as a result of new technologies such as microprocessing, fibre optics, lenses, and digitization. In many cases, there is no longer any physical property to protect and the significance of information often lies in the exploitation of the idea rather than physical access to it.[3] With the growing importance of information to wealth creation has come an increasing interest in protecting the proprietary claims to information. But owning information is like lassoing clouds or clutching jello. Moreover, society has a strong interest in access to information. How has law grappled with this problem?

Existing Legislation

A number of statutes, including the Patent Act, the Copyright Act, the Industrial Design Act, and the Trademarks Act, serve to protect the expression of new ideas. Legislators also provide specific guidelines for the dissemination of proprietary information in the hands of government bodies as provided in federal, provincial, and municipal privacy legislation. The two most important means of legislative protection of the expression of an idea are the Patent Act and the Copyright Act.

The Patent Act

The Canadian Patent Act and Copyright Act protect the authors of original works from the unauthorized use of their work by another. Both economic and moral rights are protected. There is no protection of the idea itself, but only the manner in which the idea is expressed. The Patent Act grants the holder of a patent the exclusive right to exploit the information for a given period, in return for the inventor's agreement to allow the information to be used by the public after the patent has expired. To qualify as a patent, an invention must be new, useful, and contain a new and creative element that is not obvious.[4] No patent will be granted for 'methods of doing business, newly discovered laws of nature or purely mental processes'.[5] The invention must be described clearly enough that a person with skill or expertise in the area could practise the invention on the basis of the specifications or drawings contained in the patent. Once a patent is registered, the law grants the holder of a patent the exclusive right to exploit information for a 20-year period, after which the information can be used by the public.

The registration of patents almost totally precludes unauthorized duplication of the invention. As such, the patent owner can license the patent through comparatively straightforward contracts and assignments. Since the information is a matter of public record, it is easy to trace the infringement of patent rights.

The Copyright Act

Copyright is the legal protection that exists to protect the creator or one who acquired rights from the creator of an original literary work. Copyright is the sole right to produce or reproduce a work, to perform the work in public, or to publish the work. Copyright subsists in Canada in every original literary, dramatic, musical, artistic, or choreographed work, photographs, computer programs, and collective works such as encyclopedias, dictionaries, tables, compilations, translations, newspapers, and magazines. The words 'literary work' have been interpreted to include all works expressed in written form irrespective of their literary quality or style. However, the Copyright Act does not protect ideas, procedures, processes, systems, methods of operation, concepts, principles, or discoveries.

To be protected by copyright, the work as a whole must be original. However, the originality of the parts is immaterial. Difficult questions of fact frequently arise when dealing with compilations, since they are made up of a considerable quantity of non-original material. The originality of the work as a whole is determined by the degree of labour and skill used so that the end product has some character or quality that the raw material did not possess, which differentiates the product from the raw material. A work is considered 'original' if the thought derives from the author, was not copied from some other work, and has not been in the public domain.

Copyright is acquired upon creation of the work and protection does not depend on the creator taking any formal steps to protect the work. However, if the work is not registered with the Copyright Office, it is more difficult to resolve a dispute regarding ownership of copyright. Infringement of copyright is established where there is a restricted act, such as reproduction. Generally speaking, copyright exists for a period of the life of the author plus 50 years.

The owner or creator of confidential information may prefer to register the work with the Copyright Office instead of registering a patent. Registration with the copyright office is easier and also creates a longer period of protection, but, unlike the case of patents, a work may be a copyright work and be confidential at the same time.

The expansion of the definition of types of works covered by copyright, coupled with the increased scope of protection offered to copyright holders over patent holders, may create a problem in that inventors whose work is utilitarian or of commercial use, but does not qualify for patent or other legislative protection, may be conferred a stronger right by registering their work with the Copyright Office.[6]

> The demarcation is no longer to be clear. Patents—which are subject to examination—provide relatively short but strong protection for inventions of economic and industrial significance. The patents were expressly subject—even after grant—to compulsory licensing if they were not used, or if their use was withheld, or if they were used for abusive purposes. Copyright, on the other hand, was automatic, long-term and limited in its scope because aesthetic creations—while important—were thought to be incapable of being the instruments of economic abuse, or even great economic significance. All of this has now changed, as a result of the emergence of the entertainment, com-

munication, and computer sectors as leading forces in the modern world economy in general and the U.S. economy in particular. As noted, many of the public interest checks and balances in the patent system have been removed and copyright protection now extends to such functional and industrially important subject-matters as computer programs.[7]

Information and Privacy Legislation

Freedom of information and privacy legislation provides a right of access to information so that it is available to the public, with limited but necessary exemptions, and ensures that decisions on the disclosure of government information are reviewed independently of government. Prior to the enactment of privacy legislation, there was no general right of access to government information. However, there has long been an entitlement to certain kinds of government information in specific circumstances. For example, in legal proceedings a party has been entitled to production of relevant government documents and evidence. In addition, the doctrines of fairness and natural justice in hearings before administrative tribunals may entitle disclosure of certain government information so that defendants can mount a case.

The Ontario Freedom of Information and Protection of Privacy Act ('the Ontario Act'), enacted in 1988, is applicable to bodies whose authority is derived from the law of the government of Ontario.[8] The right of access under the Ontario Act generally takes precedence over the confidentiality provisions of other legislation, unless the legislation specifically provides otherwise.[9]

Information Covered by Privacy Legislation

Information or records in the possession or control of a public institution will be provided to the person who requests them, unless the information or records fall within one of the exemptions listed in the Act. The exemptions are the same, whether the information is sought by a third party or a party about whom the information was gathered. The following types of information are exempted from disclosure:

- Cabinet records, which include documents prepared for cabinet or a record that indicates what has or will take place in cabinet;
- Advice to government that forms part of the deliberative process of government decision-making;
- Information that would interfere with law enforcement, including records that could reasonably be expected to harm the personal security or rights of a particular individual or law enforcement agency[10] or information the disclosure of which would constitute an offence under a federal statute or reveal details of the history, supervision, or release of an individual held by a correctional authority;

- Information dealing with relations between two government bodies or agencies that would prejudice the government or cause the government body to be in breach of an obligation of confidence to another government or international organization;
- Information that constitutes trade secrets or scientific, technical, commercial, financial, or labour relations information supplied by a third party in confidence where disclosure could cause harm to the party to whom the information belongs. 'Trade secrets' are defined as information contained in a product or device that may be used in a business, is not generally known in that business, has acquired economic value, and steps have been taken to maintain its secrecy. 'Harm' is defined as harm to a third party or to the institution by rendering it more difficult to continue to obtain such information where the procurement of such information is in the public interest;
- Information consisting of a communication, either verbal or written, between a client and a solicitor related to the giving or receiving of legal advice (whether or not legal proceedings have been commenced);
- Personal information about an identifiable individual. The information may relate to race, colour, religion, age, sex, educational background, medical, psychiatric, or employment history, personal opinions or views, correspondence sent by the individual, the views of others about the individual, or the individual's name;
- Information that has been or will be published by an institution within 90 days of the request; and
- A discretionary exemption from disclosure exists when disclosure could reasonably be expected to result in danger to health or safety to the person about whom the information was written unless there is a compelling public interest in the disclosure that clearly outweighs the purpose of the exemption and there is a direct link between the disclosure and the risk of harm.

Common Law Protection for Confidential Information

The legislative means of protecting information like that described above are not always suitable for the computer industry, which forms a large part of the information technology today. The traditional laws of copyright and patent provide a monopoly over the expression of the idea for a limited time. However, patent laws require a lengthy and complicated filing process that takes months and sometimes years to complete. This is not feasible for many computer innovations, which have a life span of only a few months. Furthermore, neither the Patent Act nor the Copyright Act protects the idea itself, which has become increasingly important in the high-technology industry.

Common law protection of confidential information is most often used in the computer and technology industry where risks are high and information is of value for only a very limited time. The law of trade secrets and confidential business information does not purport to grant to the owner a monopoly over the idea or expression of the idea, but only to prohibit the improper appropriation of confidential information or breach of confidence. That is, 'no restrictions should fetter an employee's right to apply to his own best advantage the skills and knowledge acquired by the overall experience of his previous employment.'[11]

Confidential business information includes trade secrets, formulae, client lists, and internal office memoranda. There is no requirement that confidential information be novel, as is the case with patents. All that is required is that the creator of the information used ingenuity in the form of human effort, skill, or money and produced a result that can only be achieved by someone who goes through the same process.[12] The information must also be unknown to others in the industry and kept in secrecy.[13]

Trade secrets have been defined by the American Law Institute as 'any formula, pattern, device or compilation of information which is used in one's business, and which gives him an opportunity to obtain an advantage over competitors who do not know to use it. . . . A trade secret is a process for continuous use in the operation of the business.'[14] Although most of the American states have now adopted the Uniform Trade Secrets Act, there is no legislative protection for trade secrets in Canada, where the only protection is through the common law. In Canada, trade secret law does not purport to grant an inventor a monopoly in the trade secret. The only protection afforded a trade secret owner is against acquisition by improper means or breach of confidence.

The common law has some advantages as compared to legislative protection:

- access to information may be restricted indefinitely unless the other party has independently discovered the same idea;
- the idea itself and not simply the expression of the idea may be protected;
- there are no costly registration requirements; and
- there is no compulsory licensing and it may never be declared to be invalid.

However, the cost of ensuring that the secret remains a secret may be high, and there is no guaranteed monopoly period. The terms and conditions in a licence of confidential business information are generally more complex than those in a patent licence and are usually accompanied by a requirement for collateral, which suggests that they are more costly to enforce. On the one hand, a truly protectable secret such as a chemical formula requires no legal protection. At the other extreme, if 'reverse engineering' is simple enough that a skilled observer looking at the product can unravel the secret, then confidential information cannot be protected even with legal assistance. However, there is, within these extremes, a spectrum of inventive activities for which legal protection of information is, to some degree, effective.

Once a plaintiff can establish that he or she has the sole right to benefit from use of the confidential business information, the defendant has wrongly appropriated the confidential business information, and he or she has suffered damages as a result, the wronged party may be entitled to claim one or more of the following heads of relief.

Breach of Contract. The court will enforce the express or implied obligations of a contracting party provided the clause in question is lawful, reasonable, and in the public interest.[15] The courts may restrict the mobility of employees and, thus, the knowledge acquired by them, and/or may prevent the dissemination of the information itself.[16] In the case of a business contract, the courts will usually only enforce the obligation not to use confidential information that belongs to another and was imparted in confidence.[17]

Breach of Confidence. An action for breach of confidence is based on the duty to act in good faith and not take unfair advantage of information obtained in confidence or use it for any purpose other than that for which it was conveyed. A person who has obtained information in confidence is not allowed to use it as a springboard for activities detrimental to the person who made the confidential communication, even when all features have become public.[18]

Equity. A wronged party may claim that there has been a breach of a fiduciary relationship where the person to whom the information was imparted has scope for the exercise of some discretion or power that can affect the beneficiary's legal or practical interests and the beneficiary is peculiarly vulnerable to or at the mercy of the fiduciary holding the discretion or power.[19]

Unjust Enrichment. The doctrine of unjust enrichment is aimed at preventing a person or other entity from retaining a benefit 'which it is against conscience that he should keep'.[20] Few unjust enrichment cases have dealt directly with business information.[21]

Criminal Action. The Supreme Court of Canada has held that confidential information should not be considered as property by the courts for the purposes of the law of theft.[22] As such, at the moment no authority can bring criminal proceedings for theft of confidential business information without an appropriation of tangible property. Section 338(1) of the Criminal Code provides that fraud may be claimed where the wronged party has consented to the disclosure of confidential information but the consent was obtained by deceit.[23] Section 387 of the Criminal Code provides that mischief is committed by anyone who 'destroys or damages property . . . [or] obstructs, interrupts or interferes with any person in the lawful use, enjoyment or operation of property.'[24]

Proposals for Change

Because it relies on precedent, the judiciary has trailed the growth in technology. There have as yet been no major legislative or doctrinal changes in the common law that would enable society to deal with problems arising with respect to confidential information, either in the form of a uniform statute or in the characterization of 'confidential information' as something entirely new.

The existing common law and equitable remedies considered by the courts fail to provide a comprehensive and predictable body of law regarding the protection and dissemination of confidential business information. The law of contract cannot be the basis for a uniform treatment of confidential information because there are many situations in which confidential information is appropriated but where there is neither an express nor an implied contract in place between the parties. The law of equity cannot be the basis for the protection of confidential information as the basis for the equitable duty is the owner's right to the intellectual property itself. This leaves open two additional possibilities: to characterize the information as a distinct form of intellectual property, or to treat it as a new and independent concept to be protected by legislation or the common law.

It is difficult to dissociate the basis of the right to confidential business information from origins of confidential information, which are derived from a long line of historical precedent. Consistency is necessary to ensure that innovators can predict legal outcomes and govern their actions accordingly. Confidential information has, for some time, been characterized, among other things, as a property right. The desire for consistency in the treatment of confidential information and predictability would seem to favour the treatment of confidential business information as a property right over the implementation of a new concept.

Property has been defined as that 'which is peculiar or proper to any person; that which belongs exclusively to one. In the strict legal sense, an aggregate of rights which are guaranteed and protected by the government . . . . More specifically, ownership; the unrestricted and exclusive right to a thing; the right to dispose of a thing in every legal way, to possess it, to use it, and to exclude every one else from interfering with it'.[25] Trade secrets and confidential business information are generally considered to be intellectual property and are, like other species of intellectual property, property rights that are frequently licensed or assigned.[26]

Many of the early cases used property law as the basis for determining liability for breach of confidential business information. For example, in *Millar v. Taylor*,[27] Mr Justice Yates held that an author's unpublished manuscript 'is, in every sense, his peculiar property; and no man can take it from him or make any use of it which he has not authorized, without being guilty of a violation of his property.' The Canadian courts have yet to recognize a property right in information. However, in the Supreme Court of Canada decision, *R. v. Stewart*,[28] Lamer J. for the majority recognized that confidential information:

> possesses many of the characteristics of other forms of property: for example, a trade secret, which is a particular kind of confidential information, can be sold, licensed or bequeathed, it can be the subject of a trust or passed to a trustee in bankruptcy. . . . Some cases have treated confidential information as property, and thus have entitled the owner to exclude others from the use thereof. . . . On the other hand, the courts have recognized certain rights with respect to confidential information in the guise of an equitable obligation of good faith. . . . No Canadian court has so far conclusively decided that confidential information is property, with all the civil consequences that such a finding would entail.

The possibility for confidential information to be considered a proprietary right in civil cases was left open when Lamer J. went on to say that 'It is possible that, with time, confidential information will come to be considered as property by statutory enactment. Even if confidential information were to be considered as property under civil law, it does not, however, automatically follow that it qualifies as property for the purposes of criminal law.' Some American courts have specifically recognized a property right in an idea that is compensable in damages. For example, in the *Belt*[29] case, the District Court held that the 'law has recognized a qualified property right in trade secrets and grants injunctive relief against their use or disclosure by a breach of contract or a violation of confidence. It is but one step further to extend to ideas at least a limited property right. . . . The law now gives effect to a property right in an idea even though the idea may be neither patentable nor subject to copyright.' On appeal, the Circuit Court of Appeal, confirming the District Court judgement, held that 'the dangers [of attributing common property to individual ownership] are sufficiently avoided to warrant the law in placing an idea among protected property rights when it is definite and concrete, new and novel, has usefulness and is disclosed for commercial purposes in circumstances which the parties ought reasonably to construe as contemplating compensation for its use.'[30]

Problems with the Property Law Concept

There are several problems with analogizing confidential information as 'property'.

Knowledge Is Infinite

It has been argued that the fact that land is physical makes it a scarce resource. Knowledge, on the other hand, is not a scarce resource. It can be shared by any number of people without depleting its value. It cannot be possessed or stolen in the traditional sense,[31] as something cannot be returned when it has not been taken away.[32]

Although information itself may be infinite, the development of confidential business information requires the use of labour and skill to develop ideas that render the information scarce, and thus valuable. Value is acquired because the information is not accessible to and cannot be enjoyed by any except those to whom the creator of the idea chooses to impart the information.

Information May Be Shared without Losing Possession

Those critical of the property theory have also argued that, in order for it to be considered as property, confidential business information must be able to be excluded from the possession of others.[33] Others may obtain copies of information while the information itself is still in the hands of the owner. Furthermore, a property right in confidential business information does not preclude the independent creation by another of the same idea, in much the same manner that it is possible for a copyrighted work to be independently created by two individuals. When information is shared, there is no permanent deprivation but only a loss or reduction of market advantage.[34]

The focus on possession is misguided since value, in all forms of intellectual property, derives from the use that may be made of the property and not in physical possession of the property itself. In any event, this concept is similar to the case where an individual with no rights to the land uses it, and the user develops rights to the land, such as easements, which thereby diminish the value of the land to the rightful owner.

Secrecy

Some courts have been sceptical of the argument that secrecy in some way creates a proprietary right to that knowledge, while knowledge that is not secret does not.[35] However, the value of the property is not acquired through secrecy. It is acquired through the labour, skill, and money spent to create confidential business information and is simply maintained through secrecy.

Public Policy

It has been argued that an inventor should not be able to obtain rights greater than those offered to inventors who register with the patent or copyright office.[36] It has also been argued that no inventor should have a perpetual monopoly over information as this would be contrary to the societal interest in the encouragement of new ideas. However, the laws governing confidential information protect only the unauthorized use of information. Those who have registered patents have an absolute monopoly over that information for the term of the patent, while the creators of confidential business information run the risk that a third party will independently discover the same information or will acquire the confidential business information by way of reverse engineering.[37] The protection of confidential business information does not provide its owner with better protection, but simply different protection than would be obtained by registering a patent.[38]

A New and Independent Concept

It has also been suggested that an action for breach of confidential information may be best treated as separate and independent.[39] In his article, 'Restitution of Benefits Obtained in Breach of Another's Confidence',[40] Gareth Jones states:

> Confidential information is conceptually very much sui generis. It is an intangible; and, consequently, it would be 'wrong to confuse the physical records with [the information] itself . . . ; for if you put them on a duplicator and produce one hundred copies you have certainly not multiplied your asset in proportion.' It has, too, the quality that it may be transmitted to a limited class without destroying its value; so, know-how 'can be communicated to or shared with others outside the manufacturer's own business,' for example under license . . . .[41]

The Supreme Court of Canada and the New Zealand Court of Appeal have recently accepted the theory of a synthesized *sui generis* wrong relating to broken confidences.[42] Use of the *sui generis* concept provides the courts with the flexibility to deal with the rights of the parties without the necessity of complying with the precedents established in property, contract, or equity, which are not necessarily best suited to deal with the peculiar problems and policy concerns governing confidential business information and would not necessarily be the best method of dealing with new problems that arise.

Trade Secrets Act

Alternatively, it may be preferable to have the *sui generis* concept drafted by legislators rather than articulated by the courts. This would enable legislators to realize policy objectives that specifically pertain to confidential information while providing a uniform code of business ethics that pertains specifically to confidential business information and could provide the predictability that might be difficult to obtain from judicial interpretation.

In 1979, the United States Commissioners on Uniform State Laws adopted the Uniform Trade Secrets Act.[43] Approximately one-half of the state legislatures have adopted this Act. The definition in that Act reads as follows:

> 'Trade Secret' means information, including a formula, pattern, compilation, program, device, method, technique or process that:

- derives independent economic value, actual or potential, from not being generally known to, and not being readily ascertainable by proper means by, other persons who can obtain economic value from its disclosure or use, and
- is the subject of efforts that are reasonable under the circumstances to maintain its secrecy.[44]

However, a Canadian Uniform Trade Secrets Act containing a slightly broader definition of trade secrets,[45] which was proposed by the Canadian Institute of Law Research and Reform, has never been implemented.

Conclusion

Little attention has been paid in Canada to the provision of one comprehensive law or statute that would be predictable yet afford the flexibility to reflect societal concerns regarding the dissemination of information and the economic incentives to encourage inventors to continue creating new ideas. The conceptualization of confidential business information as property would make it easier to resolve problems regarding sales and licences, to use both criminal and civil sanctions to protect the information from espionage and theft, and to fit information into existing taxation schemes.[46]

On the other hand, a new body of law or a statute created specifically to govern confidential information could include the necessary incentives to create new ideas by upholding business ethics and prohibiting the wrongful use of confidential information, while allowing for the dissemination of new ideas for the benefit of society as a whole when in the public interest to do so. There would be no requirement to remain within the confines of existing bodies of law. When it comes to confidential business information, Canada, ironically, has a wilder frontier than the United States. This unruly legal regime has worked reasonably well in the past, but as information becomes more important as the key source of wealth, we need both more clarity and originality in establishing a supportive framework of law and policy.

Notes

1 Arman Alchian, 'Some Economics of Property Rights', *Il Politico* 30 (1965).
2 Gary Klueck, 'The Coming Jurisprudence of the Information Age: Examinations of the Three Past SocioEconomic Ages Suggest the Future', *San Diego Law Review* 21 (1984): 1079.
3 Ibid.
4 G.F. Henderson et al., eds, *Patent Law in Canada* (Toronto: Carswell, 1994), 7.
5 *Patent Act*, R.S.C. 1985, c. P-4.
6 *Bayliner Marine Corp. v. Doral Boats Ltd* (1986), 10 C.P.R. 76 (S.C.C.).
7 G.F. Henderson et al., eds, *Copyright Law of Canada* (Toronto: Carswell, 1994), 19.

8   An exhaustive list of those bodies is set out in the regulations.

9   For example, the Municipal Elections Act provides that no person is entitled to inspect the contents of a ballot box except by court order made in connection with the prosecution of an election offence or contested election proceedings. Similarly, Section 53(1) of the Assessment Act provides that information acquired for the purpose of determining the value of real property or any assessment is protected, with limited exceptions.

10 To be exempt from disclosure, there must be a reasonable expectation of harm and not a mere possibility. Furthermore, there must be a reasonable expectation that the information would remain confidential.

11 *Jim W. Miller Construction Inc. v. Schaefer*, 298 N.W. 2d 455, 459 (Minn, 1980) quoting Reed, *Roberts Association Inc. v. Strauman*, 40 N.Y. 2d 303, 307, 353.

12 *Promotivate International Inc. v. Toronto Star Newspapers Ltd et al.* (1986), 8 C.P.R. (3d) 546; *Talbot v. General Television Corp. Pty. Ltd* [1981] R.P.C. 1 (S.C. Vict.).

13 *Pharand Ski Corp. v. Alberta* 37 C.P.R. (3d) 288 at 317.

14 Arthur H. Seidel and Ronald L. Panitch, 'What the General Practitioner Should Know about Trade Secrets and Employment Agreements', *American Law Institute* (1973): 173.

15 *Tank Lining Corp. v. Dunlop Industrial Ltd.* For example, a party cannot enforce a non-competition clause covering a geographic area wider than the confines of the business. See *McAllister et al. v. Cardinal* (1965), 1 O.R. 221, 47 D.L.R. (3d) 313, 47 C.P.R. 28. Furthermore, the offending party will not be prevented from earning a livelihood in his or her area of expertise. See *Chemical Co. v. Plastic Paint & Finish Specialities Ltd et al.* (1978), 41 C.P.R. (2d) 175; (1979), 47 C.P.R. (2d) 129.

16 Information does not become confidential simply because a contract provides that it is confidential. However, when two competently advised parties with equal bargaining power enter into a business agreement, the courts will generally accept the parties' own judgement of what may be disclosed. See *North Western Salt Co. Ltd v. Electrolytic Allkali Co. Ltd* (1914), A.C. 461 at 471. Furthermore, the idea must be sufficiently developed that the idea can be realized or used, and must be clearly identifiable. See *Fraser v. Thames Television* [1983] 2 W.L.R. 917 at 935.

17 Simon Mehigan and David Griffiths, *Restraint of Trade and Business Secrets: Law and Practice*, 2nd edn (London: Longman, 1991).

18 *Seager v. Copydex Ltd* (1967), 2 All E.R. 415 as applied by Spence J. in *Slavutych v. Baker* (1976), 1 S.C.R. 254 at 262. However, when commercial information is communicated in a business setting 'with some common object in mind', it is difficult for the recipient to argue that there is no obligation of confidence. See *Coco v. A.N. Clark (Engineers) Ltd* (1969), R.P.C. 41 at 47.

19 *Frame v. Smith* (1987), 42 D.L.R. (4th) 81, (1987) 2 S.C.R. 99, 9 R.F.L. (3d) 225, 42 C.C.L.T. 1, 78 N.R. 40. In the *Lac* case, the majority held that senior officers may not use their positions to make a profit even if the opportunity could not have been seized by the company. A possible conflict of personal interest may be enough to establish a basis for relief without proof of an actual conflict of interest. See *Lac Minerals Ltd v. International Corona Resources Ltd* (1989), 26 C.P.R. (3d) 97 (S.C.C.). See also *Canadian Aero Service Ltd v. O'Malley* (1973), 40 DLR (3d) 371; *Genesta Manufacturing Ltd v. Babey et al.* (1984), 48 O.R. (2d) 94; *Dialadex Communications Inc. v. Crammond et al.* (1987), 14 C.P.R. (3d) 145; *Alberts v. Mountjoy* (1977), 16 O.R. (2d)

682.; *Abrams v. Ross Wemp Motors* (1986), 12 C.P.R. (3d) 87 (O.H.C.); and *Profast (London) Ltd v. Wright* (1986), 14 C.P.R. (3d) 118 (O.H.C.).

20 *Pettkus v. Becker* (1978), 20 O.R. (2d) 105, 5 R.F.L. (2d) 344, 87 D.L.R. (3d) 101 (C.A.), affirmed [1980] 2 S.C.R. 834, 19 R.F.L. (2d) 165, 8 E.T.R. 143, 117 D.L.R. (3d) 257, 34 N.R. 384; and *Deglman v. Guaranty Trust Company of Canada* (1953), O.W.N. 665, Rv. (1954) S.C.R. 725.

21 *Promotivate International Inc. v. Toronto Star* (1986), 8 C.P.R. (3d) 546.

22 *R. v. Stewart*, 50 D.L.R. (4th) 1 at 5 (S.C.C.).

23 *Regina v. Kirkwood* (1983), 5 C.C.C. (3rd) 393.

24 *R. v. Turner*, (1984), 27 B.L.R. 207 (Ont. H.C.) wherein the court held that, although the physical tapes were available, the accused were convicted of mischief because they had denied the victims the right to enjoy their physical property.

25 *Black's Law Dictionary*, 6th edn (1990), 1216; F.S. Cohen, 'Dialogue on Private Property', *Rutgers Law Review* 9 (1954): 378.

26 David Vaver, 'Civil Liability: Trade Secrets in Canada', (1981) 5 C.B.L.J. 253 at 261.

27 *Millar v. Taylor* (1769), 4 Burr. 2303; 98 E.R. 201; *Abernethy v. Hutchison* (1825), 47 E.R. 1313; 1 H & Tw 28.

28 *R. v. Stewart* (1988), 50 D.L.R. (4th) 1 at 10 (S.C.C.).

29 *Belt v. Hamilton National Bank*, 108 F. Supp. 689 (D.D.C. 1952), aff'd 210 F. 2d, 706 at 708.

30 Ibid.; *O'Brien v. RKO Radio Pictures*, 68 F. Supp. 13, 14 (S.D.N.Y. 1946); *Sellers v. American Broadcasting Co.*, 68 F. 2d 1207, 1210 (11th Cir. 1982); *Smith v. Recrion Corp.*, 91 Nev. 666, 669-70, 541 P. 2d 663, 665 (1975).

31 Vaver, 'Civil Liability', 261.

32 R.J. Roberts, 'Is Information Property?', *Intellectual Property Journal* 3 (1987): 209-15.

33 Ibid.

34 A. Birrell, *Seven Lectures on the Law and History of Copyright in Books* (Rothman Reprints, 1971), 12–13.

35 *F.C.T. v. United Aircraft Corporation* (1944), 68 C.L.R. 525 at p. 534 per Latham C.J.

36 Vaver, 'Civil Liability', 266.

37 Steven Cheung, 'Property Rights and Trade Secrets', *Economic Inquiry* 20 (Jan. 1982); *Samuel Moore & Co. v. Com'r of Patents* (1979), 45 C.P.R. (2d). (Fed. Ct. T.D.), at 188.

38 Vaver, 'Civil Liability', 267; *Kewanee Oil Co. v. Bicron Corp.*, 416 U.S. 470 (1974).

39 *United Scientific Holdings Ltd v. Burnley Borough Council* [1978] A.C. 904 (H.L.) at 943; *Vokes, Ltd v. Heather* (1945), 62 R.P.C. 135 (C.A.) at 141.

40 Gareth Jones, 'Restitution of Benefits Obtained in Breach of Another's Confidence', *Law Quarterly Review* 86 (1970): 463.

41 *Seager v. Copydex* [1967] 1 W.L.R. 923 (C.A.); *Rolls-Royce Ltd v. Jeffrey (Inspector of Taxes)* [1962] 1 All. E.R. 801 (H.L.) at 805–6.

42 *Canadian Aero Service v. O'Malley* [1974] S.C.R. 592 at 606, 11 C.P.R. (2d) 206 at 218, 40 D.L.R. (3d) 371; *A.B. Consolidated Ltd v. Europe Strength Food Co. Pty Ltd* [1978] 2 N.Z.L.R. 515 (C.A.) at 520.

43 Uniform Trade Secrets Act (1979).

44 Ibid., section 1(4), (1979).

45 Uniform Trade Secrets Act (Edmonton, 1986), 43.

46 Cheung, 'Property Rights and Trade Secrets'.

Chapter 9

SEX ON THE NET: REGULATION AND CONTROL OF PORNOGRAPHY IN THE NEW WIRED WORLD

Michael D. Mehta

Introduction

It is somewhat ironic that one of the most promising information and communications technologies, the Internet, is being used to satisfy a basic human drive, sex.[1] For the individual, a computer costing thousands of dollars, with high-speed modem access through fibre-optic telephone lines, is needed to access the thousands of pornographic images and movie clips found in UseNet newsgroups and the World Wide Web.[2] Although accessing such material is mostly a private affair, the public policy implications of regulating and controlling the flow of information through the Internet are daunting, and several hotly contested issues such as censorship, privacy, surveillance, and interjurisdictional conflict arise. To make matters stickier, some individuals are using publicly funded Internet connections through universities and government offices to retrieve, and post, pornography.[3] How societies balance freedom of expression with the promotion of a new technology is at issue. Recent attempts in the United States to regulate content available to US Internet users by the Communications Decency Act[4] exemplify the strong response to what some perceive as a social problem and others as a prelude to an Orwellian nightmare.

Pornography in Western societies is not a new social problem. What has changed over the years is the mechanical, and now digital, means for producing and distributing it. What has not changed is what the word 'pornography' implies. In its simplest incantation, pornography is defined as the portrayal of persons as sexual objects for the pleasure of others.[5] Feminists, and others, maintain that pornography objectifies individuals (mostly women) in a sexualized, eroticized manner, and that it symbolizes differential levels of power in society. These differences in power can be represented in any medium, including paintings and drawings, photographs and videos, or digital images viewed on a computer screen. However, when images are sent across the Internet new issues arise. For anti-pornography writer and law professor Catherine MacKinnon:

> Pornography in cyberspace is pornography in society—just broader, deeper, worse, and more of it. Pornography is a technologically sophisticated traffic in women; electronically communicated pornography traffics women in a yet more sophisticated form. . . . As pornography comes ever more into the open, crossing new boundaries, opening new markets, and pioneering new harms, it also opens itself to new scrutiny.[6]

Computer pornography, in this view, represents the ultimate in erotic fragmentation. Not only are individuals reduced to bytes and pixels, but their images are subject to mass distribution, electronic manipulation, and commercial exploitation.

The potential of the Internet to disseminate vast amounts of pornographic material within an unregulated marketplace with a large, international audience is of great concern to those who feel that it does harm. If so, computer pornography has important consequences not because it is new or substantially different from pornographic magazines and videos, but rather because the distribution of pornography via computer networks can reduce costs dramatically, therefore reducing barriers both to publish and to receive. Access to pornography by computer represents an unexpected use for the technology of the 'global village'. For those who do not believe pornography to be harmful, the issue of computer pornography is still important because it represents a domain of deep social and political controversy, and is possibly the main point of contention over regulation of this new revolutionary information and communications technology.

The Nature of Computer Pornography

Computer pornography has moved from simple images composed of alphanumeric characters to more sophisticated digitized, moving images. A variety of computer pornography, including soft- and hard-core images of male and female models, animated serials, sexually explicit moving images, interactive sex games, and virtual reality-based types of cybersex, is available.[7] On the Internet, the most accessible pornography is on the World Wide Web and in UseNet newsgroups.

To find pornography on the Web, users need to know the address (URL) of the homepage where images are distributed. More often than not, homepages are commercially owned pornographic distribution sources that give away samples, but then require individuals to become members of their service (for a fee) to gain access to the larger sets of archived material. A credit card transaction, or an authenticated transaction involving digital currency, is often required before becoming a member of these services. A password is sent to the new member giving him/her access to the image libraries. It is claimed that this authentication system also minimizes the risk that minors (those under the age of 18 in Canada) will gain access to sexually explicit material. Some services even insist on a telephone conversation with the subscribing applicant prior to issuing access to their archives. This registration and the pay-per-use system are more easily regulated than the other primary source of pornography, UseNet.

Access to pornography through UseNet newsgroups is relatively simple and straightforward. These newsgroups are organized collections of text, images, and computer software that cater to specific users. Access to the main news menu, available through Internet service providers and with popular browsing software like Netscape Communicator and Microsoft Internet Explorer, allows users to retrieve or post text, computer programs, or graphic image files. The vast majority of newsgroups are associated with societies, organizations like universities, gopher servers, and computer-user groups. However, several thousand so-called 'alternative' (alt.) newsgroups also exist, and this is where most pornography can be found.

Pornographic images may be posted to newsgroups in two ways. Firstly, material may be posted anonymously or non-anonymously by individual users from any location in the world. Posting a message (and attaching a file) is simple, much like sending an e-mail message. Anyone who has sent an e-mail message with a text attachment can easily send a binary encoded image file in the same manner. Those with access to a scanner or digital camera can scan images from pornographic magazines or take photographs that can be posted in one or more newsgroups. Video capture boards in computers also allow for video-taped movies to be scanned and sent to a newsgroup. Secondly, images may be posted by businesses such as bulletin board services (BBS), software companies, 'sex shops', or graphic design firms. Commercial vendors view public domain space like newsgroups as a good opportunity to advertise freely their products or services. This latter group of posters stands to profit the most from wide-scale, unregulated exchanges of pornography through the Internet.

There have been relatively few studies of Internet pornography, and therefore policy issues associated with regulation and control of the Internet become muddied and, worse still, ineffective. The first study of UseNet pornography was done by Mehta and Plaza[8] in April 1994; they analysed 150 randomly selected image files from 17 alternative newsgroups. Since the National Science Foundation of the United States had just stopped administering the central 'backbone' of the Internet and new rules regarding commercial services would replace the previous 'acceptable use' policy, Mehta and Plaza were interested in seeing how commercialization influenced the type and amount of pornography available. Of the 150 images analysed, 65 per cent were of non-commercial origin, 81 per cent were images produced in colour rather than black and white, and 92 per cent were digitized images of photographs instead of cartoons or drawings. The most prevalent themes they discovered were close-ups (43 per cent), images with an erect penis (35 per cent), fetishes including lingerie and high-heeled shoes (33 per cent), and masturbation (21 per cent).

In their study they also examined themes that are illegal under Canada's Criminal Code or taboo in our society. For example, 15 per cent of their sample involved images with children. It should be noted that in all of these cases, not one image showed actual sexual interaction involving children with children or children with adults. Mehta and Plaza found that images involving children were usually nude poses or, in rare instances, simulated activity with children or young-looking models.

Other illegal and/or taboo subjects that Mehta and Plaza examined were bestiality (10 per cent), urination (3 per cent), group sex (11 per cent), and bondage/discipline (10 per cent). In these instances, there are clear prohibitions against sex mixed with coercion, violence, degradation, or appealing to the 'prurient'. Images that combine these features are deemed 'obscene' under the Criminal Code since they reflect an 'unhealthy' interest in sex and pose a threat to viewers' psycho-sexual development.

Mehta and Plaza also compared their results with pornography from other sources, including magazine and video distribution. There were some important differences in prevalence of themes among these different media, which suggests that pornography on the Internet involves different editorial considerations and a different market profile. For example, they found that fellatio was present in 15 per cent of their images, while Garcia and Milano[9] found fellatio in 8.1 per cent of erotic videos. For homosexual sex, Mehta and Plaza's study found that 18 per cent of images involved either male with male or female with female sexual interaction. Studies by Winick[10] of pornographic magazines and Garcia and Milano of videos obtained much lower results, in the 2–4 per cent range, for homosexual interaction.

Mehta and Plaza were also interested in discovering differences, if any, in kinds of material posted by individuals or commercial outlets. They analysed the prevalence of themes by source and discovered that commercial distributors of pornography used UseNet newsgroups to advertise their products and services. Advertising that gets noticed is most effective, and in that regard commercially distributed images in the Mehta and Plaza sample were, generally speaking, more explicit. For example, their study revealed that close-ups, erect penises, use of foreign objects like dildos for masturbation, fellatio, and pictures of children or young-looking models were more prevalent in commercial pornography. Mehta and Plaza conclude that commercial vendors of pornography are willing to take risks by posting explicit images so as to attract customers to their pay-per-use services. In an era of weak regulation, such activities are low in risk, while the potential benefits of free advertising in UseNet are significant.

Another study of computer pornography is the infamous Rimm[11] report. After its publication, considerable debate over the study's accuracy and originality, as well as the ethics of the researcher, were investigated. Rimm considered the descriptions given to 917,410 images found primarily on private bulletin board services rather than in UseNet or the World Wide Web. Using what he calls 'linguistic parsing software', Rimm analysed pornographic images based on their descriptions alone. His study coded only for the presence of dominant themes. Since most images contain multiple themes (e.g., oral sex with bondage and the use of a foreign object in the same image), Rimm's study tended to inflate the prevalence of certain acts and underestimate others. To code his sample, Rimm used the current issue of the *Diagnostic and Statistical Manual for Mental Disorders*, with its pedophilic (sexual attraction to children), hebephilic (sexual attraction to pubescent adolescents), and paraphilic (fetishes) categories. Rimm's paraphilic category combined a wide variety of acts, including bondage, sadomasochism, urination, defecation, and bestiality, which could account for the exaggerated amount of obscene material he claims to have found.

When the Mehta and Plaza study is compared with Rimm's, several similarities emerge. Rimm's classification system makes direct comparisons with Mehta and Plaza's results difficult. However, certain trends can be gleaned from the data. For example, Rimm reported that 15.6 per cent of images were pedophilic/hebephilic. Mehta and Plaza found very similar results, with 15 per cent in the children/adolescents category. Of the other themes common to both studies, Mehta and Plaza found bondage and discipline (10 per cent), foreign objects (17 per cent), incest (1 per cent), bestiality (10 per cent), and urination (3 per cent). The sum of these percentages is not dissimilar from Rimm's 32.8 per cent for paraphilic images. Overall, Mehta and Plaza's findings indicate that pornography in the bulletin board services studied by Rimm appears close to what they found available in UseNet.

A new and more comprehensive study on pornography has been done by Mehta.[12] In this study, he collected 9,800 images from UseNet newsgroups between July 1995 and July 1996. Since this period represents a time when strong attempts to control the Internet were implemented (e.g., passing and eventual revocation of the Communications Decency Act), the study tracks changes in content and the impact of regulation.

Mehta developed a new coding typology that is more sensitive to the way themes in images combine and less tied to any particular country's legal definitions of obscenity or child pornography. Here are some examples of how his new coding works. For images involving bondage and discipline, Mehta distinguishes between images portraying props alone (e.g., clothing and whips) and those involving pain and torture. For child pornography, he makes an important distinction between nudity, hebephilic, and pedophilic imagery. Mehta also examines two new variables in this study, number of participants in an image and interracial interactions. For number of participants involved in an image, Mehta found that 49.3 per cent are with one person, 37.6 per cent involve two people interacting sexually, 10.5 per cent are with three people, and 2.5 per cent involve four or more people. Also of interest, considering the global nature of the Internet, is that only 5.3 per cent of images involve interracial sex.

Comparing the Mehta study with the Mehta and Plaza study of 1994 reveals some interesting facts (see Figure 1). As expected, commercialization of the Internet over the past few years has accelerated. In the 1994 study, 35 per cent of images were of commercial origin. By July 1996, this number had increased to 40.5 per cent. The sample of images from the new study shows a significant decrease in bondage and discipline images, from 10 per cent to 3.5 per cent. For child pornography, the new study shows that approximately 20 per cent of images fit this category compared to 15 per cent in 1994. However, there are some noteworthy differences arising from the new classification scheme. Of the images defined as involving children, 5.1 per cent were simple nudes, 10.6 per cent were young-looking individuals (hebephilic), and 4.4 per cent were pedophilic images. The number of images depicting homosexual sex decreased over the two-year period from 18 per cent to 10.1 per cent. Images with fellatio and cunnilingus stayed virtually unchanged, as did vaginal and anal penetration scenes, while bestiality images decreased from 10 per cent in 1994 to 3.1 per cent.

This new study suggests that 'command-and-control' forms of regulation like the Communications Decency Act are ineffective means for stemming the flow of pornography through the Internet. This makes sense since regulations on a national or local level only apply to the jurisdictions involved. Unless international co-operation, voluntary initiatives, and software-based filtering are employed, pornography will continue to be readily available to anyone with Internet access. The next sections of this chapter frame these issues and examine the various options of regulation and control that have been proposed.

Controlling On-line Pornography

Contrary to common wisdom, the debate over pornography on the Internet is not primarily about the issue of controlling explicit content but about the direction this new medium takes as the forces of commercialization shape and pull it. Some, like Paul Burton,[13] argue that regulation of content would do more

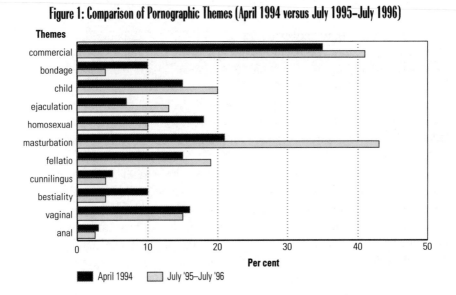

Figure 1: Comparison of Pornographic Themes (April 1994 versus July 1995–July 1996)

harm than good by damaging the free flow of information, thus crippling an important new technology. Others, including Alvin Toffler,[14] note how wealth creation has shifted from a resource- to a knowledge-based economy, and the Internet is clearly one of the main targets for developing information as a vital economic resource. Therefore, any attempts at controlling the flow of information through the new wired world will have concomitant economic repercussions beyond the social impacts generated by contentious content.

In addition to spurring the development of technical advances and promoting technology transfer, this new world has created a demand for seamless telecommunications services that traverse national boundaries. As a result, in Canada and the United States legislative proposals like the US Telecommunications Reform bill have been crafted to remove outdated regulatory structures and promote the Internet. In general, these changes involve a variety of approaches, including reforming the monopoly structure of telephone companies, encouraging private investment, building in regulatory flexibility, providing universal access, and promoting standards for interconnectivity and systems interoperability. In terms of practice, these goals have led to the deregulation of cable television rates, the introduction of V-chips for parental screening of violent television programming, allowing local and foreign telephone companies to enter the long-distance market, and relaxing the rules regarding media concentration.

The Internet is intricately tied to the forces of globalization and fits a post-industrial world-view, where profitable and progressive industries are assumed to provide more satisfying, high-paying jobs. In this post-industrial information economy, a transformation of the economic structures of industrial society supplants capital and class with technology and politics. Moreover, this transformation is expected to push Western society further along in its evolution to a service economy, where white-collar and professional workers dominate and where increased reliance on computers and information technology enhances our post-modern potential by improving quality of life (more leisure time).

This view of the liberating potential of new technologies is not held by all. Heather Menzies[15] contends that the restructuring effects of the Internet create new sets of inequalities that marginalize and displace workers. She fears that the forces of globalization are stimulating new social arrangements that encourage further concentration of corporate power and increased surveillance. Individuals who upload and download pornographic material, hate literature, pirated software, and the like are developing sophisticated cloaking techniques for maintaining their anonymity in this new 'surveillance society'.[16] For example, some users deliberately construct complex access paths criss-crossing the globe to post and download legally obscene material. Others use public and private key encryption software like 'Pretty Good Privacy' (PGP) to accomplish the same objective. Finally, some subscribe to anonymous 'remailers' like the well-known anon.penet.fi in Finland, which guarantees anonymity. In these instances, technology is being used to perform a vital function—to protect individual rights in the wake of a technological juggernaut.

For now, the Internet is regulated on a local, micro level by access providers who restrict and censor information. On a larger scale, such practices have profound implications for individuals and corporations wishing to partake in the possibilities offered by a global information infrastructure. The Internet has outpaced current rules and regulations regarding intellectual property rights, definitions of obscenity, publication bans, and government excise mechanisms. In a very real sense, pornography on the Internet is a 'sacrificial lamb' for testing the strength of new social and institutional arrangements and for holding tight to the eroding powers of the old world order (the state). For example, consider the case of Robert Thomas, who was convicted under obscenity laws in Tennessee for distributing material via his private bulletin board through the telephone lines. What makes this case unique is that the convicted individual resided in California and was extradited to Tennessee for prosecution, where obscenity laws are different.[17]

The Internet, by definition, is the opposite of centralization, and as a result a conflict between this technology and the state is inevitable. The shift from a highly centralized information and communications infrastructure to a decentralized set of interconnected networks crossing the globe has generated considerable concern about issues of jurisdiction, privacy, and censorship. There are also concerns about the effects of this new technology on self-identity and social interaction through the formation of virtual communities. For example, a group of individuals known as the Orchid Club has been trading pedophilic images across the Internet for years and constitutes a micro-society with its own rules and norms.

This new 'public sphere' of virtual communities represents an exclusive enclave of privileged, technologically oriented and enabled individuals and groups who prosper from the globalizing effects of new communications networks like the Internet. Although the benefits of the Internet are real for many, the socially dislocating effects of this technology create a global economy and culture geared towards the internationalization of labour and the erosion of some nation-states and expansion of others, and place a severe strain on governance and public accountability. Here we see the influence of globalization on economic and public policy with broad implications for citizens, governments, and markets. These effects include, but are not limited to, changes in the global economy, evolution of nation-states, and a redefinition of social contracts and associated deficits in democratic practices.

Obviously, technological innovation is not neutral but takes place within the context of existing power relations, but these power relations are presently in flux. In this sense, knowledge—or in this case, electronic technology—is shaped to offer an advantage to specific groups, individuals, or institutions. For example, Oscar Gandy[18] has admirably shown the extent to which capitalist corporations have integrated the collection and analysis of data on individuals and groups into their marketing strategies. Even pornographers could profit from better understanding the demographic profiles and tastes of their customers. Much more is at stake here than simply controlling pornography. However, the need still exists to restrict access to minors and to stem the tide of illegal pornography, most notably child pornography. The next section of the chapter examines some of the technical and social solutions proposed for accomplishing this objective.

Regulation and Control of Explicit Material

Regulation and control of content have been commonly used for promoting and protecting broadcast media for decades. In Canada, the Canadian Radio-television and Telecommunications Commission (CRTC) regulates existing telecommunications companies and broadcasters to serve a multiplicity of goals. In the interest of promoting universal accessibility and protecting Canadian culture through content regulation, the CRTC, it is claimed, protects customers from the abuses of unrestrained monopoly powers.[19] Furthermore, these powers give the CRTC, as a licensing body, the mandate to restrict the broadcasting of certain kinds of material deemed unfit for general audiences. Its American counterpart, the Federal Communications Commission (FCC), has similar powers for controlling content, but some commentators are critical of this regulator's intentions. Jonathon Emord[20] suggests that media owners are likely to seek a 'devil's bargain' with regulators to ensure monopolistic advantages. In exchange for giving away content control, media owners expect regulators to impose market controls that lead to higher profits and weaker competition. The need for regulatory reform is often attached to such critiques, and the future of the Internet is intimately tied to its status as a common carrier channel or as a broadcast medium. Recent debates over pornography have focused on this definitional issue.

A broadcaster offers a service where information is widely dispersed to an audience. Common examples include newspapers, radio, and television. This information is usually one-way in nature and non-discriminatory. Users simply tune into a channel or pick up a newspaper to receive information from a broadcaster. Once the information source is selected, the information is 'pushed' at the consumer. With the exception of changing channels or pages, consumers of broadcast media have little editorial control over what they are exposed to. As well, all ages can tap into a particular broadcast, and therefore broadcasters must maintain strict controls on content. Liability for breaches of content control, including the airing of explicit sexual messages or indecent words, rests squarely in the hands of the distributor (broadcaster). By contrast, common carriers act as conduits for the transmission of information and have minimal control over content. For example, telephone companies, couriers, and postal services transfer information (or goods) between customers. The information sent through a common carrier is generally private and directed. Common carriers act as 'pull' technologies in that consumers must make requests for information and have more editorial control over content. This distinction between common carrier and broadcaster is important, because if the Internet is simply a conduit for information, then the responsibility for 'pulling' information into one's own hands is different than if information is 'pushed' at the consumer.

The Communications Decency Act[21] treated the Internet as a broadcaster and criminalized the transmission of obscene, pornographic, or 'indecent' material. This law, if reinstated, would have far-reaching impacts on Internet service providers, who would become liable for content transmitted by their customers. The service provider would be crippled effectively by the legal requirement to scan all customers' e-mail messages, Web postings, and UseNet activities. The burden of verification would threaten the privacy of Internet users, who would be required to treat the Internet as an interactive broadcast medium. In this instance, the standards for indecent communications would apply, since the Internet has become a glorified cable company, and one's computer, an expensive television. This move towards defining the Internet as a broadcast medium has probably been encouraged by the powerful media interests who see a 'Wild West' that needs taming. Convergence between telephone companies and cable companies and recent trends towards providing Internet access through fibre-optic television cables clearly show who benefits the most from a strong content-based regulatory framework.

Alternatives to content-based regulation include software filtering and self-regulation by Internet service providers. Many countries throughout the European Union and Japan have recently decided that 'command-and-control' regulations are inefficient and probably ineffective means for minimizing the amount of illegal content on the Internet. A report prepared by a study group for the Japanese Posts and Telecommunications Ministry rules out new legal mechanisms for regulating pornography, and suggests self-regulation and software filtering.[22] Several companies make filtering programs that work in tandem with popular Web browsers.[23] These software packages, also known as 'blocking' software, work by referencing a database of Web addresses rated in advance for content. When someone (usually a child) requests information from a blocked Web page, the filtering software prevents access. Many of the programs available allow parents the option of customizing search parameters that exclude certain words or phrases from their children's browsing. This is one way parents can exercise control over their children's access to explicit, sexually oriented material. A concern raised by critics of blocking software is that many new Web pages are being put on-line daily, and some previously blocked sites will escape filtering if mirrored at different Internet addresses. A more damning claim is that filtering software companies are practising a technologically sophisticated form of censorship. There is a concern that such companies, who do not as a rule make their lists of blocked sites public, may be discriminating against Web pages that contain content politically inconsistent with the companies' orientation. For example, material discussing homosexual lifestyles or espousing anarchist views may be summarily blocked.

To avoid some of these obstacles, a more consistent and uniform rating system is needed. In theory, blocking software works best when Webmasters voluntarily rate their own Web pages. The growing number of Web sites around the world makes rating by a single company a futile task. Therefore, considerable effort has gone into developing protocols for self-rating. Two organizations have suggested independently a system of self-rating that could be built into the standards for Web-page construction, and consequently facilitate automatic detection by filtering software when the Web page is requested. The Recreational Software Advisory Committee (RSAC) developed a rating system with four levels for violence, sex, nudity, and language.[24] The other rating agency, SafeSurf, uses a scale from 0 to 16 for profanity, heterosexual themes, homosexual themes, nudity, explicit sex, drugs, violence, and gambling.[25] The integrity of self-rating systems, especially without recourse to regulatory mechanisms in the event of breach of conduct, depends heavily on the motivation of Web-based companies to participate in the filtering of content. It should also be apparent that these rating systems contain inherent societal biases that may not be echoed on an international level. For example, the Western obsession with controlling drugs, homosexuality, and gambling may generate little sympathy in cultures where the self-rating of Web pages may reflect different priorities and concerns. Despite these weaknesses, filtering software does play an essential role in thwarting overly restrictive regulatory initiatives like the Communications Decency Act and, combined with standards for self-regulation by Internet service providers, helps minimize the amount of illegal content on the Internet.

A report on 'Illegal and harmful content on the Internet', prepared for European telecommunications and culture ministers, outlines a set of minimum requirements for self-regulation by Internet service providers.[26] Firstly, a system for self-regulation must not hamper the ability to provide services on a competitive basis. That is, the costs of administration must be fairly shared, and consistent levels of self-enforcement are needed to ensure that customers are not repelled or attracted to services because of stricter or laxer rules. Secondly, self-regulation should respect fundamental freedoms such as expression and privacy for customers, unless illegal activity is discovered. To facilitate this goal,

Internet service providers are expected to develop a code of conduct with provisions for independent, external auditing when breaches of conduct are suspected. Thirdly, a hotline should be established for hearing complaints from the public regarding the activities of customers, and sufficient safeguards should be in place to minimize the risk of the complainant's identity being revealed. Fourthly, Internet service providers will not be held liable for material, either illegal or defamatory in nature, unless they fail to take appropriate action upon being informed of a violation. Fifthly, service providers should encourage their customers to rate their Web pages so as to facilitate software filtering. Finally, service providers should participate in public awareness and educational campaigns to help parents and educators learn more about protecting children from explicit, or otherwise damaging, content.

What is clear from this review of pornography on the Internet, and the various options for control, is that there are benefits to having both regulatory and non-regulatory mechanisms available. Command-and-control approaches have the benefit of being highly directive, but at the same time they are relatively inflexible. Laws, on a local or national basis, can apply to citizens within designated jurisdictions who contravene particular criminal statutes or who invoke the wrath of paying damages under civil law. However, the global nature of the Internet and the fact that individuals can set up computer accounts almost anywhere in the world make enforcement difficult and expensive. Furthermore, there are few incentives for Internet service providers to improve the services they offer to the public, since the force of law will fall on the individual customer who has, for example, posted or retrieved legally obscene material. Insisting that Internet service providers share legal liability will only stunt the growth of the Internet and push the Internet more towards being a broadcast medium. Many of the advantages of this new 'electronic agora' would be lost if this were to happen.

The other options, namely voluntary initiatives and software filtering, depend on how the following question is answered: can the Internet police itself? With the overturning of the Communications Decency Act in the United States and with countries in the European Union and elsewhere looking for solutions other than regulation, the onus is now on parents and educators to control access to potentially harmful material. At this stage, there appears to be a mix of approaches being used. For example, the state of California is now discussing a bill called the Children's Internet Protection Act of 1997.[27] This bill, if passed, would require that school districts providing Internet access to students must maintain filtering software to prohibit access to sexually explicit material, information on drugs including alcohol and tobacco, and material about illegal activities and gambling. In another example, the Orange County Library System of Florida has put blocking software on all public terminals.[28] The American Civil Liberties Union (ACLU) threatened a lawsuit against the library system on the grounds that this action may violate the American con- stitution's freedom of speech and expression provisions. These examples show how a purportedly voluntary option, namely filtering software, can be used as a tool for regulating access to content and, according to some, as a mechanism for censorship.

Codes of conduct and voluntary initiatives spearheaded by Internet service providers also have the potential to lose this 'voluntary' label. For example, the Royal Military College (RMC) in Kingston, Ontario, decided last year to install a 'firewall' for Web use by its students, staff, and faculty.[29] Not only will this fire- wall block outsiders from 'hacking' into the RMC's computer systems, but it will also monitor account holders' Web usage. Here we have an example of how internal sanctions can be applied to Internet users by their Internet service provider. Nevertheless, even though this voluntary initiative does not rely on external regulations, Internet users have been forced to sacrifice some of their freedom and privacy to their service provider.

To conclude, there are no perfect solutions to controlling access to illegal material through the Internet. A mix of regulation and voluntarism, with the aid of blocking software for protecting children, is probably best, as long as it does not, as in the last few examples, replace regulation with service provider initiatives that sacrifice privacy and freedom of expression. In this era of dereg- ulation, the race to embrace new technologies should not have such profound effects on the formal and informal institutions, and hallmarks, of democratic societies. The Internet is supposed to usher in a new golden age of democracy. Missionary zeal for cleaning up pornography should not derail us from this goal.

Notes

1   Although ironic, the use of new technologies for sexual purposes is hardly new. For example, Susan Dwyer notes that 75 per cent of video cassette sales involved pornographic content dur- ing the early years of the VCR. See Susan Dwyer, *The Problem with Pornography* (Belmont, Calif.: Wadsworth, 1995), 1–2.

2   Lower-cost equipment can be used to retrieve binary encoded image and sound files. However, to retrieve these relatively large-sized files, higher-speed telephone connections and faster central processing units help considerably. For example, a 30 kilobyte image sent over a tele- phone line using a 14.4 band modem will take approximately 30 seconds. A high-speed ISDN connection or a T1 connection will transfer the same image in less than a second. The limita- tions become most apparent when retrieving large, moving-image files (e.g., .mpg or .avi). These files are often over 1 megabyte (1,000 kilobytes) in size.

3   Physicist Blair Evans of the Department of National Defence in Ottawa was charged with pos- session of child pornography, which he allegedly obtained via his employer's Internet service. *Ottawa Sun*, 3 Jan. 1997.

4   See Chapter 7 in this volume.

5   For a more detailed discussion of pornography in general, see Dany Lacombe, *Blue Politics: Pornography and the Law* (Toronto: University of Toronto Press, 1994); Kirsten Johnson, *Undressing the Canadian State: The Politics of Pornography* (Halifax: Fernwood, 1995).

6   C.A. MacKinnon, 'Vindication and Resistance: A Response to the Carnegie Mellon Study of Pornography In Cyberspace', *Georgetown Law Journal* 83 (1995): 1959–67.

7   P. Robinson and N. Tamosaitis, *The Joy of Cybersex: An Underground Guide to Electronic Erotica* (New York: Brady, 1993).

8   Michael D. Mehta and Dwaine Plaza, 'Pornography in Cyberspace: An Exploration of What's in UseNet', in S. Kiesler, ed., *Culture of the Internet* (Mahwah, NJ: Lawrence Erlbaum Associates, 1997), 53–67.

9   L.T. Garcia and L. Milano, 'A Content Analysis of Erotic Videos', *Journal of Psychology and Human Sexuality* 3 (1990): 95–103.

10 C. Winick, 'A Content Analysis of Sexually Explicit Magazines Sold in an Adult Bookstore', *Journal of Sex Research* 21 (1985): 206–10.

11 M. Rimm, 'Marketing Pornography on the Information Superhighway: A Survey of 917,410 Images, Descriptions, Short Stories, and Animations Downloaded 8.5 Million Times by Consumers in over 2000 Cities in Forty Countries, Provinces, and Territories', *Georgetown Law Journal* 83 (1995): 1849–1934.

12 Michael D. Mehta, *Pornography on the Internet: Censorship in the New Wired World* (in progress).

13 Paul Burton, 'Regulation and Control of the Internet: Is It Feasible? Is It Necessary?', *Journal of Information Science* 21 (1995): 413–28.

14 Alvin Toffler, *The Third Wave* (Toronto: Bantam, 1981).

15 Heather Menzies, *Whose Brave New World? The Information Highway and the New Economy* (Toronto: Between the Lines, 1996).

16 David Lyon, *Electronic Eye* (Minneapolis: University of Minnesota Press, 1993), examines the issues of privacy and surveillance in the Information Age. As well, a paper by Michael D. Mehta and Éric Darier explores how Foucault's work on the Panopticon can be used as a metaphor for exploring new forms of power and electronic governmentality. See Michael D. Mehta and Éric Darier, 'Virtual Control and Disciplining on the Internet: Electronic Governmentality and the Global Superpanopticon', *Information Society* (forthcoming).

17 J. Wallace and M. Mangan, *Sex, Laws, and Cyberspace* (New York: Henry Holt and Company, 1996).

18 Oscar Gandy, *The Panoptic Sort: A Political Economy of Personal Information* (Boulder, Colo.: Westview Press, 1993).

19 Robert E. Babe, *Telecommunications in Canada: Technology, Industry, and Government* (Toronto: University of Toronto Press, 1990).

20 Jonathon W. Emord, *Freedom, Technology, and the First Amendment* (San Francisco: Pacific Research Institute for Public Policy, 1991).

21 The Communications Decency Act was part of the larger US Telecommunications Reform bill put into law in February 1996. The US Congress voted to amend Section 1462 of Title 18 of the US Code (Chapter 71) to make sending the following over the Internet illegal: (a) any text, graphic, or sound that is lewd, lascivious or filthy; (b) any information telling about how to obtain or make abortions and drugs, or obtaining or making anything that is for indecent or immoral use.

22   This announcement was made by the Kyodo News Service of Japan on 26 Dec. 1996. The announcement can be found at the following address: http://netday.iworld.com/business/NATW/archive.shtml

23   Some of the popular filtering software available includes NetNanny, CyberSitter, CyberPatrol, SurfWatch, and Net Shepherd. For a comprehensive review of these packages, see *Internet World* (Sept. 1996): 48–58.

24   For sex, RSAC uses the following system: level one is for passionate kissing, level two for clothed sexual touching, level three for non-explicit sexual activity, and level four for explicit sexual activity or sex crimes. For more details about RSAC rating, see the homepage at http://www.rsac.org

25   More details about the SafeSurf rating system can be found at http://www.safesurf.com

26   This report was presented at the council meeting of the European Union in Bologna, 24 Apr. 1996. For an on-line copy of the report, see: http://www2.echo.lu/legal/internet/content/wpen.html

27   The Children's Internet Protection Act of 1997 is an amendment to Section 51870.5 of California's Education Code.

28   This story can be found on the Web at http://www.wired.com/news/story/1289.html

29   A memo by Paul Allard, Dean (Academic Services) at RMC, dated 5 Feb. 1997, states: 'As a result of a number of incidents involving the Internet, I have felt obligated to inform RMC's senior management of the security risks to RMC from the Internet.' Dean Allard is referring here to the arrest of Department of National Defence physicist Blair Evans in January 1997. The firewall to be set up would require RMC users to log into a UNIX account prior to browsing the World Wide Web. Dean Allard goes on to state, 'Web surfers should also be aware that a log of activity for auditing purpose is maintained by the firewall software.' In other words, this software will track users and provide evidence regarding any suspicious or illegal browsing activities.

Chapter 10

PRIVACY-ENHANCING TECHNOLOGIES: TRANSFORMING THE DEBATE OVER IDENTITY

Ann Cavoukian

Privacy and Freedom

There is a fundamental relationship between privacy and freedom: simply put, you cannot have one without the other. The ability to remain free from surveillance—free from the prying eyes of the state, as portrayed in various dystopias such as George Orwell's *1984*—is only possible in a world that respects privacy. Professor Gary Marx noted that the common thread running through free and democratic societies was the presence of privacy, while its absence characterized a totalitarian state: 'The protection of privacy says something about what a nation stands for. It is vital to the protection of individual liberty. A thread running through all totalitarian systems is lack of respect for the individual's right to control information about the self.'[1] Respect for human rights must remain at the core of any free and democratic society.

Individual control, freedom of choice, self-determination: these are the terms commonly associated with privacy. These are also the terms associated with freedom and liberty. In most countries of the Western world, privacy is considered to be a fundamental human right, one especially cherished by European countries that have experienced threats to their freedom or the complete loss of their freedom for a period of time. Thus, it should come as no surprise that Germany stands as the world leader in privacy and data protection. This is neither an accident nor a product of mere coincidence. It is directly related to Germany's experience during World War II. The subjugation by a totalitarian regime the likes of the Third Reich, which used information to find and persecute classes of people, made the return of freedom all the more precious. The Germans readily understood that freedom depended in large part on informational self-determination or, in other words, the right to privacy.

The concept of privacy is a broad and all-encompassing notion that subsumes a number of interests. On the surface, it tends to be very subjective in nature and thus is associated with a variety of meanings. Definitions of privacy range from the simple—'the right to be let alone', as framed by Justice Louis Brandeis of the United States Supreme Court in 1890—to the complex, as in the following definition by Arnold Simmel:

> Privacy is a concept related to solitude, secrecy, and autonomy, but it is not synonymous with these terms; for beyond the purely descriptive aspects of privacy as isolation from the company, the curiosity, and the influence of others, privacy implies a normative element: the right to exclusive control of access to private realms . . . the right to privacy asserts the sacredness of the person; . . . any invasion of privacy constitutes an offence against the rights of the personality—against individuality, dignity, and freedom.[2]

Other definitions of privacy have included:

The extent to which we are known to others, the extent to which others have physical access to us, and the extent to which we are the subject of others' attention.[3]

A degree of inaccessibility of persons, of their mental states, and of information about them to the senses and surveillance devices of others.[4]

The claim of individuals, groups, or institutions to determine for themselves when, how, and to what extent information about them is communicated to others.[5]

We can be certain of one thing: privacy is a highly subjective concept, focusing for some on human dignity and respect, for others, on freedom from interference or intrusion, and for still others, on the preservation of personal autonomy and anonymity. One important component of all of these is the individual's ability to maintain control—to control various realms of one's life and to be able to make choices about which aspects of it you wish to reveal, and which you wish to keep private. In an age fuelled by information, control over the uses of your personal information—information that is circulating about you—takes on a heightened sense of importance for those who value their privacy. This type of privacy, 'informational privacy', or data protection as it is known in Europe, will form the basis of this chapter.

Germany has the strongest data protection laws worldwide, but it is also unique in creating a constitutional right to privacy in the form of 'informational self-determination'. In 1983, the German Constitutional Court entrenched the ability to determine the fate of one's personal information in ruling that all Germans had the right of informational self-determination. In doing so, the Court recognized the individual's right to determine the uses of his or her information. Privacy scholar and former German Data Protection Commissioner, Spiros Simitis, stated: 'Since this ruling . . . it has been an established fact in this country that the Constitution gives the individual the right to decide when and under what circumstances his personal data may be processed.'[6]

The federal Privacy Commissioner of Canada, Bruce Phillips, has noted that information is not just a single substance or entity, but far more: 'It is not just data; it is not a product or a commodity . . . information is the expression of all that we know and are. Personal information expresses the substance of individual lives; in short, all the things which distinguish one human being from another, which certify the uniqueness of each individual.'[7] Phillips believes that the preservation of a private life in this day and age depends largely on our ability to retain some control over what others know about us.

Informational privacy will assume even greater importance as we move from a resource-based economy to a knowledge-based economy. The world is on the verge of a massive paradigm shift—from an economy based on material resources to one based on knowledge, where ideas and information fuel the economic engines. The growing web of networked communications, linking millions of databases of information and making them easily accessible in seconds to anyone, anywhere in the world, is the underlying bedrock of this new economy. With this shift will come new demands for the protection of this knowledge, starting with its most basic element—electronic bits of data. In a knowledge-based economy, the exchange of information and ideas becomes the new capital, the new commodity, that requires protection. In a very short period of time, the Internet has become the enabling exchange medium.

The primary cause of this transformation is the increasing use and reliance by organizations, in the conduct of commerce, of electronically transmitted information through networked computers and information systems. Similarly, individuals will increasingly come to conduct their commercial affairs in front of a keyboard, be it for banking, information gathering, or electronic purchases. As electronic commerce and communication systems are further implemented, organizations and individuals alike will be confronted with unprecedented challenges to their privacy and the security of their information holdings.

With the transformation of capital from a tangible to an intangible in the form of bits and bytes, the opportunities for electronic commerce and trade are enormous, as are the opportunities for fraud and misappropriation. Information can now be stolen, altered, accessed, copied, and distributed without the originating party having any awareness of it, let alone gaining any value from it. What is more, the ability to assume another person's identity, without that person's knowledge or consent, presents itself as a new threat to privacy, perhaps more sinister than those known to us. The reason for this arises out of the medium's ability to allow for the unauthorized access to one's personal information, which at a minimum is a nuisance and, at the extreme, can cause devastating harm to the individual, both financial and personal.

Privacy and Identity

Identity is at the heart of privacy—one is intertwined with the other. The theft or impersonation of one's identity by a third party is becoming a growing concern. 'Identity theft' is a term we will become increasingly familiar with in the coming years, as we function more and more in a networked world. It is one of the reasons why privacy advocates will need to rethink their traditional opposition to identifying oneself in various forms such as paper documents and identity cards. The means by which positive identification is achieved will become critical, but the need for it will only strengthen with time. But before exploring this further, I will briefly review the historic opposition to identity documents such as identity cards, service cards (i.e., a driver's licence), and benefits cards (providing benefits such as health insurance), followed by a discussion of the changing face of identification in a networked world, and ending with a possible solution in the form of privacy-enhancing technologies.

The resistance to compulsory identity cards stems largely from the potential for surveillance that such cards and identity schemes foster. Since identity cards carry with them a unique identification number, the potential for data linkage is greatly facilitated (with other pieces of personal information), which in turn leads to the development of detailed personal profiles in the form of electronic dossiers. In effect, an individual's identity becomes converted to a unique and communicable surrogate through his or her unique number. Consequently, mandatory identity cards increase the power of government to engage in surveillance. They represent the encroachment of the state and the potential usurping of our freedoms and liberties. Accordingly, they are perceived as a grave threat to privacy.

One example of a government identity card was the Australia Card—attempts to introduce this identity card in Australia in 1985 generated a great deal of opposition. The Australia Card was viewed as another tool of the state to track the activities of its citizens. People did not want to be reduced to mere numbers and strongly opposed the card, leading to its ultimate withdrawal by the government. Ironically, however, it was only to be replaced with a 'tax number', which in effect served the same purpose but was given a different name.

Identity cards have also been regarded as internal passports, used to track the movements of people within the borders of their own country. The arguments in favour of identity cards, such as their convenience, improved administrative efficiency, fraud reduction, and their capability of serving as an aid to law enforcement, must be balanced against the harm they may engender. One cannot forget Hitler's fond use of identity cards as a means of identifying and tracking individuals of Jewish origin, or the use of Social Security numbers (SSNs) in the United States to locate and intern the Japanese during World War II. One can only imagine the potential for abuse in today's world of networked communications and data linkage with a unique and communicable digital surrogate of one's identity—the ease with which targeted individuals could be located and their activities monitored is staggering. Next to the mandatory nature of identity cards, the potential for discrimination that they may foster is another major concern associated with these cards.

Let us not, however, limit the realm of privacy-snatchers to government alone. In the past, government may have been the prime contender for intrusions into the private lives of its citizens, but the private sector can now lay equal claim to peering into our lives through the massive amounts of transaction-generated information it gathers. The term 'dataveillance' has been coined to describe the use of amassing bits of data, instead of using cameras, to do the watching. Roger Clarke, who originated the term 'dataveillance', argues that surveillance through the use of data is now 'supplanting conventional surveillance techniques'.[8] Thus, the use of identifiable data by the private sector may be just as invasive of privacy as the government's use of various means for identifying people. Both public and private sectors will search increasingly for reliable methods of positive identification; both will be capable of using such methods to peer into the private lives of the public.

Here is the dilemma we face: While people will no doubt continue to resist having their identities reduced to mere numbers and object to having their actions monitored, governments and commercial enterprises will no doubt continue to introduce new ways of identifying people. Fraud associated with stolen identity or the impersonation of multiple identities to access services, such as credit cards, cellular phones, bank accounts, or government benefits, is said to be the growth industry of the nineties. The electronic infrastructure built around the digital world has enabled fraud to grow exponentially in the last decade. And fraud is nearly 100 per cent profit. Worldwide markets are demanding better and more secure ways of identifying people in order to deal with the growing problem of fraud. How can these opposing views be reconciled? Therein lies the challenge.

Returning to government for a moment, it is important to differentiate between two types of government cards—a multi-purpose identity card (i.e., 'show me your papers') and a purpose-specific identification or 'service' card, used for the purposes of obtaining a specific service (i.e., social assistance) or for certifying your ability to perform a particular operation (i.e., driving a motor vehicle). This distinction is a very important one. In the case of the former, a compulsory government identity card, state officials could compel production of the card at any time, requiring that it be carried on one's person at all times. This would understandably conjure pictures of a police state, with visions of the East German Stasi demanding to 'see your papers'.

The second type of card, a purpose-specific service card, is different in several ways, not the least of which is that it may be viewed in a positive light— as authenticating an individual's right to access certain benefits, such as health care, or permitting one to engage in a desirable activity (in most Western countries), namely, driving a car or other activities such as hunting or fishing. While privacy commissioners have consistently spoken out against the former type of all-encompassing identity card, this has not been the case with purpose-specific cards. This reflects an acceptance that some types of documents authenticating a user's eligibility for benefits or certification for various activities are a necessary part of life and need not be considered a threat to privacy. But could we take this one step further and argue that the ability to identify oneself accurately will become highly desirable in the years to come?

At some basic level, I suspect that we all accept the need to identify ourselves for one purpose or another; the question is, where along the continuum of 'needs' for identification do we draw the line? For example, it is desirable for a bank teller who does not know you to ask for identification before allowing you to withdraw money from your bank account. It is desirable for a front-desk clerk to ask an alleged husband for identification before giving him the key to a room his wife had checked into earlier in the day. Any time that you engage in a variety of activities ranging from writing a cheque, accessing your voice mail, and entering a secure building to accessing your computer, you are required to identify yourself for your own benefit. In all of these activities, it is to your advantage to be able to identify yourself uniquely so that you and only you can engage in that activity. In these circumstances, the ability to identify oneself positively serves to enhance one's privacy. We do not wish to have someone else mistaken for ourselves.

What differentiates the above examples, where it is in an individual's self-interest to identify oneself as uniquely no one else, from the earlier ones where having a uniquely identifying number acts as an instrument of surveillance, capable of tracking one's activities? A number of factors, all of which hinge on freedom of choice, must be considered. The former is voluntary: it is either self-selected and chosen by the individual (selecting a PIN to gain access to an ATM), or consented to (showing identification to be allowed to write a cheque or enter a hotel room). In the case of a mandatory government identity card, no choice is involved. It is created and imposed by the state for purposes over which you have little control; it is also highly visible and identifiable. The former is nei-ther—it is invisible in that it is known only to yourself (kept secret) and is intended to do the opposite of serving as an identifier that facilitates data link-age—its purpose is to keep everyone out; the latter is intended to let them in. One puts you in control, the other causes you to lose control.

Identity schemes such as those used for identity cards are also universal in nature—they apply the same numbering system to the entire population (e.g., in Canada a nine-digit SIN—social insurance number—for all). Applied univer-sally to the entire population, such numbers act as your surrogate in uniquely identifying you to the world. A personal identification number (PIN) does the opposite—it consists of a variable number of digits, determined by the indi-vidual, and serves to lock everyone else out. One forces you to have a public face, the other permits you to keep your identity to yourself. One can be likened to your public key (see below), which is widely distributed, the other to your private key known only to yourself. The difference, of course, is that your public key is of no value in decoding information without your private key. That is not the case with a universal identification number that is identifi-able on face value.

On-line Issues: Encryption Will Be Key

When communicating on-line via the Internet, senders and recipients need to be assured of the authenticity of their respective identities. In the case of elec-tronic commerce, both vendors and customers must be assured that they are dealing with legitimate parties (i.e., paying clients and real vendors who will deliver the goods ordered). Therefore, the need for on-line identification is heightened since one has no recourse other than to have satisfied oneself at the outset that you are dealing with a legitimate, bona fide party at the other end. The only way to be assured of this is through a system of encryption or coding of information.

Encryption is a mathematical process that disguises the content of a message transmitted on-line. It provides a means of locking and unlocking information so that only the intended parties can gain access to it. Cryptography is the study of encryption and the development of mathematical algorithms. Whittfield Diffie, a veteran cryptographer and the inventor of public key encryption, has referred to cryptography as 'the only technology that can protect privacy . . . it is indispensable to protecting privacy in networked communications.'[9] A system of encryption known as 'public key' is among the most advanced systems developed.

In a public key cryptosystem, two different keys are created for each person: one private, one public. The private key is known only to the individual, while the public key is made widely available. Someone can send you a confidential message in code by using your public key to encrypt it. However, only the corresponding private key, known only to yourself, can be used to decrypt or decode the message. What is encrypted with one key may only be decrypted with the corresponding key in the pair.

Public key encryption not only shields the content of one's on-line communications, keeping them confidential, but it also provides a means of authenticating them in a manner similar to one's signature—just as a handwritten signature serves to authenticate the document to which it is attached, so does a digital signature attached to an electronic communication. In the absence of encrypted transactions that promise both confidentiality and authentication of identity, one is left wide open to numerous forms of fraud.[10]

It is in this area where we are beginning to see the growing convergence of public and private sectors: controlling fraud in the areas of finance, electronic commerce, and benefits disbursement has become an overarching priority for both governments and businesses alike. Fraud has become a major source of losses in both sectors, and with shrinking dollars competing for a greater number of deliverables, reducing waste in the form of fraud has become a primary objective. Privacy advocates can no longer shrug off the issue of fraud—we must meet it head on and offer solutions that protect privacy.

Accepting the need to combat fraudulent activities and enlisting information technology towards that end is one thing, but must this take place at the expense of privacy? In order to answer this question, one must first understand that there is a built-in predisposition towards surveillance in the existing information infrastructure—it has been designed to identify. Professor Phillip Agre of the University of California at San Diego, who speaks extensively on this subject, states that existing information systems are designed precisely to make information available in identifiable form. The concept of protecting anyone's privacy is completely foreign to those designing these systems—it simply does not exist in the architecture. And the concerns associated with surveillance and the electronic tracking of people's activities rests on this one key point: the identifiable nature of the information.

One's name or a uniquely identifying number such as a SIN or SSN is a personally identifying piece of information that links the content of any other information relating to one's transactions and communications with an identifiable individual. The definition of personal information is 'recorded information about an identifiable individual'. The removal, however, of the identifiable portion of the record greatly enhances privacy since most threats to privacy lie with the personal identifier attached to various pieces of information. Once the identifier is either removed or made unintelligible through encryption, any information attached to it can no longer be linked to the individual, thereby rendering it 'non-personal'—it cannot be linked to an identifiable individual. Therefore, any technology that serves to de-identify and anonymize personal information is considered to be privacy-enhancing, as opposed to simply advancing security.

Is there much difference between privacy and security? Yes. While privacy is often used interchangeably with security, let me assure you they are not the same. Privacy subsumes what is implied by security but goes much further—it is a far broader concept involving the right to be free from intrusions, to remain autonomous, and to control the circulation of information about oneself.

Privacy entails restrictions on a wide range of activities relating to personal information: its collection, retention, use, and disclosure. Security, however, is only one means of protecting information, by safeguarding it from unauthorized disclosure to third parties. Security only comes into play after the information in question has already been obtained.

Privacy-Enhancing Technologies

Privacy-enhancing technologies (PETs) not only provide for heightened security but also total privacy, in that such encrypted systems preclude the central retention of identifiable data—no more central databases of personal information linked together to form detailed personal profiles. The anonymization of personally identifiable data is the objective. Contrast that with present-day practices such as data-mining and warehousing. However, things are beginning to change. Privacy-enhancing technologies that provide authentication without divulging identity in the process not only address privacy concerns but also provide much needed assurances to organizations regarding the authenticity of the individuals they are doing business with.

Two examples of anonymizing, privacy-enhancing technologies may be found in Appendix A. The important feature of both is that they rely on the 'blinding' of identity through anonymizing techniques made possible by encryption. It is now possible to enlist technology in the support of privacy instead of its demise. Technologies of privacy enable users to minimize or eliminate dramatically the amount of identifiable data collected and stored, while still meeting the needs of those collecting the information. They allow for authentication of identity without divulging identity. They provide both government and business alike with the necessary assurances that they are interacting with legitimate users of their programs or services without giving away privacy in the process.

Privacy-enhancing technologies meet the needs of both organizations and individuals. While organizations claim they need access to identity information, on careful analysis their true needs usually lie in being able to authenticate the eligibility of those they are doing business with—to ensure they are legitimate users of a program or eligible recipients of benefits.[11] PETs provide much needed information to organizations to assist them in combating fraud, but they do so in a way that preserves individual privacy, thus creating a true win/win scenario. These privacy-enhancing technologies exist today. However, awareness of their existence is minimal since they are in their infancy. And it is unlikely that they will be championed by organizations of either the public or private sector, which presently view their interests through the prism of a 'more is better' mentality.

Recognizing these limitations, the privacy commissions of Ontario and the Netherlands issued a joint report in 1995 encouraging the widespread adoption of privacy-enhancing technologies and urging their counterparts to do the same. They agreed. A resolution was passed at the 1995 meeting of the European Union data protection commissioners to heighten public awareness and promote the use of anonymizing technologies of privacy over the tracking technologies of surveillance. Realizing that the greatest challenge lay in getting the word out to the public, they accepted this task, which, quite naturally, would fall on the shoulders of privacy commissioners. As the Ontario-Netherlands report indicated:

> Among the challenges that lie ahead will be the reluctance of both public and private sector organizations that wish to collect more, not less, identifiable information (until the benefits of collecting less are understood and organizations come to realize that identifiable information is not always necessary for their activities). Add to this a public which generally lacks awareness of the benefits to be had through the use of anony-

mous technologies, and the challenge grows even larger. To help meet these challenges, we make the following recommendations.[12]

Five recommendations were made in total (see Appendix B), all aimed at reducing the amount of personally identifiable data collected by organizations and
encouraging the adoption of privacy-enhancing technologies wherever possible. The Ontario-Netherlands report was surprisingly well received by the data
protection commissioners, as were the recommendations.

Conclusion

Privacy is a fundamental human right being jeopardized by identifying technologies that track the movements and activities of the public. Given the fundamental relationship between privacy and freedom, the loss of privacy could
also signal losses to our other freedoms. Preserving the ability to control the
uses of our information, or informational self-determination, will grow in
importance as the ability of others to gain electronic access to our information
grows; so will the ability to protect our identity. Being able to identify ourselves
accurately will assume far greater importance in an increasingly networked
world, and as long as we do so voluntarily, this will become highly desirable.

Technology need not be viewed exclusively as an evil force poised to
threaten privacy. Privacy-enhancing technologies that serve to de-identify and
anonymize personal information achieve the opposite effect: they protect privacy by anonymizing personal information. This serves the needs of both individuals and organizations: privacy is preserved through the anonymity afforded
by such technologies, while organizations are assured of the authenticity of the
individuals they are doing business with—a case in point that competing interests can, at times, be reconciled.

Appendix A: Two Examples of Privacy-Enhancing Technologies

Blind Signatures

The blind signature, created by David Chaum of DigiCash (Amsterdam,
Netherlands), is an extension of the digital signature—the electronic equivalent
of a handwritten signature. Digital signatures are an extension of public key
encryption. Just as a signature on a document is proof of its authenticity, a digital signature provides the same authentication for electronic transactions. It
provides the necessary assurance that only the individual who created the signature could have done so, and permits others to verify its authenticity.

While a digital signature provides proof of authenticity (that a transaction
originated from a particular sender), it reveals the identity of the individual in
the process. The blind signature is an extension of the digital signature but with

one additional feature: it ensures the anonymity of the sender. While digital signatures are intended to be identifiable (to serve as proof that a particular individual signed a particular document), blind signatures provide the same authentication but do so in a non-identifiable or 'blind' manner. The recipient is assured of the fact that a transmission is authentic and reliable without knowing who actually sent it.

Biometric Encryption

Biometric measures provide irrefutable evidence of one's identity since they offer biological proof that can only be linked to one individual. The most common biometric measure is the fingerprint. Identifiable fingerprints have historically raised concerns about privacy. The central retention of fingerprints and multiple access to them by different arms of government invoke images of Big Brother.

The fundamental problem with identifiable biometric measures has been that, once obtained, they are stored in identifiable form together with other personal information in a central database. This may be accessed by a number of third parties and used for a variety of unintended purposes. All of this facilitates surveillance—making it easier to track your movements and compile detailed personal profiles. Thus, the threat to privacy comes not from the positive identification that biometrics provides best, but from the ability of others to access this information in identifiable form and link it to other personal information. This can only occur, however, if the biometric information is kept in identifiable form. All of that changes if the biometric measure is used only to encrypt the information to be stored.

Therein lies the paradox of biometrics: a threat to privacy in identifiable form, a protector of privacy in encrypted form; a technology of surveillance in identifiable form, a technology of privacy in encrypted form. As noted earlier, reliable forms of encryption can anonymize data and prevent unauthorized third parties from intercepting confidential information. In the case of encrypted biometrics, authentication is made possible without identification of the user.

A Canadian company, Mytec Technologies of Toronto, founded by George Tomko has developed a new technology called 'biometric encryption' that will transform the way we view fingerprints: from posing a threat to privacy to becoming its protector. Fingerprints encrypting information will now be used to protect people's privacy instead of invading it. Through the 'bioscrypt', a compound of biometrics encryption, user eligibility is authenticated without divulging identity. Further, the bioscrypt bears no physical resemblance to the user's actual fingerprint—no record, image, or template of the individual's print is retained. Therefore, a copy of the fingerprint cannot be kept on file. Instead, a number or set of characters encrypted by the finger pattern is retained in the form of the bioscrypt. Nor can the bioscrypt be converted back to its corresponding fingerprint from which it originated because it is not a fingerprint. Rather, one's finger becomes one's uniquely private key with which one can lock or unlock information in an anonymous, privacy-enhancing manner.

Appendix B: The Path to Anonymity: Recommendations of the Ontario-Netherlands Report

1. International information systems design standards should be developed incorporating the need to examine whether an individual's identity is truly required for the operation of various processes within the system. Attention should be explicitly directed to the introduction of an identity protector, which functions to separate the identity domain from the remaining pseudo-domains.

2. At the design stage of any new information system, or when revising an existing one, the collection and retention of identifiable personal information should be kept to an absolute minimum. Only that which is truly needed should be collected and maintained in an identifiable form (as opposed to a pseudonymous form).

3. Consistent with the privacy principle that information systems should be transparent and open to view to data subjects, they should also provide users with the ability to control the disclosure of their personal information. Data subjects must be placed in a position to decide for themselves whether or not their identity should be revealed or maintained in an information system.

4. Data Protection Commissioners, Privacy Commissioners and their staff should make every effort to educate the public and raise levels of awareness in the area of privacy-enhancing technologies. The use of privacy technologies by public and private sector organizations should be also encouraged. The message that it is now possible to preserve an individual's anonymity during service delivery should be included in all public outreach efforts. The benefits to be derived to individuals from the use of anonymous technologies are far-reaching and will ensure the continuation of privacy protection in a fully networked world.

5. Data Protection and Privacy Commissioners should ask the parties involved to review the use of identifiable data in light of privacy protection principles and make use of privacy-enhancing technologies wherever possible. The unnecessary collection of identifiable data, where appropriate, should give rise to further action to promote compliance with existing statutes.

Notes

1   Gary T. Marx, 'Communications Advances Raise Privacy Concerns', *Christian Science Monitor*, 2 Jan. 1992.

2   Arnold Simmel, quoted in David H. Flaherty, *Protecting Privacy in Surveillance Societies* (Chapel Hill: University of North Carolina Press, 1989), 9.

3   Ruth Gavison, quoted in Ferdinand D. Shoeman, ed., *Philosophical Dimensions of Privacy: An Anthology* (Cambridge: Cambridge University Press, 1984), 379.

4   Anita Allen, quoted in Sheri Alpert, 'Smart Cards, Smarter Policy: Medical Records, Privacy and Health Care Reform', *Hastings Center Report* 23, 6 (1993): 19.

5   Alan F. Westin, *Privacy and Freedom* (New York: Atheneum, 1967), x.

6   Spiros Simitis, quoted in Flaherty, *Protecting Privacy in Surveillance Societies*, 377.

7   Bruce Phillips, *Annual Report of the Privacy Commissioner of Canada, 1994–5* (Ottawa, 1995), 2.

8   Roger A. Clarke, 'Information Technology and Dataveillance', *Communications of the ACM* 31, 5 (May 1988): 498–512.

9   Whittfield Diffie, speech given at the Security and Privacy Workshop, 17 Feb. 1995, Industry Canada, Ottawa.

10 For an introductory explanation of encryption and public key systems, see Ann Cavoukian and Don Tapscott, *Who Knows: Safeguarding Your Privacy in a Networked World* (Toronto: Random House, 1995), ch. 10.

11 Joint Report by The Office of the Information and Privacy Commissioner/Ontario and The Netherlands, 'Privacy-Enhancing Technologies: The Path to Anonymity', Aug. 1995.

12 Ibid., 19.

Chapter 11

THE CUTTING EDGE? GENDER, LEGAL, AND ETHICAL IMPLICATIONS OF HIGH-TECH HEALTH CARE

Cynthia J. Alexander and Sue P. Stafford

Introduction

While public policy-makers are devising alternative reform initiatives in the health system, consultants with re-engineering methodologies and informatics expertise are themselves reconceiving and restructuring all facets of health care systems, from administration to service delivery, to the allocation of scarce human, fiscal, and other resources. The rapid adoption of information, communication, and knowledge-based systems facilitates changes in the health care system that affect everyone, from patients and health professionals to policy-makers. These changes will in turn affect: the quality of care; the costs of care; labour force structures; the workplace environment; patient-professional interactions; management systems and procedures in health care organizations; and the administration of different levels of health care systems.

Information and communication technologies (ICT) can support the following functions in health care settings:

- data acquisition, including medical imaging;
- record-keeping, increasing the comprehensiveness, accuracy, and speed of the processes and reducing labour intensity;
- information storage and retrieval, improving archiving functions, as well as enhancing bibliographic retrieval systems such as Medline;
- data analysis, offering more sophisticated and clearer analysis;
- communication and integration, supporting the concept of a health care team;
- monitoring, by identifying and flagging test results;
- decision support, complementing the reporting and interpretation of data and information;
- expert diagnosis and prognosis, offering complex analysis;
- education, supporting continuing knowledge services through the establishment of new information and communication flows as well as sophisticated computerized simulations.

While important benefits can be gained from the adoption of computers and other ICT in health care, 'this does not mean that we must expect the benefits to flow automatically and without a great deal of effort and concerted attention by highly motivated groups and individuals. There is a need to discuss and reflect upon the more pessimistic or cautious side of these issues.'[1] From this vantage point, and with a primary emphasis on the Canadian policy environment, this chapter looks first at the forces driving the adoption of ICT in health care and then focuses on two sorts of applications, information-intensive and knowledge-intensive systems.

The first section of the chapter offers an examination of some of the organizational, human resource, and privacy challenges and choices that may arise with the adoption of information and communication systems. Information systems are introduced to assist with information-intensive tasks, such as record-keeping and inventory. The computer's ability to organize, store, retrieve, display, and manipulate information is much greater than that of human beings, and the result of the introduction of information systems can contribute to an increase in productivity, a decrease in administrative costs, and an overall improvement in the delivery of care. Existing communication processes in health care systems can be enhanced with the ability to share large amounts of information quickly and inexpensively. New communication flows can also be facilitated that enhance the roles of different actors within the health care system, from the patient to the isolated health care practitioner. However, with the adoption of the powerful new information and communication systems, there may be important negative implications. Gender inequities embedded in the system may be aggravated. Confidentiality requirements may be subverted. Inaccurate records may contaminate data banks that, with the 'halo' effect of computerization, may appear to be flawless. The first section reveals the need to identify and assess such non-technical issues in any informatics initiative.

The second section provides an exploration of the promise of computers as 'intelligent' partners in medical decision-making, moving the analysis beyond the domain of computers as information systems into the less familiar domain of knowledge-based systems. Computerized decision support systems that are knowledge-based have been introduced into a variety of health care settings; such systems support activities such as patient monitoring, the approval or denial of insurance coverage or treatment, fraud detection in claims, and patient diagnosis, treatment, or prognosis. A knowledge-based system for patient monitoring must know the current status of each patient being monitored, as well as the meaning of any deviation from that status along a myriad of data dimensions. A computerized system for approval or denial of insurance coverage must know the coverages allowed under various policies. An expert system for diagnosis must know the symptoms of disease. The most knowledge-intensive applications diagnose disease, prescribe treatment, and make prognoses for recovery. To illustrate some of the ethical and legal challenges that such systems pose to policy-makers, a case study is offered of the Acute Physiology Age Chronic Health Evaluation, otherwise referred to as the APACHE III system; the system is designed to predict patient mortality in hospital intensive care units (ICUs).

The questions posed in this chapter will be useful to those who seek to assess technological changes in the other helping professions, such as education and social welfare. How, if at all, does technological change affect the people, processes, and institutions through which public goods and services are designed and delivered? Further, how does it affect the recipients of technologically mediated public goods and services, if at all? As the chapter illustrates, there are few clear-cut answers to such questions. There are no technological silver bullets to solve the crisis of health care. Instead, there are increasingly complex legal and ethical questions, fewer fiscal resources, overworked and, some will argue, underpaid health professionals, among other challenges. Without consideration to the political and policy context of health care systems, technological change will, as Shoshana Zuboff reminds us, follow the path of least resistance, aggravating instead of alleviating old problems, and creating some new ones.[2]

A Contextual Framework: 'Re-engineering' Public Services

One of the enduring beliefs of the twentieth century is in the power of scientific and technological developments to 'solve' complex physiological, organizational, and sociopolitical problems.[3] Belief in scientific rationality and technological wizardry provides the foundation for the new 'wired era'. Jeremy Rifkin observes that 'Intelligent machines are already invading the professional disciplines and even encroaching on education and the arts, long considered immune to the pressures of mechanization.'[4] How are such professional endeavours changing, both in terms of the nature of the work and in the quality of service delivery? Within specific policy fields such as health care or social services, is there a strong predisposition to adopt technological change—given the current fiscal climate—and if so, what are the implications?

Technological change does not occur in a vacuum; it is influenced by the political, economic, and social climates at the organizational level as well as at the broader societal level. In a study of the adoption of technological change in the Canadian public sector, it is important to acknowledge, then, that innovation in the eighties and nineties has occurred in a period of persistent economic recession when neo-conservatism has prevailed. In an ongoing period of budget cuts throughout the Canadian public sector, if technological 'solutions' promise significant cost efficiencies then we might expect that the question posed by decision-makers tends not to be, 'what might the implications be for . . .' but rather, 'how quickly can the system(s) be introduced?' The trend to use technology to increase service efficiency (defined in narrow economic terms) and increase standardization was examined in Alexander's 1990 comparative study of three provincial governments' applications of the new electronic technologies in the social welfare field: 'When computers are used in government to maximize the measurable, people become inputs, targets, and products, lost in the labyrinths of computer systems.'[5]

As in social services, budget consciousness continues to redefine the health care sector in significant ways. Cuts in health care budgets are evident across Canada. In Alberta, since 1993 the annual health care budget has been cut by

$550 million, resulting in: the loss of 15,000 health care jobs; closure of over half of the hospital beds in Edmonton and Calgary; a rise in health care premiums by 25 per cent; a growing list of de-insured services, including eye examinations; the emergence of for-profit ventures such as the Hostel de Health, private eye clinics that charge patients directly. There is concern in Alberta and elsewhere that a two-tier health care system is already emerging. The emerging tiers will be based on economic and social distinctions. For example, in Ontario an internationally renowned hospital, Toronto's Women's College Hospital, recognized by the World Health Organization as the first collaborating centre in North America in women's health, has been targeted for closure by the Ontario government. From a policy perspective, it is important to consider that:

- The chiefs of medicine of 36 of Metro Toronto's 41 hospitals are men.
- The chiefs of surgery of 40 of Metro Toronto's hospitals are men.
- The chairs of the board of 35 of Metro Toronto's hospitals are men.
- The CEOs of 28 of Metro Toronto's hospitals are men.
- Even though 37 per cent of students at the University of Toronto's medical school (the largest in Canada) are women, only one hospital has anywhere near that percentage of women doctors. In fact, at Women's College, women doctors are in the majority.[6]

Federal reductions in transfer payments have created a critical revenue shortfall for the provinces. The report from a conference of provincial and territorial ministers of health, *A Renewed Vision for Canada's Health System*, states: 'Federal funding reductions are forcing the acceleration of change beyond the system's ability to absorb and sustain adjustments.'[7] Without adequate cash transfer payments throughout the 1990s, the federal government has been unable to maintain national standards in health care via the Canada Health Act. While the National Health Forum recommended that cash transfers not fall below $12.5 billion, in its February 1997 budget the federal government chose to continue cutting the cash transfers until they hit a low of $11.1 billion. Dr Judith Kazimirski, the CMA president, stated: 'As a result of progressive cuts, there will be a 50 percent reduction in the federal government's CHST [Canada Health and Social Transfer] cash contribution between fiscal 1995 and 2000.'[8] The federal contribution equals less than 10 per cent of total health expenditures in Canada.

It is in this fiscal context that the promise of technological change to bring economic efficiencies—to do more with less—is particularly enticing to hospital administrators, government officials, politicians, and citizens alike. As health care systems in Canada deteriorate, a new market for medical entrepreneurs offering faster access for paying patients is emerging. Similarly, a new market is growing for the health care informatics sector, which promises to bring greater cost-effectiveness to health systems.

Policy Implications of Computerized Information Systems in Health Care

Information is literally the lifeblood of any health care system; whether we are talking about a human as a biological information system or about the American or Canadian health care system as a whole, information is the heart of the matter. It is therefore surprising that health is one of the few policy areas—in Canada, the United States, and elsewhere—that has only begun to make substantial investments in computer technology. James M. Gabler states: 'Health care has accomplished a great deal with computers, but compared to other industries, health care is only beginning to take real advantage of information tools.'[9] Electronic data interchange, automated patient records, medical expert systems, and other technological systems are currently being introduced in the US and Canada. The motivation is the promise of realizing new cost reductions and decreasing personnel expenditures. The situation is not unique to Canada. In the United States, 'Competition is reducing HMO industry margins, and consolidation has begun. Survivors must make effective use of innovative HCIS [health care information systems] to provide demonstrably high-quality health care at competitive cost.'[10]

The health care sector has been slow to adopt such technologies for reasons that include: the resistance of a highly independent group of professionals—physicians; the reluctance of nurses, who like physicians resisted computers because of the new skill requirements and other considerations; concern for the potential dehumanizing effects of computer techniques on the art-like aspects of health care; the lack of good software in the field; the distinctive cultural settings of individual health care organizations. Further, close study of the lack of standardized data and information within hospitals and between hospitals and of other health care reform debates highlights some persistent problems: enormous administrative cost savings; the lack of accurate, timely, and comparable data within and between health care organizations; the lack of a national health information system; inefficient work processes. These observations hold true in Canada and the United States. In the mid-1990s, there is a strong interest among health professionals and policy-makers in the promise of information technologies to support reform initiatives that would address such problems. Given the lucrative health care market, a savvy informatics industry has been marketing its solutions to health officials, offering the twin engine power of re-engineering methodologies and technological systems.

What kind of return might be expected from the strategic technology applications? Information technology could support some public policy officials' and hospital and health administrators' efforts to collect more data and more information about the recipients of health services. Even in the midst of the Information Era, there is a dearth of comparable data and information in the health care community to inform policy-makers, health professionals, and other interested observers. Such data are necessary to evaluate, from a comprehensive comparative perspective, the outcomes of the array of health procedures. The following assessment was made in a 1996 report from Alberta Health:

> Up to date, comprehensive information is key to making improvements in health. You simply can't make good decisions without knowing what works and what doesn't or what the impact of changes or new treatments is on the quality of care. Health care providers need to share information about patients so they can make the right decisions.
>
> Right now, we have many pieces of information, lots of records and data, but no consistent approach that gives comparable information to regional health authorities and government. The technology is there to improve health information and the care patients receive, whether it's new networks or other ways of sharing and tracking information. What's needed is leadership and coordination.[11]

Given that the term the 'Information Society' was coined in the mid-1970s, it may be surprising that in the mid-1990s the above quotation describes the state of information holdings and databases existing not in a lesser developed nation or in one of Canada's 'have-not' provinces, but in a 'have' province such as Alberta. The move towards a comprehensive health information system reflects a major policy shift—of paradigmatic proportions—towards an evaluative model of health care, comparable perhaps to the shift from 'medical care', which reflects a reactive approach to illness, to 'health care', which seeks to be preventive in its approach and to foster wellness rather than a primarily curative approach. Such a model requires a comprehensive health information system; without the appropriate data, it is difficult to evaluate the performance of medical procedures and practitioners. It is readily apparent that addressing concerns about the high costs of health care requires financial information about administrative costs. Less readily apparent to politicians, the media, and other agenda setters is the crucial need for clinical information to facilitate evaluation of the procedures and of the health practitioner. As the quotation above indicates, Canadian provincial health databases do not support the evaluation of outcomes. Currently, a patient is likely to have several records, one for each site of care. Data entries into each record are often widely divergent, with little or no standardization. Often, no data are available on ultimate outcomes because the record ends when the patient leaves the hospital or physician's office.

In the collection and use of information, the health care community has been less efficient than other sectors; what is needed is complete, accurate, legible, accessible information based within a national and, eventually, international health information system. Such information would be of interest to clinicians, administrators, researchers, policy-makers, and patients. Such a database would be important for undertaking the following activities: quality assurance; outcomes research; technology assessment; practice guideline development; and cost management. In 1998 information-gathering is often local, fragmented, and incomplete. In health care systems, of course, the lack of information can have life and death implications. For example, federal officials in the US became concerned about the scant information available on the use of nuclear resources in health care only after the media investigated the misuse of radiation therapy. Similarly, scant information and research exist on the side-effects of pharmaceuticals: 'Many serious problems appear only after the drug is approved and marketed more widely.'[12] Charles Silberman observes that:

> physicians do not know the scientifically correct way to practice medicine—not because of personal ignorance or indifference, but because nobody knows; the ignorance is collective, not individual . . . medical science has enjoyed spectacular success in developing new diagnostic tests and treatments but has failed to evaluate the usefulness of those tests and the consequences of those treatments.[13]

Outcomes data are rare and little unbiased research information exists to help physicians decide on which drugs to 'base their choice of therapy'.[14] The need for more and better information is clear, given, for example, deficit-conscious politicians who assert that unnecessary and/or inappropriate services are provided that do not improve health outcomes. Silberman states that there 'is, in fact, remarkably little scientific basis for much of what physicians do; medical science has enjoyed spectacular success in developing new diagnostic tests and treatments but has failed to evaluate the usefulness of those tests and the consequences of those treatments.'[15] How much progress have we made? What will it take to improve the collection and assessment of what should be considered basic 'operational' information?

Improving the quality of care and reducing expenditures are strong incentives to address the dearth of information available to all decision-makers, including the practitioner, the administrator, and the policy-maker. There is no coherent, longitudinal record for most patients. This situation appears to be changing. In 1979 a British physician, Archie Cochrane, criticized the medical profession for failing to establish a system for producing up-to-date summaries of the results of reliable research about the effects of health care procedures; it took over a decade, but in 1993 an international initiative, the Cochrane Collaboration, was founded to respond to his challenge. While 'a massive effort is required to build, maintain and disseminate the database of systematic reviews of health care which Cochrane envisaged, it has become clear that the collaborative spirit required to make efficient progress already exists.'[16] The Canadian

Cochrane Network, a consortium of Canadian health care researchers, promotes and co-ordinates Cochrane Collaboration research activities in Canada. Government agencies seeking to provide health care information in support of policy decisions include the Canadian Co-ordinating Office for Health Technology Assessment (CCOHTA) and the Canadian Institute for Health Information. However, CCOHTA has also been subject to budget underfunding: 'Despite the dedication of its staff, the CCOHTA has been fairly described as a fax machine in a broom closet. . . . Given their budgets and scope, however, all these organizations put together can barely scratch the surface when it comes to conducting evaluations or diffusing their results to decision-makers.'[17] It is one thing to establish agencies mandated to achieve certain policy objectives; it is another to fund them adequately so they can do so.

A comprehensive information network would have the potential to ensure more complete and richer information sources to support better decision-making. In the Canadian federal system, in which there are as many health care systems as there are provinces and territories, interjurisdictional co-operation and co-ordination will be among the most difficult challenges facing the success of such a centre, currently established at McMaster University in Hamilton, Ontario. The challenge is that such an information system requires an unprecedented partnership between the health care community set within an increasingly decentralized federal system. Such a system would also depend on well-developed individual database sites with interconnectivity compatibility.

> Beyond the initial [patient] contact, the organized health care delivery system needs patient care information systems at all inpatient and outpatient locations of service to collect clinical data in standardized formats, using a standardized nomenclature for diagnosis and procedures. . . .
>
> This computer-based patient record will be the integrated regional health care system's most valuable asset, because it is the principal resource for facilitating care of individual patients and informing the *continuous* quality improvement efforts of the system as a whole.[18]

Although the language usage varies greatly in the health informatics literature, there are three main categories of information and communication technologies: (1) transaction systems—such as admission, scheduling, order entry, results reporting, and laboratory systems—which permit real-time updates of electronic databases or patients; (2) analytical or decision support systems, which depend on large databases of patients' records to facilitate interrogation of the data to discover important trends in outcomes and processes of care; (3) communication systems, using local- and wide-area networks (LANs and WANs) that permit the electronic transmission of data (including images) among any number of geographically disparate but connected sites.[19] Together, transaction and communication systems could realize the kinds of fiscal, management, and planning reforms required to improve Canada's health care system.

Reform initiatives that seek to address the interwoven fiscal, administrative, and planning issues must consider the lack of comparable, timely, and accurate information in the health care field. Computer links within health facilities are being established and links between sites are slowly being developed. Throughout North America, newly developed open architecture systems provide health professionals with varying levels of access to direct treatment protocols, patient encounters, reference libraries, and a myriad of data and information from a variety of health providers. The systems being designed will allow data received at one site to be easily transmitted to another location. Such a network will be particularly important for isolated rural areas and Canada's northern communities. The development of a comprehensive electronic information and communication system may be impeded by: the lack of standards; the lack of infrastructure and leadership, both within and between health facilities and across provincial jurisdictions; the costs, including non-technical costs such as education, required to develop, implement, and operate compatible systems for an open architecture infrastructure; legal and regulatory considerations; and resistance to change by those who seek to maintain control over their information domains.

Large-scale hospital information systems became more widespread in the late 1980s. For example, Vancouver General Hospital in British Columbia was one of the first large-scale integrated hospital information systems. Developed in 1986 for the 1,000-bed hospital, it linked together a range of hardware within a large Ethernet local-area network. However, many of those systems remain administrative and managerial systems; movement towards more truly care-oriented systems will likely increase in the late 1990s. The fiscal investment for more sophisticated networks is heavy. For example, St Joseph's Hospital and Medical Centre in New Jersey plugged in its new hospital system in April 1994. The network consumed three years of planning, preparation, and employee training and $25 million in computers, software, and fibre-optic cable.[20] St Joseph's added an artificial intelligence protocol program later in 1994, which compares past patients and procedures with facts in the current case. St Joseph's is unusual in the United States (let alone in Canada, which tends to lag in every sector in the adoption of informatics) in its comprehensive move to a full-blown wired facility. A professor at Indiana University who studies hospital technologies, Dr Clement J. McDonald, states: 'I don't think there's a hospital in the country that doesn't want this—but there's some caution. It's like a brain transplant—that's what it's like putting in a medical records system—hundreds of millions of nerves, all those sources of input.'[21] Sensitive to prevailing cultures and traditions, physicians will not be required to use the system if they do not want to; paper records and charts will still circulate. Further, cognizant of and sensitive to confidentiality issues, some functions will not be wired into the system; for example, tests for HIV will not be entered on the network because of the recognition that the system cannot be fully secure. In wiring across existing information and communication gaps ICT can, knowingly or not, short-circuit privacy and other legal requirements.

Several technological initiatives in Canada have sparked some public debate. There have been a number of provincial efforts to fill some of the information gaps in provincial health systems. One such initiative involved the development of a 'service encounter system', the Ontario Encounter Card Pilot Project. It was designed to provide the means by which standardized information on patients' encounters throughout the health care delivery system could be collected and aggregated. Such information would allow analyses to be undertaken that should enable better policy planning and research. To fill the information gap, the system would record patients' health care uses, including visits to physicians, hospitals, and other professionals such as pharmacists and physiotherapists. The pilot project was tested in the Rainy River district of northwestern Ontario and included the towns of Fort Frances and Emo. The participating agencies were: a hospital; two clinics/medical centres; four pharmacies; a district health council; two homecare groups; laboratories; and an optometry group. The project was designed to test 'the collection of service encounter information using advanced card technology (the so-called 'smart card'). . . . This smart card is portable, ensures confidentiality, and can be used to provide current vital medical information and encounter history'.[22] Various health care providers in Fort Frances and Emo, Ontario, were invited to participate in a six-month project using a sample population of 2,000–3,000 patient volunteers from their communities. Significantly, one of the project's objectives was to examine professional and societal issues surrounding the collection of health information using smart-card technology. The card contained three levels of information: biographical information, including emergency contact information; health status information, including significant test results and family illnesses; and service encounter history, including medications, optometry, and other health service provided. The premise and promise of the project included:

- empowering patients by giving them an accurate, timely record of their health problems;
- improving the communication within and among provider groups;
- enhancing the planning capabilities of the public policy-makers;
- providing to professional bodies the information needed for quality assurance and the development of new standards and guidelines for caregiving;
- providing higher-quality information needed for health care research.[23]

While there is the potential for improving information to policy-makers, administrators, and physicians, as well as for patients themselves, the potential also exists for a slow erosion of the standards and freedoms we may take for granted, such as the privacy of information, controlled access to patient information, the evaluation of the reliability of information sources, and the protection of professional autonomy. Of these issues, privacy is afforded the greatest media attention.

Privacy Considerations

Sensitivity to privacy and access issues was a high priority in the Fort Frances project, and Ontario's Office of the Privacy and Access Commissioner worked with the project planners. The Fort Frances project was only one of several smart-card pilot projects; others include the Canadian Forces Individually Carried Medical Record, the Green Shield Smart Card Project, and the New Brunswick Health Card Project. The Alberta provincial government estimated that the card would save between $25 and $30 million in laboratory costs alone by allowing patients to 'carry' the results of previous medical tests with them, thereby avoiding unnecessary duplication. In June 1995, it was expected that the system would involve approximately '6,000 sites (largely at doctors' offices, pharmacies and hospitals), it would cost about $30 to $40 million a year in technology and telephone line charges. . . . On top of that, cards for 2.5 million Albertans would cost Alberta Health from $1 to $5 each depending on how sophisticated they [the cards] are.'[24] Like the Fort Frances pilot project, different health officials would have different levels of access to a patient's medical record. Like the Ontario pilot project, privacy became a public issue, and across the country, smart cards were dubbed 'Big Brother's little electronic helpers'. The first words of a *Calgary Herald* editorial stated that the 'problem with smart cards is that they are anything but' and cautions: 'It's not the technology Albertans should be concerned about, but the reasons why government—and anyone else interested in your personal health—is eager for that information . . . it's also a window for the government on the relationship between you and your doctor.'[25]

The concern about privacy is an issue that crosses borders. A US National Research Council panel reported in March 1997 that the 'computerized medical records of millions of Americans are vulnerable to misuse and abuse, but few people recognize the extent of the problem and little is being done to improve the security of those files'; importantly, the chairman of the panel stated that 'Efforts must focus on finding ways to maintain privacy rather than opposing the use of information technology in health care.'[26] Reports of privacy invasions abound, and they are not always maliciously guided; for example, in March 1997 a woman who purchased a used IBM PC found 2,000 patient records when she turned on the computer.[27] Such security concerns and policy implications exist in a world in which individual health information is becoming an increasingly profitable commodity.

In Canada, the federal government and most provincial governments have privacy and access legislation covering government data banks, both electronic and paper; there is, however, some debate as to whether adequate resources are given to privacy and access officers. For example, on 29 September 1993 a proposal from the New Brunswick government to save $300 million in health care costs was reported in the *Globe and Mail*. Premier Frank McKenna proposed to relinquish the administration of the provincial health system to insurance companies in the private sector. The processing of private health information would be facilitated by issuing residents 'a personal identification card with a magnetic stripe containing basic health information'.[28] The Premier offered assurances that confidentiality would be guaranteed. Past experience does not reinforce one's confidence. We live in an age when privacy is for sale. If the Canadian health care system becomes more exposed to the involvement of insurance companies, then personal health records may become less secure. In a wired health community, the lines between right to access and right to privacy become increasingly blurred. Equally problematic is the fact that computerized information systems make it difficult to determine violations of a patient's privacy, since one can obtain personal information without anyone knowing.

Ownership of one's patient record is clear after a decision by the Supreme Court of Canada on 11 June 1992. Until then, only health practitioners directly involved in a patient's treatment had legal access to the patient's record. *McInerney v. MacDonald* resulted in the Court's ruling that 'a patient is entitled to examine and copy all information in his or her medical records which the physician considered in administering advice or treatment, including records prepared by other doctors which the physician may have received.'[29] This ruling gives patients the opportunity to ensure that their records contain accurate, complete information. Medical information is increasingly valuable. In the workplace, more is monitored than key strikes, e-mail messages, and phone calls. Employers are now interested in one's ability to concentrate, one's predisposition to error and to health risk, and one's truthfulness; the electronic era is one in which employers want to measure employees' brainwaves and undertake drug testing, genetic screening, and polygraph tests. Large corporations in the United States are finding that their investment in 'wellness centres' (health and medical facilities provided to employees) is reaping rewards beyond healthier and happier employees; in addition, they are able to access the physiological and psychological records of their employees. In this new context the privacy of computerized patient records must be considered.

Access Considerations Arising from Information Systems

An often overlooked decision-maker in the health care process is the patient. A comprehensive database would be useful in moving towards a new paradigm of health care whereby the role of the patient would change from passive recipient of treatment to one in which the patient plays an important role in decision-making. The new information and communications environment is giving individuals an opportunity to take control over their health. Much has been written about the ability of the World Wide Web to reduce temporal and spatial barriers. In the realm of health care, this means that if a person wants to know the benefits and drawbacks of different treatment options, she or he can now turn to a flood of health information available on-line; hundreds of hospitals, universities, medical groups, and government research organizations have created health-related sites on the Web. The popularity of on-line health sites is rising, according to a senior associate, Dr Tom Ferguson, at the Center for Clinical Computing at Harvard University Medical School; further, health-related chat groups offer support, empathy, and the opportunity to share personal experiences.[30] As in any study of the potential of ICT, there are negative implications to consider as well. Anyone who surfs the Net knows the importance of checking the site carefully to determine the source, the accuracy of the information, and its timeliness. In the new electronic frontier:

> Anyone can put information on the Internet stating or implying that they are a qualified doctor, but there is no way to be sure. . . . Unverified stories abound regarding pharmaceutical producers going online anonymously to promote their drugs and bring discredit on their competitors' products, or of spiritually driven self-healing groups spreading their beliefs.[31]

In addition to these concerns, the ease of access of the Internet to such information resources should not be assumed to be widely shared among the population. In the post-industrial society, information 'of all kinds and forms is increasingly being made into a commodity for sale.'[32] Concerns about the emergence of a two-tier health system in Canadian provinces focus attention on access to health care services; in the Information Society, we must also consider equitable access to health information.

Gender Considerations in New Digital Health Processes

There may be fiscal savings to be gained from investment in such technologies. One argument, for example, is that 'when occupational health nurses are earning $25,000 to $35,000, it is expensive to not use a computer. . . . Over time, the computer would pay for itself in freeing the nurse to provide professional service rather than manipulate data.'[33] However, in *Vanishing Jobs*, the authors state that while such systems can introduce new cost efficiency measures, the 'downside is the increased percentage of professional time spent on record keeping, rather than on patient care.'[34] Professional autonomy may be on the cutting edge. The fiscal imperative, scientific management, and technological dynamism may mean that fragmentation and loss of control are part of a more sweeping transformation of the hospital labour process. Sociologist Jerry White maintains that an 'intensification' of the labour process in health care has affected everyone, from the patient whose 'turnaround time' is reduced to the decrease in the number of nurses being employed for patient load. He states: 'The final change in intensification has been in the monitoring of "productivity," with computers used to keep track of the procedures done, and the time it takes to execute them. This creates a "for productivity" rather than a "for care" orientation, a setup the nurses have found totally unsatisfactory.'[35]

Nurses are asked to do more with less, and faster, too. 'The new technologies, which are part of the patient classification, and machine-generated "care" plans contribute to a change in what the nurse does. Particularly important is the reduction in the skilled judgements that nurses were trained to carry out.'[36] Marie Campbell's concerns a decade ago remain valid in 1997; she carefully explains why trying to establish a 'minimum data set' of nurses' knowledge is neither a rational nor a trustworthy undertaking. Nurses across the country would likely agree more than ever in 1997 that their 'work and the time, energy, individual skills and sensitivity it takes are overlooked in systematic accounts.'[37] Such systems need to capture nursing's product; however, what is recorded in the system is only that part of their labour that is a quantifiable and visible result of the patient care they deliver. It is important to note that the definitions of 'nurses' labour', upon which new ICT systems are based, tend to focus solely on the quantifiable result; too little effort has been made to recognize the qualitative aspects of the caregiving nurses provide.

As in other professional settings such as social work, computerization tends to emphasize and value that which is quantifiable. In a decade in which narrow economic notions of efficiency are paramount, that which cannot be objectified or standardized tends to be undervalued. Further fragmentation and loss of autonomy are not unique to health care. Resistance may arise since health providers, like other 'helping professionals' such as social workers, have high degrees of pluralism and non-conformity. 'Professional groups and program units develop their own definition, language and, to some degree, procedures. Attempts to bring these features into a single format suitable to the information system can generate strong resistance.'[38] Can professionals organize to resist the standardization of their work processes? Will the introduction of computers into the 'helping professions' such as health, education, and social work become all high-tech and no-touch? Without attention to considerations such as those explored here technology can compound existing human resource, structural, and procedural problems and, as indicated, may introduce new problems, constraints, and even inequities. Technology is not an easy 'quick fix'.

Putting the Byte on Medical Know-how: A Case Study of APACHE III

Just as there are some serious concerns within the nursing community about the adoption of ICT, so, too, are there reservations about the implications of automation for the patient-physician relationship. The most serious questions arise with the introduction of expert and knowledge-based systems, computer systems that are claimed to embody the knowledge and expertise of physicians. Medical expert systems are designed to offer explicit diagnostic and therapeutic advice. A typical expert system is built on the following three foundations: (1) a knowledge base containing commonly agreed-upon facts that are general to the policy domain, and heuristics (the rules of good judgement within the domain); (2) a strategy for knowledge representation to encode the knowledge within the domain; (3) an inference engine or a problem-solving methodology. Systems such as MYCIN and INTERNIST are early successes that represent the enormous (and costly) efforts undertaken in the past 30 years to mimic human experts. MYCIN diagnoses meningitis and blood infections and recommends treatment. INTERNIST is an instructional system developed by a doctor to diagnose disease; his motivation was that written communication was too limiting a medium for sharing his expertise.

The use of knowledge-based and expert systems in health care settings introduces a new set of complex issues. One of the problems evident with both MYCIN and INTERNIST has been how quickly such systems become outdated. In addition, if it is agreed that the practice of medicine is as much an art as a science, then dependency on rule-based expert systems may not be wise. As with other computer systems, too often medical expert systems are still considered to be neutral, objective, and fail-safe, yet there are reasons to question each of these alleged features. Assessing the reliability of expert systems in most policy domains, including defence expert systems, is difficult since there are no procedures available 'to test all constellations in all environments'.[39] Wyatt and Spiegelhalter caution that 'only about 10 percent of the many medical knowledge-based systems that have been described over the years have been tested in laboratory conditions.'[40] So-called 'fuzzy logic' systems reflect the attempt to imitate physicians' subjective and judgemental decision-making processes. David Gerlernter, an expert in artificial intelligence at Yale University, offers the following assessment:

> The cases in the database are simulations of the memories of particular cases or experiences that are stored inside a human expert's head. Weak and feeble simulation: When an expert remembers a patient, he doesn't remember a mere list of words. He remembers an experience, a whole galaxy of related perceptions. . . . For human beings, in other words, remembering isn't merely retrieving, it is re-experiencing. . . .

> We want our Mirror Worlds [artificial universes] to 'remember' intelligently—to draw just the right precedent or two from a huge database. But human beings draw on reason and emotion when they perform an act of remembering. An emotion can be a concise, nuanced shorthand for a whole tangle of facts and perceptions that you never bothered to sort out. . . .
>
> Mind-stuff consists of rational and emotional strands densely interwoven. Your intellectual faculties depend on your emotions and not merely your 'reason.' And these are issues that AI (artificial intelligence) rarely confronts.[41]

That said, there are also potential benefits from the use of this technology, such as: reduction of errors in physicians' practice; standardization of the medical practice, which, as stated earlier, varies significantly; faster, more consistent decisions about therapy; and delivery of expert decision-making to environments where human expertise is lacking (rural areas, Third World countries). Because knowledge-based and expert system technology is relatively new, information concerning the impact of its introduction into health care settings is sparse. One notable exception is the APACHE III system for predicting mortality of patients in hospital intensive care units.

APACHE III, which stands for Acute Physiology Age Chronic Health Evaluation, is a computer system designed to assist physicians in predicting outcomes of adult critically ill patients. It is not a typical expert system with rules and an inference engine but is claimed to function equivalently to human physicians. Begun in 1978 and now in its third version, APACHE III looks at 27 pieces of information for each patient: patient origin (direct admissions, ICU readmission, operating room), admissions diagnosis, physiology variables (temperature, heart rate, blood pressure, glucose levels, etc.), chronic health, age, and surgical status (elective or emergency). These pieces of information are mapped into a database of 17,440 real-life profiles of intensive care patients. The system produces a daily mortality projection for each patient. For example, if Sally Smith is a patient in the ICU and her mortality projection for today is 75 per cent, this means that 75 per cent of patients in her situation died in the ICU. Trends are important and are shown as a graph. If yesterday's mortality projection for Sally was 83 per cent, this means that her status is improving; she is benefiting from care. APACHE III's projections have been shown to be reliably accurate. In one study, the system predicted that 20 per cent of 850 critically ill patients would die, while physicians predicted that 25 per cent would die. The actual death rate was 21 per cent.[42] Another study reports that 'within 24 hours of an ICU admission, 95 percent of patients admitted to ICUs have a risk estimate [made by APACHE III] for hospital death within three percent of that observed. The remaining 5 percent of ICU admissions have mortality projections within 19 percent of observed.'[43] These studies suggest that the computer system is able to make projections with an accuracy comparable to that of humans.

APACHE III is currently being used in 41 hospitals in the United States and in 38 hospitals outside of the US; it is not currently used in Canada. The primary reason for its adoption is to control costs. In the US, critical care accounts for one-third or more of hospital costs for mid- to large-size hospitals and costs three to five times more than care provided on a medical/surgical floor. It is expected to exceed 50 per cent by the year 2000. Critical care in the US consumes nearly US $50 billion annually, with elderly critical care patients comprising the fastest growing group. With costs soaring, there is increasing demand for use management, that is, for matching true patient need with diagnosis and treatment and for monitoring the outcome. According to Charles Watts, head of the ICU at St Joseph Mercy Hospital in Michigan, which is using APACHE III, the system can help ensure that patients get the treatment they need, and no more. 'We want to define entitlement to critical care as the ability to respond to treatment.'[44]

APACHE III exemplifies one sort of knowledge-based system. The goal of the system is simply to produce reliable projections of mortality; system designers do not claim a correlation between the algorithms of the system and the mental processes of physicians making projections of mortality. Expert systems are another sort of knowledge system. The process of inferencing or chaining of rules is claimed to be functionally equivalent to the mental processes that human experts go through as they solve problems in a particular domain. While these two sorts of knowledge-based systems represent different approaches to providing computerized decision support, they share a common attribute of being designed and developed to provide knowledgeable assistance to decision-making domains that are knowledge-intensive. Thus, their design, development, marketing, and use raise similar issues.

Ethical Implications of Medical Expert Systems

As computerized decision support systems such as APACHE III proliferate in clinical settings, questions are being raised about their proper use. Who is responsible for a decision that has an undesirable effect, when the decision was made with computerized assistance? What is the appropriate division of labour between human and machine? Are there any health care domains in which computerized decision support is inappropriate? To address such questions, Figure 1 identifies the participants involved in the process of computer-assisted decision-making in health care settings and itemizes what it is that they do; the systems under consideration are on the knowledge-intensive end of the scale.

Firstly, a team conceives, designs, and develops knowledge-based systems. Knowledge engineers are responsible for working with those who have the relevant knowledge (usually physicians) and structuring that knowledge so that it can be programmed into a computer. Programmers write the code that runs the computer. A software company funds and manages the development project.

☐ Figure 1: Participants in Computer-Assisted Decision-Making

	Knowledge Engineers	Experts	Programmers	Software Companies	Vendors	Consumers	Hospitals	Physicians	Patients
Concept & Design	•	•	•	•					
Programming	•	•	•	•					
Marketing Selling Purchase					•	•	•	•	
Installation Customization				•	•	•	•	•	
Use				•		•	•		•

Vendors market, sell, customize, and install the knowledge-based system for general consumers, hospitals, and physicians. This large group of participants makes it especially difficult to answer questions concerning moral responsibility in specific instances.

The conception and design of knowledge-based and expert systems raise a number of troubling questions. Firstly, human expertise is largely tacit.[45] Physicians who have developed clinical expertise through years of experience know a lot, but they are notoriously poor at articulating that knowledge; that is, they do not know what they know.[46] This suggests that the knowledge represented in expert systems is likely to be incomplete. Secondly, physician expertise is limited and fallible. Thus, even if developers are able to elicit all of a physician's or group of physicians' expertise, the computer's knowledge base will be inherently incomplete. Thirdly, while the goal of knowledge-based and expert systems is to function in a manner equivalent to the thought processes of human experts, the knowledge representation in the computer system does not—and cannot yet—replicate those processes, despite the fact that an IBM-developed computer, Deep Blue, defeated world chess champion Gary Kasparov on 11 April 1997; the computative aspect of thinking is only one facet of human intellectual currency.

The systems being designed and developed are therefore known to be fallible because the knowledge they contain is fallible. Who, then, is responsible for a medical decision that has an undesirable effect, when the decision was made with computerized assistance? It is the role of the physician using the system to make diagnostic decisions, but responsibility for the system assisting in that decision is distributed across a large group of players: system designers, programmers, vendors, health care organizations, and the numerous individuals involved in the delivery of health care services—nurses, physicians' assistants, and the physicians themselves. Bearing in mind the complexities of assigning blame to those who conceive, develop, install, and customize decision support systems, as well as that the use of such systems can result in better decisions, greater access to medical care, and cost reductions, let us look to the user of such systems as the final locus of responsibility.

If computers are to serve as partners in medical decision-making, the manner in which human beings use such computers will be critical from a moral perspective. The difference between computer decision-making and computerized decision support is of critical importance, but the line between them is not always clear. There is an easy, but potentially invisible, transition from (1) consulting a decision support system such as APACHE III for a projection considered as 'one more piece of information', to (2) placing greater emphasis on the system's projection than on other pieces of information, to (3) basing a decision primarily on the system's projection, and finally to (4) letting the system 'make the decision'.

APACHE III Revisited

A careful look at the specifics of the experience with APACHE III may help us begin to answer some of the questions we have raised. APACHE III was designed to be the ideal partner in decision-making. It has knowledge of the facts and an ability to recall and use the facts appropriately. APACHE III is impartial—colour-blind, sex-blind, age-blind, and insurance-blind. In addition, it is immune to illness, fatigue, and stress. Indeed, William Knaus, the developer of APACHE III, insists that the human and machine together are more powerful than either alone.[47] Bearing in mind that machines already make many decisions for us— just think about the automatic transmission on your car, or the controls of the last airplane you boarded—exactly what is the outstanding problem with APACHE III? A strong argument can be made that the only significant ethical issue is how the system is used; practices can be designed that will go a long way towards ensuring that APACHE III and systems like it are used in an ethically responsible manner.

APACHE III knows and remembers a lot—27 facts concerning each of approximately 18,000 patients—and the accuracy of the projections the system makes is impressive. However, there are many facts that APACHE III does not know. It does not know what might be called 'the look and feel' of the patient. Martin Vessey, professor of social and community medicine at the University of Oxford, expresses this by suggesting that intensive care medicine is as much an art as a science, and that physicians develop a clinical acumen that cannot be duplicated by a computer program.[48] Alistair Short, director of the ICU at Broomfield Hospital in Chelmsford, England, is more emphatic. 'Forget it. . . . With APACHE you can give a probability, but you can't give a prediction. All you are doing is being a bookie.'[49] In addition, APACHE III does not know its own limitations; it does not know what it does not know. None the less, this situation may be acceptable as long as the physicians who use the system are aware of these limitations and as long as the system is used as it was designed to be used, as a decision support system. In other words, if the system is properly positioned, we may be able to rely on humans to remember and factor in the limits of APACHE III's knowledge.

The projections of APACHE III are numbers, and 'there are times when personal numbers can be reassuring', according to Thomas Gravelyn, a pulmonary specialist involved in the management of the patients of the ICU of the Catherine McAuley Hospital in Ann Arbor, Michigan.[50] While this may be true, it is also true that numbers must be interpreted by both physicians and their families. Families bring their own interpretive contexts—their hopes, their fears, and their biases—and they must be helped to understand what the numbers mean. We must even question our own understanding of what the numbers mean. There may be a significant difference in being told that 70 per cent of the patients who have been in your spouse's situation have died and being told that 30 per cent of the patients who have been in your spouse's situation have lived. Research indicates that the way predictive percentages are worded or 'framed' can significantly affect decision-making.[51] And why are we so eager to hear a number? While a number may simplify an exceedingly complex situation, it also opens the door to oversimplification. All of these considerations reinforce the importance of maintaining a human/machine decision-making team with an appropriate division of labour. Physicians must learn to 'read into' APACHE III's projections and apply their own judgement accordingly. This can be done, as evidenced by physicians who report a case in which the life of a patient with a low APACHE III score, a 4 per cent chance of not dying in the ICU, was saved after her condition deteriorated rapidly. 'The lesson in a case like this is: Don't ever get lulled into complacency by a low number. Four percent is a real number. It has magnitude', comments the ICU director at Catherine McAuley Hospital.[52]

APACHE III is a tool, at least by design; it was not designed to be a decision-maker. As William Knaus puts it, 'It isn't thinking. It's remembering.'[53] Be that as it may, do we really know what we are doing when we use this tool? Remember Gerlernter's claim that computer memories in this domain are 'feeble'. As noted earlier, a tool is just a tool, but it can be used for good or ill. While it is easy to see how some tools are used, it is not so easy with APACHE III because decision-making goes on in the privacy of the mind. We can take some comfort from the fact that most physicians are initially sceptical of the APACHE III projection, and all indications are that use of the system is currently accompanied by thoughtful discussion.[54] It seems fair to ask, however, what will prevent the invisible progression from consulting the system for one more piece of information to letting APACHE III 'make the decision'. Turning the decision-making responsibility over to a machine, without public discussion, is surely an abdication of our moral responsibilities.

Perhaps we can create an ethically appropriate niche for APACHE III and all systems like it, a niche that would make decision-making 'public' and thereby ensure an ethically appropriate division of labour between human and machine. One way to do this would be to require 'public' rationales for decisions to alter or terminate care. Rationales would include consideration of what information is known and used in the decision, and what sorts of information are not known and therefore not used in the decision. Rationales would be written and discussed with all parties involved in or affected by the decision—ICU physicians and family members, at the very least. In critical care decision-making, there is a need for as much information as possible, and the APACHE III projection is an important and useful piece of information. Requiring 'public' rationales is one step towards ensuring that all information is used appropriately and that no information is given more weight than it deserves.

Conclusion

There are few comprehensive analyses of the non-technical issues that arise with the increasingly widespread use of powerful, sophisticated information and communication systems in health care. Study of the public policy, legal, ethical, organizational, professional, gender, and other issues tends to be fragmented and case-specific. Many questions merit examination. For example, will a new class of information worker arise within health care facilities to act as a buffer? If so, they could become new guardians or gatekeepers of data, information, and knowledge about sophisticated systems. What will be the potential impact of the increasing use of expert systems in medical education? How are heavy investments in costly expert systems affecting the allocation of scarce resources? While attention in this paper has been on some of the negative side-effects that may accompany the adoption of powerful technology in health care, the promise of the technology is enormous. The need for more and better information and communication at all levels in the health care system could be supported by the technology. The concern is that there is a tendency for the technology to aggravate existing organizational, gender, and other problems. Strategic initiatives are needed to place issues such as those discussed in this chapter at a priority level at least comparable with the objective of attaining greater cost efficiencies. The rapid development of medical informatics must be accompanied by timely public policy responses that reflect thoughtful attention to the legal, ethical, gender, and other considerations.

Notes

1 Dr Mike Nelson, NHN Consulting Group, 'Health Promotion and New Information Technologies', submitted to Health Canada.
   http://hppb1.hwc.ca/healthpromotion/pube/infotech/infotech4.htm [5 Mar. 1997.]

2 Shoshana Zuboff, *In the Age of the Smart Machine: The Future of Work and Power* (New York: Basic Books, 1984).

3 See, for example: Jennifer Daryl Slack and Fred Fejes, eds, *The Ideology of the Information Age* (Norwood, NJ: Ablex, 1987); Edward Wenk, Jr, *Tradeoffs: Imperatives of Choice in a High-Tech World* (Baltimore: Johns Hopkins University Press, 1989); Langdon Winner, *Autonomous Technology: Technics-out-of-Control as a Theme in Political Thought* (Cambridge, Mass.: MIT Press, 1977); Langdon Winner, *The Whale and the Reactor* (Chicago: University of Chicago Press, 1986).

4 Jeremy Rifkin, *The End of Work: The Decline of the Global Labour Force and the Dawn of the Post-Market Era* (New York: G.P. Putnam's Sons, 1995), 158.

5 C.J. Alexander, 'Putting the Byte on Canadian Social Welfare Agencies', *Computers and Society*, Special Issue (Oct. 1990): 18.

6 Robert Ramsay, 'What if it were called Men's College Hospital?', *Globe and Mail*, 8 May 1997, A21.

7 Canadian Medical Association, *Highlights from CMA News* (Mar. 1997).
   http://www.cma.ca/news/cmanews/vol-7mar06e.htm [5 Mar. 1997.]

8 Ibid. (Apr. 1997). http://www.cma.ca/news/cmanews/vol-7/apr04a-e.htm [5 Mar. 1997.]

9 James M. Gabler, 'Caught with Your LAN Down: Security Issues in an Age of Networks', *Health Care Informatics* (Feb. 1993): 26.

10 Samuel C. Fleming and Ho Seung Joun, 'Opportunities in Health Care Information Systems', *Spectrum: Information Systems Industry* 91 (31 Dec. 1996), on-line abstract, no page number.
   http://www.dresources.com/abst.htm [5 Mar. 1997.]

11 *Edmonton Journal Online*, 'Issues', drawn from the Alberta Department of Health report, 'Action on Health', 26 Nov. 1996. http://www.southam.com/edmontonjournal/issues/edhealth/11269 6report.html#tech [3 Feb. 1997.]

12 Raymond L. Wesley, 'A Prescription for Better Prescriptions', *Issues in Science and Technology* (Spring 1994): 60.

13 Charles E. Silberman, 'Providing Patient-Centered Care', *Health Management Quarterly* (1992): 12.

14 Wesley, 'A Prescription for Better Prescriptions', 59.

15 Silberman, 'Providing Patient-Centered Care', 12.

16 The Cochrane Collaboration Informatics Methods Group and the Health Information Research Unit, McMaster University, *The Cochrane Collaboration*, Overview, last updated 16 Sept. 1996.
   http://hiru.mcmaster.ca/cochrane/overview.htm#The_Need_for_More_Reliable_Reviews_of_Re [5 March 1997.]

17 Michael Rachlis and Carol Kushner, *Strong Medicine: How To Save Canada's Health Care System* (Toronto: HarperCollins, 1994), 112.

18 Marshall Ruffin, M.D., 'Medical Informatics', *Health Care Forum Journal* (Mar./Apr. 1993): 49. Emphasis added.

19 Ibid.

20   Kirk Johnson, 'Like a Light Bulb Going On, Hospital to Computerize', *New York Times*, 8 Apr. 1994, B2.

21   Ibid.

22   Ontario Ministry of Health, 'Backgrounder on Planning and Managing Health Care', no date, 3.

23   For an assessment of the Fort Frances project, see Christel A. Woodward and Lynn Curry, 'The Health Encounter Card Pilot Project: An Innovation in Health Care', in S. Mathwin Davis, ed., *Health Care: Innovation, Impact and Challenge* (Kingston, Ont.: Queen's University, School of Policy Studies/School of Public Administration, 1992).

24   Robert Walker, '"Smart Cards" To Cut Health Costs', *Edmonton Journal Online*, 15 June 1995. http://www.southam.com/edmontonjournal/archives/0103sma9.htm [5 Mar. 1997.]

25   *Calgary Herald*, editorial, 'Mind Your Business: Beware of Trusting Your Health History to So-Called "Smart Cards"', *Edmonton Journal Online*, extra section, 12 Nov. 1995. http://www.southam.com/edmontonjournal/archives/0103sma1.htm [5 Mar. 1997.]

26   Warren E. Leary, 'Panel Cites Lack of Security on Medical Records', *New York Times* online, Cybertimes section, 6 Mar. 1997.

27   John Markoff, 'Patient Files Turn Up in Used Computer', *New York Times* online, Cybertimes section, 4 Apr. 1997.

28   'Private Sector to Run N.B. Medicare System', *Globe and Mail*, 29 Sept. 1993, A11.

29   Jeffrey Sack and Georgina Pickett, 'Supreme Court Addresses Patient Access to Records, the Nature of the Physician/Patient Relationship', *Ontario Medical Review* (July 1992): 53.

30   Susan Gilbert, 'On-Line Tips about Health Offer Mountains of Gems and Junk', *New York Times* online, Cybertimes section, 10 Apr. 1996.

31   Bruno Guissani, 'Searching for Reliable Medical Information on the Web', *New York Times* online, Eurobytes section, 8 Apr. 1997.

32   Nelson, 'Health Promotion and New Information Technologies'.

33   Eileen Nosko Lukes and Joy E. Wachs, 'Use of Computers among Occupational Health Nurses', *American Association of Occupational Health Nurses Journal* 40 (Aug. 1992): 369.

34   Lars Osberg, Fred Wein, and Jan Grude, *Vanishing Jobs: Canada's Changing Workplace* (Toronto: James Lorimer, 1995), 144.

35   Jerry White, 'Changing Labour Process and the Nursing Crisis in Canadian Hospitals', *Studies in Political Economy* 40 (Spring 1993): 109.

36   Ibid., 110.

37   Marie L. Campbell, 'Productivity in Canadian Nursing: Administering Cuts', in David Coburn et al., eds, *Health and Canadian Society*, 2nd edn (Richmond Hill, Ont.: Fitzhenry & Whiteside, 1987), 467.

38   Richard Caputo, *Management and Information Systems in Human Services: Implications for the Distribution of Authority and Decision Making* (New York: Haworth Press, 1988), 119.

39   K. Piwernetz and U. Fischer, 'What Are Computers and Models Good For? Pros and Cons', *Computer Methods and Programs in Biomedicine* 32 (1990): 174.

40   J. Wyatt and D. Spiegelhalter, 'Evaluating Medical Expert Systems: What to Test and How?', *Medical Informatics* 15 (1990): 206.

41   David Gelernter, *Mirror Worlds or: The Day Software Puts the Universe in a Shoebox . . . How It Will Happen and What It Will Mean* (New York: Oxford University Press, 1991), 149–51.

42   Rachel Nowak, 'A Matter of Life and Death', *New Scientist*, 18 Dec. 1993, 12–13.

43 C. Watts, 'Calculating the Odds: Patients, Outcome Probabilities and ICUs', *Health Care Informatics* (Sept. 1992): 40.

44 Susan FitzGerald, 'When a Computer Can Calculate a Critical Patient's Chances', *Philadelphia Inquirer*, 7 May 1992, A1.

45 Michael Polanyi, *The Tacit Dimension* (Garden City, NY: Doubleday, 1966).

46 See, for example, E. Carroll, 'The Role of Tacit Knowledge in Problem Solving in the Clinical Setting', *Nurse Education Today* 8 (1988): 140–7; G.M. Goldman, 'The Tacit Dimension of Clinical Judgment', *Yale Journal of Biological Medicine* 63 (1990): 47–61.

47 Kay Schwerzler, 'Help in the ICU', *Physicians and Computers* (1992): 30–2.

48 Nowak, 'A Matter of Life and Death', 12–13.

49 Ibid.

50 D. Brown, 'Computers' "Second Opinions" Help Guide Medical Treatment', *Washington Post*, 1 Jan. 1992, A1, A8, A9.

51 Barbara McNeil, Stephen Pauker, and Amos Tversky, 'On the Framing of Medical Decisions', in Raiffa Bell and Amos Tversky, eds, *Decisionmaking* (Cambridge: Cambridge University Press, 1988).

52 Brown, 'Computers' "Second Opinions"'.

53 D.N. Staff, 'The 2nd Opinion', *Detroit News*, 24 Feb. 1992, 11A–12A.

54 FitzGerald, 'When a Computer Can Calculate a Critical Patient's Chances'.

Chapter 12

INFORMATION TECHNOLOGY FOR INDIGENOUS PEOPLES: THE NORTH AMERICAN EXPERIENCE

James H. May

It was once said that freedom of the press belongs to those who own one. Democracy for the indigenous is elusive. Democracy, and with it literacy and productivity, demands that the tribes and small nations take control of their information resources. That requires governmental support in enhancing indigenous information systems, including publishing, multimedia production, library service, and links.

External information systems have developed and are continuing to develop that intrude on Native cultures with or without Native input. External information systems can destroy indigenous cultures if information fails to be tailored to meet community needs and support the survival of individual cultures. Indigenous peoples must join the Information Age.

Historical Context

Contrary to what most people assume, indigenous peoples in the Western hemisphere are not new to libraries, publishing, literacy, or education. Nor, for that matter, are indigenous peoples throughout the world. It is just that the form may be different. In the Americas a long tradition of library, information, and communication services exists. The Mayans, Aztecs, and Incas had excellent information and communication systems, superior in numerous respects to what the Europeans had at the time. The Mayans had libraries of printed materials. Indians used foot power where now electronic means are available. Coded messages were carried by relay runners among the Incas. In North America, Aboriginal people had distance communication through the often caricatured smoke signals. They were, in reality, one of the first digital communication systems with 'on/off' signalling. In more recent times Native Americans also had substantial publishing systems.

Cherokees, for example, began a newspaper over 160 years ago. Using a syllabic spelling system developed by Sequoyah, their publishing continued and still continues today. Other tribes have published in their own languages and in English. By 1826 Cherokees as a whole had better than 90 per cent literacy in their language while the Euro-Americans surrounding them had a far lower rate; the Keetoowah band of Cherokees still uses this language today. Over the 20-year period after the forced removal to Indian Territory (today's Oklahoma) and before the American Civil War, one Cherokee press alone produced more than 14 million pages, including 250,000 schoolbooks. Sadly, hardly a page is to be found in any US library. The Cherokee Nation established the first women's college west of the Mississippi in 1851 and had one of the best school systems in the country. With statehood began a literacy decline both in English and in Cherokee.

The Cree and Inuit peoples of Canada have had considerable success with Native language literacy and publishing as well, for reasons very similar to those of the Cherokee. They also have syllabic spelling systems that are well adapted to their languages and are, in fact, simpler and easier to learn than that of Sequoyah.

A resurgence of Native publishing for small nations of the indigenous is occurring around the world. In the United States the Native American Language Act has helped.[1] It requires that any federally funded program provide equal treatment for indigenous languages in areas where they are spoken. A small but growing body of Native writers is also developing. Many tribes now have their own regular publications in their own languages or, more typically, bilingually in English and the Aboriginal language.

Only recently has there been a global recognition of the information needs of indigenous peoples. Some of this has been sparked by the declaration of 1993 as the International Year of the World's Indigenous People by the United Nations to address the plight of an estimated 300 million people in more than 70 countries. Yet, one has to look hard to ferret out any mention of information technology as a vital tool in the survival of small peoples and nations. The Draft United Nations Declaration on the Rights of Indigenous Peoples was last revised in 1993 but discussion continues on a number of fronts.[2] A Decade of the World's Indigenous People (1995–2004) proclaimed by the General Assembly in its resolution 48/163 was launched on 8 December 1994. Under the theme 'Indigenous people: a new relationship—partnership in action', the main goal is to further cultivate the partnership promoted between indigenous people and the international community during the International Year.[3] It will provide a time-frame to build on the results and lessons of the International Year. Remarkably, the proclamations and progress reports of these efforts make little or no mention of the need for technological infrastructure, access, and support.

The one area where discussion does occur is around the protection of the intellectual property of the indigenous. A few relevant statements are found in one UN document entitled 'Principles and Guidelines for the Protection of the Heritage of Indigenous People', published in 1995. Of these, two are most important:

> 17. Governments, international organizations and private institutions should support the development of regional and global networks for the exchange of information and experience among indigenous peoples in the fields of science, culture, education and the arts, including support for systems of electronic information and mass communication.

> 29. National laws should ensure that the use of traditional languages in education, arts and the mass media is respected and, to the extent possible, promoted and strengthened.[4]

In North America, Canada has taken a great lead over the United States in its use of information technology in support of Aboriginal populations. Aboriginal Business Canada is a good example. It has no real equivalent in the United States in terms of a unified approach to technology in support of Aboriginal enterprises. Another example is the support of the National Film Board. The Smithsonian Institution's National Museum of the American Indian held a Film and Video Festival in New York City in the fall of 1997. What was remarkable was that Canadian entries, especially those in Native languages, dominated the proceedings, followed by Latin American entries. American entries were a distant third. Particularly absent from the American scene were Native dramas. Native American Public Telecommunications in the US is just beginning to address that deficit.

Not only is Canada's leadership evident in North America, it has also taken a lead in exploring support for indigenous peoples worldwide. In the summer of 1997, the Prime Minister of Canada and the president of the World Bank co-sponsored the landmark Global Knowledge '97 conference in Toronto with the participation of 124 countries. Also participating were the UN Secretary-General and the directors of UNESCO, ILO, and other UN agencies along with the presidents of Costa Rica and Uganda. Canadian Aboriginal presence was at centre stage from the welcoming Native dancing to the closing. The president of the Canadian International Development Agency noted the revelance of Canada's experience to world indigenous information technology development:

> In Canada's Northwest Territories in the land that will soon be known as Nunavut the tools of modern communication are being well-used by the Inuit people who, barely a generation ago, knew little about them. A northern broadcasting system, set up originally by the Canadian Broadcasting Corporation, is now run by local, indigenous people. Using radio, TV, the Internet, and video-conferencing, in local languages, from six programming centres across three time-zones, they link scattered settlements, overcome isolation, and deal with matters of shared concern. They are using the media to do what they have decided to do and, incidentally, have become, quickly, a potent political force highly capable of defending and advancing their interests. Even more significantly, a younger generation is becoming comfortable and skilled with the new technology. Schools are becoming community access centres, where Inuit students and others, too, can interact with their counterparts in other northern settlements or, just as easily, with students in Soweto, or aboriginal people in Australia.[5]

The Problem

Television, computing networks, publications, telephones, and telecommunications all are taking a toll on traditional indigenous cultures. In most countries they provide inroads into Native communities to instil the national language. Often that is English, Spanish, or other European languages. However, if properly used, these information technologies have the capability of preserving

Native cultures. In fact, to slow or reverse the erosion of cultures, the indigenous must start using these technologies immediately and to a far greater degree than heretofore. Small indigenous populations really do not have a choice. These technologies are simply too enticing to Native youth and provide too many advantages for competitors. Fortunately, costs have plummeted, making publishing, video production, and electronic communication feasible for the smallest of Aboriginal groups.

Indigenous people have two major information needs. The first is internal. They need to preserve Native languages, literature (both oral and written), art, and home-grown science. The second need is external. Native people need to have access to information from outside, whether for medical services, education, culture, economic development, or other community pursuits. They need to share information with other Aboriginals as well as have access to government, industrial, and educational storehouses of information. How can indigenous peoples begin to use such information, and what results can be expected?

Several studies have documented the need of Native peoples for technology. In 1995 the US Office of Technology Assessment issued a landmark report on the status of, impact on, and potential for telecommunications technology among Native American (i.e., American Indian, Alaska Native, and Native Hawaiian) communities and organizations in the United States.[6] The study included effects on culture, community-building, sovereignty, and telecommunications policy. The report notes a number of success stories as well as problems. Already in 1995, when it was published, a rapid expansion in use of the Internet was beginning to emerge among Native American communities. Several tribes, starting with the Oneida Nation in New York state and including the Navajo and Cherokee, put up homepages that provided public information about the tribe, samples of tribal language, and marketing of tribal products. The Nation of Hawai'i and a Hawai'an language homepage were also described. Apple Computer's Library of Tomorrow program, which was noted in the report, produced a laptop computer language learning centre for the Zuni, a Project Jukebox to preserve cultures in Alaska, and others. However, in spite of these successes the report noted that serious problems remain for most tribes. In a section entitled 'A Pessimistic Year 2000 Scenario' it notes that 'the inadequacies of rural Native American economies and telecommunications infrastructure continue to prove too great to overcome. . . . Absent some kind of policy interventions, Native Americans are unlikely to catch up with, and probably will fall further behind, the majority society with respect to telecommunications.'

Internal Needs: Preserving Cultures with Information
How well are indigenous cultures preserved, even in the industrialized West? Little material about tribes is recorded in a form easily available to their own

members and much less to others outside the tribes. Walk into any American or Canadian bookstore, even in Indian country, and you are likely to find a wide variety of foreign-language phrase books, but virtually never one for an indigenous language except an occasional one made for a local tribe. Often when an indigenous phrase book or dictionary is found, it is either poorly done and simplistic or geared to the needs of a professional linguist. Where indigenous people have control over their own small nations, as in the Pacific Islands, one does see a presence of language aids not only in that country but throughout the world, principally as a support to tourists. Fijian language aids, for example, are available in bookstores in many major cities in the English-speaking world.

One is also unlikely to find Native histories, Native medical knowledge, or books on the many contributions they have made and can make to the broad American society. However, when books are found they usually are by non-indigenous authors and cover only Native arts in general ways. Such publications, while useful, are just too limited to provide much of an indicator of cultural richness. Aboriginal peoples have excellent oral traditions but much of this has not been captured for posterity.

The shortage of published information extends beyond books or other printed materials. *Dances with Wolves*, a major motion picture in the early 1990s, was a landmark, not only because it was culturally sensitive (unless you happen to be a Pawnee) and well done, but also because the film evoked a sense of reality with the extensive use of the Lakota language. It was, possibly, the first major motion picture ever to use a Native language for a significant portion of the film, which, in a way, is outrageous. *Black Robe*, produced in Canada, and then *Last of the Mohicans* followed with Native language playing a significant role, albeit not always the language of the tribe portrayed. More recently, Disney worked with a museum director, who did his doctoral dissertation on Eastern Cherokee, to produce a Cherokee version of Pocahontas. Of course, Pocahontas was not Cherokee.

Film and now video-making by Indians has been limited in the United States. A project in the 1960s trained Navajo to produce documentaries and a few short ones were developed. There have been few films, however, developed by Indians in Indian languages and these have usually been for specialized audiences. Thankfully, this situation is changing. Each year the Native American Public Telecommunications (NAPT), the Native public broadcasting arm for the US, has more Native-produced or Native-involved film projects to review and has embarked on a new initiative to develop a for-profit subsidiary to support Native productions. In Canada there is much greater support by the government, and that is reflected in more production there than in the US. For example, at the 1996 and 1997 Native American Film Festivals in San Francisco, Canadian films dominated the entries.

Lack of indigenous language printed material and video materials is symptomatic of a much larger problem. Tribes are not doing a good job either of getting information about themselves to the outside world or of spreading information among themselves, whether it be languages, cultural values, medical information, resource development, employment, or social services. They are not competing adequately against information from non-indigenous viewpoints and the latter are touching lives, especially impressionable children.

There is little point to acquiring publications and developing information systems if the information they need to use has not been collected and published or produced. A major consideration, therefore, for the indigenous in joining the Information Age is recording (i.e., publishing, producing, or putting on line) and disseminating knowledge.

External Needs: Tapping into Resources

The National Information Infrastructure Advisory Council (NIIAC) in the US in early 1996 published its final reports.[7] Most importantly, they recommended that schools, libraries, and community centres be connected to the Internet. The impetus for adding community centres came directly from input by Indians because often on reservations there are no schools or libraries under tribal control. This is often true among indigenous or Aboriginal peoples elsewhere in the world as well.

Increasingly, workshops and conferences are bringing together technologically talented indigenous people, often sharing ideas with non-indigenous experts. An important one of these was a multimedia planning meeting held in the spring of 1996.[8] The Tribal Information Infrastructure Planning Project, funded by the US Department of Commerce and administered by NAPT, looked extensively at six tribes with a view to all aspects of the technology and its potential and made recommendations on their needs.[9] Tribes in the study were the Campo band of Mission Indians, the Eastern band of Cherokee Indians, the Sisseton Wahpeton Sioux tribe, the Southern Ute Indian tribe, the Standing Rock Sioux tribe, and the Turtle Mountain Chippewa tribe. The study found a variety of experiences. The Sisseton Wahpeton experience was considered exemplary in many ways. 'It formed a telecommunications committee which issued a comprehensive plan that included sound planning and implementation provisions. Following on the plan, some parts of the network have been activated. It is a worthy model for other tribes and small communities to consider as they make plans for similar telecommunications infrastructure development.'[10] The report also observed that many tribes have formed 'infrastructures of technology opportunity' or core programs that include local community colleges and tribal departments or programs that have incorporated telecommunications for their respective areas. These were recommended as pilot projects for tribes to observe, monitor, and learn from before moving into larger or more expanded operations. Several considerations in outcomes for cost-benefit analysis are also given.

Academic institutions are an important part of the equation as well. Universities can offer a number of things for indigenous people in their regions. Firstly, most in North America and many throughout the world are now linked to Internet. They provide access to library catalogues, indexing services, databases, and the like all over the country. The existence of these disbursed gateways, close to many tribes, should not be overlooked in planning. These networks could provide vital information in health, economic development, and a host of other areas as well as provide opportunities for communication with compatriots who have relocated elsewhere in the world.

How does an indigenous community tap into these networks? Universities and colleges will not normally add to their burden of populations served, especially outside the institutions, without incentives in the form of funding or legislative mandate or both. The potential for universities and colleges to provide information technology support and training is substantial. The California Technology Project recently tested new multimedia modes of learning for schools. Why not explore similar use of technology for solving Native population needs? Tribes need some very basic support. Many do not have computers, modems, faxes, or printers, and they need a basic set-up to contact the rest of the world. Some need to contact other parts of their reservations. Of those who do have some equipment, many have no place to go for technical support or information on how to make use of the equipment. Universities do this on a routine basis now. Why not provide them with incentives to do this? An alternative to using the universities is to set up special Native regional technology centres. The trade-offs between the two approaches should be studied.

The scattering of the various indigenous peoples has, in the past, made communications difficult. Ground telecommunications infrastructure is lacking in many areas. Where it exists it should be used, of course. These communities need, however, a much more integrative approach to providing information resources that uses whatever infrastructures exist and then supplements these as needed.

Not only are indigenous peoples not publishing significant numbers of materials about themselves, but also they do not have adequate access to reliable information from the outside world. This is a serious problem since it affects health, economic development, education, and almost all those aspects of daily life that Native peoples have in common with all people. Tribes miss out on opportunities to improve their lot by not being connected to electronic resources. Tribal libraries often contain misinformation, especially about the very people served. These libraries are frequently recipients of discards from other libraries. Occasionally these materials are useful but often they are outdated. Sometimes that outdated information, especially in areas such as law and medicine, can be outright dangerous if relied on. More often, however, they simply do not have nearly enough information resources in any area.

Most Native peoples are very poorly served by public library systems. California, an advanced state in terms of information resources and the American state with the largest Indian population, is all too typical. The state's reservation Indians, the most diverse indigenous population in the United States, if not the world, are described by the California State Library as being 'the public library's most underserved population'. They were also described as having the lowest educational level of any minority ethnic group in the 1990 US census. This low service level, however, is not matched by low demand for information. Quite the contrary. When relevant resources are made available as, for example, from the California Indian Project at the University of California at Berkeley, information requests pour in from reservation people.[11]

Vast files of valuable Native language materials and information relevant to tribes are in files at the Smithsonian Institution, the Newberry Library, the National Archives, indigenous museums, anthropology departments, and private collections waiting to be made accessible to these populations and the outside world. Fortunately, technology has progressed to the point where it is economically feasible to make these materials available to these populations. Europe, Canada, Australia, and New Zealand also have large collections of materials relevant to indigenous peoples in the Americas and elsewhere in the world. A few years ago a California Pomo went to the Soviet Union to inventory Pomo artefacts and documents related to the Pomo at libraries and museums there. The Russians had a settlement in the mid-1800s at Fort Ross in California and dealt extensively with the Pomo, especially the Kashaya Pomo.

How does a tribe know about relevant resources and get copies of the documents? In regard to art objects and museum pieces, how do they provide video or photographic documentation to bring back when the actual objects cannot be retrieved? These are questions that need to be explored.

Trends Likely To Benefit Indigenous Communities

Native needs are matched by a number of trends that are likely to enhance an indigenous community's ability to solve the information transfer problems. Below is a list of a few of the more important of these trends.

1. The break-up of the Soviet Union and end of the Cold War have brought a renewed urge for sovereignty among individual tribes and small nations.
2. The United Nations Decade of the World's Indigenous People (1995–2004) provides a current opportunity to direct concerns for information technology support of indigenous peoples.

3. Support from national governments around the world has begun to be extended to minority languages within national borders. In the US the Native American Language Act accords special status for Native languages.
4. Finally, there is a growing trend toward lifelong learning and with it distance learning. Because many who need college courses cannot leave jobs to attend school at distant locations, electronic delivery of classes via land-based and satellite-delivered systems has developed. With this has come the need for interactive educational services at a distance to support these students.

In addition, various technological trends can support political and policy objectives that seek to wire indigenous communities. Among such trends are the following:

1. Computers are now almost entirely based on graphics and can be set up to support any language. This means training by others is greatly reduced, and in many cases actually eliminated.
2. Information technology is rapidly dropping in cost. This trend has existed for years and is likely to continue.
3. Printers, computers, and graphic displays have combined to allow low-cost desktop publishing to occur anywhere. Publishing and printing no longer require the huge capital investment of former times, which dictated that publishing take place in larger cities, especially New York since Mergenthaler and other print factories were there. Photo composition and desktop publishing have changed all of that. Publishing is increasingly done purely electronically on the World Wide Web.
4. Networks are becoming ubiquitous, especially in the United States and Canada, so that sharing resources with groups at a distance is greatly facilitated. Throughout these countries a very good and rapidly expanding communications infrastructure, in the form of satellite uplinks and downlinks, cellular phones, cable TV, and telephone lines, has developed.
5. Electronic media offer multimedia, interactivity, and non-linearity. This means that one will be increasingly able to react to the machine much as one does to another person. One talks and gets feedback from other humans. That same capability is beginning to be available with machines.
6. Most publishing is now done in multimedia. While optical disk technology, along with digital telecommunications and integrated multimedia work stations, has allowed integration of formats, interactivity is now ubiquitous because of the Internet and the World Wide Web. Text, video sequence, and keyword search capability are common.

7. Information input options are expanding, making creation of electronic collections simpler and more feasible. Character recognition of scanned documents eliminates typing in materials, and this technology will continue to improve with programs that increase in accuracy through self-learning. For English-language materials voice recognition improvements within this decade will allow for speaking what you want recorded, thereby bypassing typing.

8. Another opportunity that technology has created is multiple-dimensional access. Information seekers have probably always wanted access tools to lead them to logical units of relevant information within books, reports, and articles, and not to the physical units of books and periodical issues themselves. Computers allow the long-range opportunity of organizing information as needed rather than physically.

The Solution

Capturing Information: Publishing

Timely and effective technical opportunities exist for indigenous information production. Data input has been the primary bottleneck in the large-scale conversion of text to machine-readable form, and only a few specialized collections of monograph materials are currently available in machine-readable form. Direct keying of even a core of widely used reference books used to be prohibitively expensive, even if done on a national scale.

New text is increasingly available as a by-product of automated publishing. Full text of recent issues of thousands of journals is now available on-line. Also, direct conversion of printed text to an electronic form is now possible for a wide variety of type fonts. Scanners offer the potential for such conversions, even for non-English materials. Much information should and will remain in non-textual form. Facsimile storage of text provides an economical alternative for text whose individual words have little need for extraction. Combined systems of machine-readable indexing and text stored in page form on optical disks are likely to predominate for older material.

Projects are needed to convert the vast archives that already exist on Native peoples into electronic form for easy reproduction, packaging, and distribution. Archivists are naturally reluctant to let these out of their hands for fear of their being lost. Scanning and other new techniques for information capture, optical disk technology for storage and retrieval, and expanding telecommunications head the list of technologies that can be used on site to reduce archivists' anxiety.

Having little of an information infrastructure can be an advantage. The ability exists to design systems from scratch using the latest technology and appropriate formats. Technology has opened the way for new formats of information that surpass the book's capabilities in many ways and pave the way for its partial replacement. The book has no audio capabilities or potential for animation. A computerized animated 'article' on how a car works can clarify processes in ways a book cannot. Graphics cannot be zoomed in or out in a book. As neat as the scanning of a book is, it is no match for rapid random retrieval, especially when an entire collection of books is involved. Interaction that contributes to the content is not possible with books, either. Electronic media offer numerous other advantages, such as fast shuffling of materials, multiple ways of organizing information, on-line access to other collections, sharing of resources, savings in printing costs, and rapid updatability.

The new technology for publishing provides the potential but not the assurance of access to organized, accurate, retrievable, concise, and precise information. Libraries and booksellers historically wove tight partnerships with publishers. These publishers were few in number and acted as quality screeners between authors and readers. Publishers, with their editors and scholarly referees, continued to act as filters to ensure quality and relevance. They also provided many access tools. A book has a table of contents and an index. Secondary publishers filled in access gaps with abstracts, book reviews, and the like. Recording of knowledge must be matched with access to it.

Networking: Opportunities for Access

An enormous amount of activity is going on in distance learning in terms of innovative uses of technology for access. Much of what is used in these systems can be transferred to support for information services. There are, in fact, compelling arguments for information dissemination to be part, if not the core, of these systems. Big Sky Telegraph, a project funded by US West (the telephone operating company for the intermountain West) based at the Western Montana College of the University of Montana, linked rural communities with conferencing, bulletin board, and electronic mail. Sharing of full colour art and other graphics occurs as well. The Rural Alaska Network, developed out of necessity, provides a wide variety of interactive learning services to Alaska Natives and other Alaskans living in remote locations. Another interesting project is the Alaska Telegraphics Project, in which digitized images on TV screens are shared and interactively changed across distances.

Access to a wide variety of fully integrated and scientifically organized on-line databases could reduce the likelihood of serious misinformation. For this, integration of computerized services is needed at the creative stage of information resource development. The indigenous peoples must see their role as author and publisher of materials and information. What quickly becomes clear is that they must hook into national and international electronic networks. That may not be as difficult or as costly as might be assumed; it will, however, take support on a national or international scale to gain access to those resources already being used by universities and research companies. International networking may be more important to Native populations than one might think. They have much in common with what is often termed the Fourth World, or small tribes throughout the world ruled by alien majorities. As one pioneering example, the Navajo are using electronic mail to market crafts to 40 countries.

Overcoming Obstacles

Obstacles to upgrading services are many: cost of on-line services, distances, little money for new programs, small local collections, training difficulties (lack of instructors and facilities), lack of hardware, lack of awareness of what is available, and little co-ordination with other institutions of government, Aboriginal and other. Fortunately, those working in technology are learning ways to overcome these problems. A few examples are instructive. An excellent resource on conserving cultural resources in digital form is *Research Agenda for Networked Cultural Heritage.*[12]

The cost of technology is often raised as an objection to its use. What is often not appreciated is that maintaining the status quo is also expensive, both in fact and in terms of lost opportunity. Books are expensive and are increasing in price, and publishers have escalated these costs far beyond inflation. In contrast, technology continues to decline dramatically in cost per unit of performance. There comes a point throughout the information spectrum where a line is crossed beyond which technology is cheaper. Registering an Internet Web site costs only US $100 and provision of access is increasingly becoming affordable for First Nations. The Native American Resources Home Page maintained by Lisa Mitten at the University of Pittsburgh lists about 70 tribes of the 300+ tribes in the United States.

New low-cost technologies provide new opportunities. Local information resource units such as libraries can fill informational gaps by becoming publishers or inputters of information themselves. Ties with local presses can be forged. Tribal interests can be represented. Data from national databases can be extracted to generate locally tailored packets of information. At the Pine Ridge Reservation in South Dakota, the Oglala Lakota College Library functions as both a college library and a public library. The college is not typical in being a distributed college with courses and services delivered to nine district college centres. Faculty, as well, travel over a 110-mile stretch. Using US $95,000 received from the US Department of Education's College Library Technology and Cooperation Grants program, microcomputer stations with modems were purchased for each centre's library to provide access to the state library and the college's central location. For bibliographic service a multiplatter CD-ROM system was purchased, giving access to many databases. CD-ROM systems such as this have the advantage of unlimited searching without the timed line charges of services such as DIALOG or BRS. The cost of calls made to the central location is limited to the phone charges, which often can be discounted on a regional basis.

Several other locations are in various stages of planning and implementation of public library services to Indians using outside resources. The Oneida Community Library in Wisconsin and many other tribal libraries, through the use of statewide networks or regional public library systems, now access not only bibliographic records but also a variety of Internet services. Gonzaga University in Spokane, Washington, developed a multifaceted long-distance delivery system spanning two countries well over a decade ago. Operating an on-site electronic information centre at Camin Lake Reserve 500 miles away in British Columbia, this system made use of the Western Library Network's LaserCat CD-ROM bibliographic database containing, on three optical disks, records of about 2.5 million books and serials in the network's 300 member libraries. Also available were on-line database searches of commercial services, fax document delivery, parcel delivery of books, and electronic messaging. Existing resources need to be used in new ways. It is important to break from common divisions of libraries by type to find the best arrangement for each community.

While the European information tradition has tended to emphasize text, American Indians have historically used oral traditon, graphics, and activity to convey meaning. Electronic networks until recently have been almost exclusively textual, which has blocked use for sharing non-text information. This is changing rapidly. The trend towards allowing graphics and motion to be part of newer networks will open up ways of improving communications from Native peoples. What may impede this movement somewhat is the lack of standards. The now defunct Memex Research Institute, formed to create a massive electronic library on a national scale, addressed the development of standards for electronic information as one of its first projects.[13]

Funding: Planning and Resource-Sharing

Success through government support can be substantial. While a few programs in the US and Canada support Aboriginal technological programs directly, they are, with few exceptions, small in scope. One promising effort is Aboriginal Business Canada. It has made remarkable strides in the development of Native enterprises, including some that foster Native communications and technology. The Canadian experience with Aboriginal Business Canada's Information Highway Initiatives illustrates this dramatically:

> To attain economic self-sufficiency, Aboriginal entrepreneurs need to adapt fully to a marketplace which thrives on electronic and interactive communications. Limitations formerly imposed by remote locations, 'niche' products, and small business ventures

are increasingly irrelevant in light of today's communications technologies. 'Information Highway' opportunities will give Aboriginal firms access to expanded markets, new technology, and increased sources of financing. Aboriginal business is increasingly ready for the interactive information age: Over half of the program clients studied in 1995, as part of the 'Goss Gilroy' survey, own and use a computer, with 11 percent accessing the Internet. Thirty-three Aboriginal environmental firms form part of the award-winning Canadian Environmental Solutions CD-ROM information source. Four hundred Aboriginal communities working jointly with Industry Canada's SchoolNet Initiative will have gained Internet access by 1997 and be able to tap into business information. An introduction to technology and communications opportunities has been provided by program-sponsored Internet seminars.[14]

Aboriginal Youth Business Council (AYBC) was established in 1994 under the sponsorship of Aboriginal Business Canada to encourage young Native entrepreneurs. It has been particularly effective in that it is more directly centred on information technology use, particularly the Web. One of the strategic goals set out in the organization's plan was to have participants use the latest communications technology to deliver services. The AYBC sees itself as a facilitator of information exchange. In a press release announcing the official launch, the AYBC president, 24-year-old Cree/Métis Jason Rock, stated, 'We elected to deliver all of our support programs and services over the Net because of its global reach and cost effectiveness. We are in essence a virtual organization. More and more native youth are going on-line through school and other community resources and it was our first choice for setting up a communications and support network.'[15] Such a communications system allows Aboriginal youth throughout Canada to get access to current information on business and entrepreneurial support programs.

In the United States federal support for information systems for Native Americans often comes from sources not specifically geared to them. Native share of Library Services and Construction Act funds, Higher Education Act titles, tribal revenues, foundation grants, and business partnerships is small, but so is the total pot. One strength Native people have developed is proposal writing. They have to beg to a degree far greater than the general population. They need to broaden their targets. Too often, efforts are wasted trying to compete for crumbs from a national government. Sometimes other support is available and far less competitive.

A tribe or indigenous nation cannot benignly expect that a national government will fund any significant portion of its needs for information technology in the near future without a real battle. This leaves them largely to their own resources and economic development. Partnership with industry can be an added way to meet this need. They can start, for example, by insisting that information communications capabilities be included in agreements signed with industry. Often these can be added at little extra cost to these firms and will benefit both parties. They also should participate in pilot projects.

Conclusion: Literacy, Democracy, and Productivity

If ethnodiversity and literacy are to survive, the problem must be attacked on two fronts. Those knowledgeable and literate in the particular culture must prepare and educate the youth—as well as some older people who have missed out in the past—in their culture and language. Many more projects like the Library of Congress Federal Cylinder Project[16] ought to be funded. Technology is ideally suited for this now, although it was not when many promises were made years ago. Information necessary for functioning in the broader society must also be provided.

Technology is a two-edged sword. On the one hand, it provides access to information from all over the world quickly and at low cost. On the other, it is susceptible to dividing the population into 'haves' and 'have-nots' unless funding is provided for computer terminals and video at locations convenient to everyone. The difference between how costs are covered for printed materials and computerized services is quite marked. Books and other printed matter are usually provided free. Even with interlibrary loan, cost is limited to materials actually wanted. On-line services cost per transaction and often that transaction yields little or no useful material. The cost in user time to find and copy printed material, however, can be considerable, while automation can reduce that significantly. Plans must take these realities into consideration.

Locally, the tribal library needs to be restructured into an integrated information centre. The tribal library's role must change. It can no longer sit back and purchase a few books, take some discards, and subscribe to a handful of journals. Practically, a people can no longer count on public library services to meet any significant proportion of its information needs. Many public library systems are struggling to stay alive and most are ill-equipped to serve rural populations typical of Native North Americans. A bookmobile with a handful of books simply will not cut it when people are faced with the need for information gleaned from massive resources. One must, instead, use books where one can but forge broader networks for both hand and electronic delivery of materials. Native peoples must look beyond the public library sector to foundations, institutes, specialized networks, business, government, and, most importantly, their own generated publications and productions.

American tribes and Canadian First Nations must deal with information much more directly, including collecting and publishing it when it has not been published or is not currently in a distributable form. Taking a much broader role is essential if they are to survive against the onslaught of materials from the outside, many of which are unfriendly to their cultures and sometimes to their health. Publishing must include more than printed matter; indeed, perhaps 'publishing' is not the proper term. Videos, graphics, and sound recordings must be integrated with print and made available electronically, hopefully to the home. Indigenous peoples must be ingenious in finding both the most efficient and the most effective ways available today to communicate. They must look at all available resources. If an extensive telephone system is not present in a community, perhaps packet radio or use of a transponder on a satellite can be used to transmit data to remote areas.

The US Office of Technology Assessment's report, mentioned earlier, identified eight major components to a comprehensive policy framework for Native American telecommunications. The first four address actions internal to the Native population, emphasizing the role played by Native governments and groups; the second four address US federal policy, external to the Native populations. These eight recommendations are summarized and globalized below.

Empowering Native Telecommunications (the internal component)
- Grassroots tribal/village/community empowerment: identify and develop local sources of telecommunications expertise and a local telecommunications plan.
- Native leadership: strengthen Native leadership on telecommunications policy on the regional, national, and international scales through participation in organizations setting policies likely to affect Native telecommunications. Work with universities, especially for education and training.
- Integrated infrastructure development: install technologies and systems that are compatible, complementary, and cost-effective with existing local sites. Local schools, community colleges, libraries, cultural centres, clinics, and tribal offices might be adaptable as multiservice delivery centres to provide videoconferencing, computer networking, multimedia, and other services.
- Native entrepreneurial activity: form Native-owned and -operated business, especially in telecommunications, to (1) develop grassroots expertise and leadership, (2) create new jobs locally, (3) stimulate the Native economy, and (4) increase the prospects for Native businesses to compete regionally, nationally, and internationally.

Refocusing the UN and Federal Roles (the external component)
- Interagency strategy and funding: set up an interagency strategy to alleviate fragmented and unco-ordinated efforts. These could include a task force or working group on Native telecommunications—an electronic clearinghouse to provide relevant information on programs and projects accessible to both Native technologists and leaders as well as to UN and federal personnel.

- Telecommunications policy: include in telecommunications policy recognition of sovereignty and self-determination, universal access, and strategic partnerships.
- Information policy: in formulating information policy, government leaders and bureaucrats should consider Native perspectives. Two areas requiring particular sensitivity are (1) controlling access to selective religious, spiritual, and ceremonial information transmitted electronically and (2) protecting the integrity of the information content (e.g., Native artwork or traditional healing) from alteration, misrepresentation, or misuse.
- Further research and development: encourage the development of centres of telecommunications expertise in Native organizations and universities that serve Native populations. Telecommunications and information technology, in general, are changing rapidly so that policies need continual review and updating.[17]

In summary, the indigenous must network resources so that they not only know where something is but also what it is. Document access via the World Wide Web, fax, and electronic mail to a computer and programming to a TV are here now and must be part of the plan. Centres to train indigenous producers and publishers and to develop materials could help. Finally, the indigenous peoples need to inventory existing information tools at their disposal—radio, TV, video, cameras, fax machines, satellite dishes, personal computers, etc.— and plan for effective implementation of these into an integrated program to help to bring them out of the current levels of economic and information poverty.

Notes

[1]   US Congress, Senate, Native American Language Act, 101st Cong., 1st sess., 1989, S.1781 (now Public Law 101–477, 20 Oct. 1990).
[2]   United Nations, Economic and Social Council, E/CN.4/Sub.2/1993/29, annex I, GE.93–85003 (E), 23 Aug. 1993, Commission on Human Rights, Subcommission on Prevention of Discrimination and Protection of Minorities, Forty-seventh session, Forty-fifth session, Agenda Item 14, Discrimination Against Indigenous Peoples: Report of the working group on Indigenous populations on its eleventh session. Chairperson/Rapporteur of the Subcommission, Mrs Erica-Irene Daes. http://www.halcyon.com/FWDP/drft9329.html
[3]   United Nations, Economic and Social Council, Indigenous People: International Decade 1995–2004. Published by the United Nations Department of Public Information, DPI/1608/HR— Dec. 1994. http://www.un.org/ecosocdev/geninfo/indigens/dpi1608e.htm
[4]   United Nations, Economic and Social Council, E/CN.4/Sub.2/1995/26, annex 1, GE.95–12808 (E), 21 June 1995, Commission on Human Rights, Subcommission on Prevention of Discrimination and Protection of Minorities, Forty-seventh session, Item 15 of the provisional agenda, Discrimination Against Indigenous Peoples: Protection of the heritage of indigenous people,

elaborated by the Special Rapporteur of the Subcommission, Mrs Erica-Irene Daes.
http://www.halcyon.com/pub/FWDP/International/heritage.txt

5 Huguette Labelle, president, Canadian International Development Agency, Plenary Session on 'Global Knowledge and Local Culture', Global Knowledge '97 Conference, Toronto, 24 June 1997. http://www.globalknowledge.org/graphics/labelle.html

6 US Congress, Office of Technology Assessment, *Telecommunications Technology and Native Americans: Opportunities and Challenges*, OTA–ITC–621 (Washington: US Government Printing Office, Aug. 1995).

7 National Information Infrastructure Advisory Council, *KickStart Initiative: Connecting America's Communities to the Information Superhighway* (1996).
http://www.benton.org/Kickstart/kick.home.html; National Information Infrastructure Advisory Council, *A Nation of Opportunity: Realizing the Promise of the Information Superhighway* (1996). http://www.benton.org/Kickstart/nation.home.html

8 Native American Public Telecommunications, Multimedia Planning Meeting, Lincoln, Nebraska, 8–9 Apr.1996.

9 Native American Public Telecommunications, Tribal Information Infrastructure Planning Project, Final Report, Dec. 1996.

10 Ibid., 88.

11 Lee Davis, 'California Indians and Libraries', *California State Library Foundation Bulletin* 27 (Apr. 1989): 10–12.

12 The Getty Art History Information Program, *Research Agenda for Networked Cultural Heritage* (Santa Monica, Calif.: The J. Paul Getty Trust, 1996).
http://www.ahip.getty.edu/ahip./home.html

13 Edwin Brownrigg and Brett Butler, 'An Electronic Library Communications Format', *Library Hi-Tech* 31 (1990): 21–6.

14 Aboriginal Business Canada, 'Aboriginal Business Canada Four Priorities for Growth', 2. Encouraging the Widespread Use of Technology, Information Highway Initiatives as of June 1997.
http://strategis.ic.gc.ca/sc_mangb/abc/engdoc/abc_pri2.html

15 Aboriginal Youth Business Council, 'Aboriginal Youth Business Council—Fall Update', Press Release, Fall 1996.

16 A brochure on the project from the Library of Congress states: 'From 1890 to 1942, the cylinder phonograph was used by ethnographers, travelers, and other interested researchers to record live performances of Native American music and spoken word in the field while many traditions were still actively practiced and taught.' For example, included in the project are 254 cylinder recordings by an Omaha, which document the traditions of the Omaha, Osage, Kansa, Quapaw, and Ponca.

17 US Congress, Office of Technology Assessment, *Telecommunications Technology and Native Americans*, 6–14.